The "New Heavens and New Earth"

Hope for the Creation in Jewish
Apocalyptic and the New Testament

David M. Russell

Studies in Biblical Apocalyptic Literature **1**

The "New Heavens and New Earth"

Hope for the Creation in Jewish
Apocalyptic and the New Testament

David M. Russell

Visionary Press
Philadelphia

The "New Heavens and New Earth":
Hope for the Creation in Jewish Apocalyptic and the New Testament
©1996 by David Michael Russell

Published by Visionary Press, Philadelphia
All correspondence should be addressed to:
42 Steelecrest Ln. Granite City, IL 62040 USA
or via e-mail: 745-6330@mcimail.com

ISBN: 1-896400-17-5

Library of Congress Catalog Card Number: 96-60935

Cover Illustration: Beltasar's Feast, Used with permission from Kregel Publications.

Printed in Canada
Edited and Designed by Alan Lenzi

All Scripture quotations, unless otherwise noted, are taken from the New
American Standard Bible. © 1960, 1962, 1963, 1971, 1972, 1973, 1975,
1977 The Lockman Foundation (La Habra, CA).

TO MY NANCY
Sine Qua Non

PREFACE

This study represents the culmination of interest that began in a doctoral seminar at Southwestern Seminary in Old Testament theology under Dr. Ralph Smith in 1984. During this period of study I was introduced formally to the writings of Bernhard W. Anderson, Langdon Gilkey, Karl Barth, Gerhard von Rad, Walther Eichrodt, and other influential scholars who have written extensively on the doctrine of creation. This topic is of special concern to one who as a young boy watched the strip mining operations mercilessly decimate the beautiful mountains of my East Tennessee home. Even now after most mining activities have ceased the land has not yet fully recovered. Unfortunately, the sermons that came from the pulpits of the churches in my home town addressed only the issue of spiritual salvation without saying anything significant about God's redemptive plan for the creation. In fact, this is generally true of the modern church even though our world and society is challenged constantly with environmental disaster. While one hesitates to elevate concern for creation over humanity; nevertheless, the lack of attention regarding the former requires a reconsideration which seeks to balance cosmic and soteriological considerations rooted firmly in the biblical texts.

My interest in the biblical understanding of creation was rekindled in 1988 in a seminar at Texas Christian University on apocalyptic under Dr. M. Eugene Boring who encouraged this writer to examine the apocalyptic perspective of creation and its ultimate redemption. It is thus against this background of academic and personal experience that this study is offered in an attempt to clarify the apocalyptic and biblical concept of creation and the motif of the "new heavens and new earth" or cosmic hope.

I would like to express my appreciation most especially to my wife Nancy whose unwavering love, encouragement, and support made the completion of this task possible. I also wish to thank Dr. Bruce Corley of Southwestern Seminary who encouraged me to apply my studies in apocalyptic to the NT concept of creation and cosmic hope. A debt of gratitude is certainly owed to Dr. Jim Gilbert who carefully read this manuscript and was always available with a word of encouragement and of course *constructive* criticism. While each of those mentioned contributed in various ways, the claims, conclusions, judgments, and misjudgments for that matter, belong entirely to this writer. Appreciation is also expressed to Dr. Susan Pigott whose expertise on matters of style and form was indispensable and permitted this writer freedom to concentrate on content and research.

In matters of style I consulted Kate L. Turabian, *A Manual for Writers of Term Papers, Theses, and Dissertations*, 5th ed., ed. Bonnie B. Honigsblum (Chicago: University of Chicago, 1987). Abbreviations conform to the standards in the *Society of Biblical Literature* handbook 107 (September 1988): 579-96. Additional sigla are provided by the writer. Greek word searches were made possible through the data base of texts provided by the *Thesaurus Linguae Graecae Pilot CD ROM #C* (Irvine: University of California, 1987). For the sake of simplicity all biblical citations unless otherwise noted are from the New American Standard Bible (La Habra, CA: Lockman Foundation, 1975). While I have attempted occasionally to update the bibliography and footnotes, the text appears for the most part as submitted in 1991.

David Michael Russell
August 1996

TABLE OF CONTENTS

ADDITIONAL SIGLA

Periodicals, Reference Works, and Serials

BES	Biblical Encounter Series
CSR	*Christian Scholars Review*
CTJ	*Calvin Theological Journal*
DG	*The Drew Gateway*
EncR	*The Encyclopedia of Religions*
ETB	Environmental Theology Book Series
GGNT	Robertson, *A Grammar of the Greek New Testament in Light of Historical Research*
IBT	Interpreting Biblical Texts
L/N	Louw and Nida, *Greek-English Lexicon of the New Testament Based on Semantic Domains*
NABPR	National Association of Baptist Professors of Religion

v

NBD	*New Bible Dictionary*
NIDNTT	*New International Dictionary of New Testament Theology*
PSB	*Princeton Seminary Bulletin*
QRev	*Quarterly Review: A Scholarly Journal for Reflections on Ministry*
RefR	*Reformed Review*
RWP	Robertson, *Word Pictures in the New Testament*
RTR	*Reformed Theological Review*
SVF	J. von Arnim, ed., *Stoicorum Veterum Fragmenta* (cited by vol. and para.)

Commentary Series

BCNT	Black's Commentaries on the New Testament
ITC	International Theological Commentary
JPSTC	Jewish Publication Society Torah Commentary
TBC	Torch Bible Commentaries
TNTC	Tyndale New Testament Commentaries
WPC	Westminster Pelican Commentaries
WEC	Wycliffe Exegetical Commentaries

INTRODUCTION

The expressions, "the new heavens and a new earth" and "new creation," are rare in the biblical traditions. Yet the idea of a world renewal is widely attested in Jewish apocalyptic writings and is known even in the targumic and rabbinic traditions.[1] The early Astronomical Book of 1 Enoch reveals that nature is to hold its order "till the new creation which abides forever is created" (1 Enoch 72.1). The apocalyptic concept of a renewed world appears in the first century AD work of the Similitudes. This work envisions a radical transformation of creation on the eschatological day of the Lord: "On that day, . . . I shall transform heaven and . . . I shall (also) transform the earth and make it a blessing, . . ." (1 Enoch 45.4-5). Jewish synagogue interpretation also betrays this tradition. A targumic paraphrase juxtaposes creation and renewal: "I, God, created the world from the beginning, says the Lord: I, God am about to renew the world for the righteous" (*Tg. Jer.* 23.23). Moreover, in the NT this concept blossomed into the Christian affirmation of a new world order

---

[1]The idea of world renewal was widespread in the ancient world but differed significantly from the Hebrew and Christian concept discussed in this investigation. See Mircea Eliade, *The Sacred and the Profane*, trans. Willard Trask (New York: Harcourt, 1957), 104-113 and his more thorough discussion in *The Myth of the Eternal Return*, trans. Willard Trask, Bollingen Series, no. 46 (New York: Pantheon, 1954). The targumic and rabbinic texts will be omitted from consideration due to the limitations of space and the complex problem of dating. See Str-B 3:842-47 for references.

"in which righteousness dwells" (2 Pet. 3.13).

What is the source of this conviction concerning cosmic redemption? The Hebrew *locus classicus* for this concept is undoubtedly Isaiah's promise of the "new heavens and a new earth" (Isa. 65.17; 66.22). But how and under what circumstances was such a statement of historical nationalistic hope transposed into an apocalyptic key that announced a radical replacement of the present world by a new creation? Further, what significance do the terms relating to the concept of cosmic redemption have for the writers? Do they denote the abolition of creation and an entirely new created order *ex nihilo*?

These questions reflect important theological and historical issues which have frequently entertained biblical scholarship.[2] The last query in particular immediately raises an equally significant and contemporary interest that is often overlooked, namely, the biblical and apocalyptic perspective toward the *present* created order in anticipation of the new heavens and a new earth. In other words, what is the future of *this* world in view of the promise of a new creation? Does this hope implicitly depreciate the present created order? Can one accurately speak of the "fall" of the present creation which can be remedied only by universal, catastrophic judgment and a total re-creation of the material order? Are the biblical writers and apocalyptists actually interested in the creation or has it become superfluous in view of humanity's salvation? Is there any hope for the present natural world? These questions clarify the focus of the present study which has implications not only for biblical studies but for contemporary society as well.

The Relevance and Focus of the Study

The future of the world has become an important topic of

---

[2]See, e.g., G. C. Berkouwer who addresses many of the issues related to the concept of the new creation in Protestant theology. *The Return of Christ*, trans. James Van Oosterom, Studies in Dogmatics (Grand Rapids: Eerdmans, 1972), 211-34. Regarding the development of apocalyptic eschatology, see especially Paul D. Hanson, *The Dawn of Apocalyptic: The Historical and Sociological Roots of Jewish Apocalyptic Eschatology*, rev. ed. (Philadelphia: Fortress, 1979).

discussion as political and ecological concerns have made its "end" a present reality. At no other time has humankind been able and it would often seem willing to destroy the creation--the very basis of the existence and endeavors of the human race. Unfortunately, the prospect of world annihilation especially by nuclear destruction has been viewed by some Christian groups and interpreters as a welcome event precipitating the battle of Armageddon and the return of Christ. This perspective has even served to promote the nuclear arms race.[3] Of course, many who hold this view expect to be rescued from this doomed world before such a catastrophe occurs.[4]

A nuclear holocaust is not the only menace encouraged by such an attitude. Equally frightening is the impact upon the environment.[5] The intensity of the present environmental crisis persuaded the editors of *Time* in 1989 to name the "Endangered Earth" as the planet of the year in lieu of the usual man or woman of the year. The cover picture displaying a globe wrapped in polyethylene washed up on a deserted beach portrayed poignantly the vulnerability of the earth.[6] Indeed, the Persian Gulf conflict brought these two dangers into a disturbing close relationship as military endeavors reaped environmental havoc. The fact is that for many people a longing for the new heavens and new

---

[3]See Gordan D. Kaufman's discussion, "Nuclear Eschatology and the Study of Religion," *JAAR* 51 (March 1983): 3-14. An equal danger noted by Kaufman is an extreme view of providential care which expects God to intervene before nuclear or ecological devastation can occur. See also Brian Russell, "A Nuclear End 'Would God Let It Happen?'" in *Theology Against the Horizon*, ed. Alan Race (London: SCM, 1988), 103-16.

[4]Hal Lindsey's popular treatment of this *sensational* dispensational view has appeared under such provocative titles as *The Late Great Planet Earth* (Grand Rapids Zondervan, 1970) and *There's a New World Coming* (Santa Ana, CA: Vision House, 1973). See the critique by Robert Jewett, "Coming to Terms with the Doom Boom," *QRev* 4 (Fall 1984): 9-22.

[5]An enlightening and startling inference of this interpretative view is reflected in a statement by the former Interior Secretary James Watt before a U.S. House of Representatives Committee on the environment. He opined that he was not so concerned about the earth's resources since, "I do not know how many future generations we can count on before the Lord returns." Cited by Grace Halsell, *Prophecy and Politics: Militant Evangelists on the Road to Nuclear War* (Westport, CT: Lawrence Hill, 1986), 8.

[6]*Time Magazine*, 2 January 1989.

earth invites also a radical pessimism toward the present world. Unfortunately this sense of hopelessness has often led to the abdication of Christian responsibility believing that the present creation is without hope and therefore without significance.[7] This perspective advocates an irresponsible and more importantly a potentially dangerous prospect for human existence as well as for the environment. Hanson's comments in this regard are worthy to be cited in full.

> For many, hope and joy in life have been banished by the mushroom cloud and television portraits of nuclear winter. The resulting moral paralysis has reached the extent where the danger increases that it will abet the pernicious process of self-fulfilling prophecy. Here the situation is exacerbated by the argument of some Christians that biblical texts in Ezekiel, Daniel and the Book of Revelation foretell an imminent Armageddon in which nuclear weapons will be God's chosen instrument for ending this evil age, thereby behooving American Christians to press on aggressively with the U.S. arms buildup, so as to do a complete job. The popularity of this view . . . cries out for a much more serious effort on the part of those drawing very different conclusions from the apocalyptic texts of the Bible to explicate the central meaning of these texts in a way that is persuasive and capable of reaching far more people that has been the case in years of the "Jerry Falwell offensive."[8]

Is there any doubt that the present world era stands at the brink of disaster and thus can be appropriately labeled apocalyptic? The affirmation of the present created order and its continuity with the new creation speaks a word of warning to those preaching the destruction of the world and longing for an escape to a heavenly realm--a modern day Gnosticism. Such a perspective can never serve as a basis of responsible Christian living nor will it foster joy and perseverance while awaiting with

---

[7]Frank Moore Cross observes that the longing for the new heavens and new earth leaves many "free to exploit the old heavens and earth with all our might." "The Redemption of Nature," *PSB*, n.s. 10 (July 1989): 103.

[8]Paul D. Hanson, "Biblical Apocalypticism: The Theological Dimensions," *HBT* 7 (December 1985): 16-17.

anticipation God's pronouncement, "Behold I am making everything new" (Rev. 21.5). This hermeneutic therefore not only constitutes a danger to human existence; it actually enervates the richness of the present. The motif of the "new heavens and new earth" promises hope for the present as well as the future. Berkouwer correctly observes that "when the expectation of a new earth is denied or relativized, the meaning of life *on this earth* breaks down." Furthermore, he states that "only with an eye to God's future can one understand the richness of life in the present."[9]

The pessimistic views referred to above are admittedly popular and extreme. However, in academic circles recognized scholars of apocalyptic also have *unwittingly* fostered a negative attitude toward nature in apocalyptic writings. No doubt this is because some writers often have failed to distinguish explicitly between the apocalyptists' view of the present world *age* and the created order. Nevertheless, the emphasis upon the "new heavens and new earth" for which the apocalyptists longed unfortunately has led to the mistaken conclusion that they had little or no interest in the present creation. The apocalyptists believed that evil had so permeated the present world order that nothing had been left untainted including the realm of nature and was indeed unworthy of concern.[10] Consequently, some modern writers with environmental interests have identified apocalyptic Judaism and its concept of humanity's estrangement from nature as the root of Christianity's failure to properly address the pre-

---

[9]Berkouwer, *Return of Christ*, 227, 230.

[10]Leon Morris notes that "this present world is full of evil and hopeless, the apocalyptists abandoned it." *Apocalyptic* (Grand Rapids: Eerdmans, 1972), 48. Cf. the comments of D. S. Russell, *The Method and Message of Jewish Apocalyptic, 200 B.C.-A.D. 100*, OTL (Philadelphia: Westminster, 1976), 280 and Hanson, *Dawn of Apocalyptic*, 376. On the general pessimistic perspective of Jewish apocalyptic see Wilhelm Bousset, *Die Religion des Judentums im neutestamentlichen Zeitalter*, HNT, no. 21, ed. Hugo Gressmann (Berlin: Reuter & Reichard, 1906), 508-10; R. H. Charles, *Religious Development Between the Old and New Testaments* (New York: Holt & Co., 1914), 19-22. This tendency in apocalyptic scholarship was raised initially by Donald E. Gowan, "The Fall and Redemption of the Material World in Apocalyptic Literature," *HBT* 7 (December 1985): 83-103.

sent ecological crisis.[11] Donald Gowan argued that the familiar negative reflections upon the natural order often exhibited in apocalyptic scholarship, that is, a theology of the fall of creation, merits reconsideration. His brief survey of apocalyptic works revealed that the theme of a degenerate and thus hopeless creation was not always as pronounced as usually assumed.[12]

In light of these observations, a reassessment of the created world and its redemption is indeed appropriate in apocalyptic especially as it relates to the NT idea. It is one thing to catalog the negative comments regarding the present world in apocalyptic literature--this is often done with some relish--but quite another to penetrate the essence of the language for a more enlightened and balanced view concerning the created order. This is the challenge of this study: to demonstrate that the apocalyptic motif of the "new heavens and a new earth" preserves an important and positive role for the *present* creation. To accomplish this aim, this investigation is developed along two foci: one evaluates whether the biblical works, and most importantly the apocalyptic writings, evince any interest in the created order itself. The other attempts to determine whether the anticipation of the new heavens and new earth is actually a call for an escape from this world.

An important consideration in the study involves the relationship of the OT view with the apocalyptic and NT perspective. Therefore, the investigation presents a brief review of the OT theme. Particularly significant in this regard is avoiding the anthropocentric approach of previous studies. An additional concern relates to those texts that depict the creation as suffering under the weight of sin and experiencing eschatological redemption along with the nation.[13] This is followed by an examination

---

[11]See the discussion of H. Paul Santmire, *The Travail of Nature: The Ambiguous Ecological Promise of Christian Theology* (Philadelphia: Fortress, 1895), 1-3.

[12]Gowan, "The Fall and Redemption of the Material World," 88. A varied portrayal of the creation was revealed.

[13]The term "eschatology" usually denotes the doctrine of last things, namely, death, resurrection, judgment, and immortality. Since in reality the biblical concept did not mean the *end*, it is more appropriate to use the term and its cognates to denote the Jewish and Christian hope for the future of the entire creation including the nation, individual, and the world. For the variety

of Jewish apocalyptic writings prior to and contemporaneous with the NT. An analysis of general statements regarding the creation and particularly those reflecting eschatological renewal yields appropriate information for an adequate determination of the apocalyptic view of creation. Finally, pertinent creation themes and passages from the Gospels, the Pauline tradition (and deutero-Pauline), 2 Peter 3, and the role of creation language and motifs in Revelation are discussed with a view toward clarifying the NT understanding of the natural world and its ultimate redemption. The concept of cosmic hope thus serves as a "prism" to reveal the writers' view of the present material order in anticipation of the new heavens and a new earth.[14]

The reader may note the rather obvious observation that each passage considered in the biblical and apocalyptic literature possesses its own unique critical problem. To address each issue in depth, especially in a work as ambitious and *limited* as the present one, would seriously detract from the presentation. Such issues therefore are addressed only as they relate to the central theme under consideration and often it is necessary to relegate many of the critical comments and discussions to the notes. Additionally, while we have opted for a "survey" organization for the study, it nevertheless provides the best approach in the accomplishment of the thesis relating to a variety of material.

Creation, Nature, and Humanity

The environmental concerns of the past several decades have encouraged theologians to call for a "new theology of nature" or "ecological theology" which will appropriately address the realm of nature apart from humanity.[15] Although the motif of

---

of uses for the term see I. Howard Marshall, "Slippery Words: Eschatology," *ExpTim* 89 (June 1978): 264-69. Note also Hanson's terminology below, n. 45.

[14]Allan D. Galloway's early contribution presents a brief historical background of the concept of cosmic hope but fades into existential philosophical discussion without attention to the various texts. *The Cosmic Christ* (New York: Harper & Row, 1951).

[15]Aside from the plethora of articles and essays, important recent monographs include: Eric C. Rust, *Nature--Garden Or Desert? An Essay in Environmental Theology* (Waco: Word, 1971); Joseph A. Sittler, *Essays on Nature and Grace* (Philadelphia: Fortress, 1972); John B. Cobb Jr., *Is It Too*

the "new heavens and a new earth" has profound implications for environmental concerns, this study does not purport to be a "theology of nature." Such a systematic elaboration is better left to those more qualified in that field of study. Further, although the new theology of nature is a "child" of creation theology and therefore has many of the same theological interests, it nevertheless represents an enlargement and further refinement of those concerns normally considered under the rubric of "creation theology." According to Stewart, it centers upon the ecological motif; is "methodologically and substantially" more concerned about the relation between science and religion; and is directed by the attempt to clarify the nature of the "subhuman" creation and its relationship to humanity and deity.[16] Inasmuch as theology of nature is governed in part by the attempt to clarify the nature and significance of the nonhuman creation there will be certain affinities.

This brief caveat presents the opportunity to address additional related issues. This investigation assumes the importance of creation or the material order *in its own right*. This statement attempts to clarify the focus of the discussion regarding the physical creation apart from humanity. When this study refers to the "material, created order," or "natural order" it is with the realization that the term "nature" might serve appropriately in this regard; it has in the past.[17] However, the ambiguity of the term as it has developed within the discipline of theology and philosophy and its resultant conceptual baggage warns against using the term indiscriminately. As Kaufman observes, in some cases the terms "nature" and "natural" carry entire traditions of

---

Late? A Theology of Ecology (Beverly Hills, CA: Bruce, 1972); H. Paul Santmire, *Brother Earth: Nature, God and Ecology in Time of Crisis* (Beverly Hills, CA: Bruce, 1970); idem, *Travail of Nature*; George S. Hendry, *Theology of Nature* (Philadelphia: Westminster, 1980); Claude Y. Stewart Jr., *Nature in Grace: A Study in the Theology of Nature*, NABPR Dissertation Series, no. 3 (Macon, GA: Mercer University, 1983); Richard Cartwright Austin, *Hope for the Land: Nature in the Bible*, ETB, no. 3 (Atlanta: John Knox, 1988).

[16]Stewart, *Nature in Grace*, 14-15.

[17]Note the section on "God and Nature," in H. Wheeler Robinson, *Inspiration and Revelation in the Old Testament* (Oxford: Clarendon, 1946), 1-48.

meaning and interpretations.[18] Nature is often used in modern discussions to denote that which is "contrasted with that made by human contrivance" or nature *versus* human history and culture. Thus, humanity and nature stand in stark polarity.[19] "Nature" is further used to mean the "totality of all powers and processes conceived as a systematic whole." These two meanings especially reflect the vagueness which the term engenders.[20] Does "nature" include or exclude humanity? What is God's relationship to nature within this conceptual matrix? The term "nature" thus raises two vital issues. First, the term conceals an implicit metaphysic concerning the referent which provides the meaning of ultimate reality--nature as an infinite and self-determinative system inclusive of deity or God the creator and sustainer of all things both natural and human. Nature understood in the all-inclusive sense leaves no room for the idea of God as the independent creator. Extreme care is required, on the one hand, to affirm the intrinsic value of creation, but on the other, to avoid slipping into a linguistic or even an expressed conception of naturalism.[21] This study thus endeavors to use such terms as "creation," "created order," "physical or material order," "natural order," and the like to identify the nonhuman creation as the focus of the study. This recognizes, of course, that it is all but impossible to separate humankind from creation as the discussion below reveals. Significantly, the avoidance of the term

---

[18]Gordan D. Kaufman lists ten often confusing arrays of uses among them: the contrast of the natural with the artificial; the contrast of nature with grace; the view of nature (as the totality of the nonhuman) in contrast with history or culture; the contrast between natural theology and revealed theology. "A Problem for Theology: The Concept of Nature," *HTR* 56 (July 1972): 339-40.

[19]Ibid. It has been argued that the Christian doctrine of creation with its monarchial model effectively separated God from nature and moreover distanced humanity leading to a domineering and exploitative attitude toward the natural world. For the classic statement of this view see Lynn White Jr., "The Historical Roots of Our Ecological Crisis," *Science* 10 (March 1967): 1203-1207. White called for a return to the Franciscan view.

[20]Kaufman, "Nature," 345. Stewart's analysis of the use of the term among contemporary writers illustrates the vexing problem. *Nature in Grace*, 238-44.

[21]Kaufman, "Nature," 342-48. See also *EncR*, s.v. "Naturalism," 10.314-18 by Jeffery Stout.

"nature" attempts not only to eschew the abstruseness of the concept as it is used in contemporary writings, but rejects any implicit ascription of ultimate value to nature apart from God. The fundamental axis for the created order in the biblical and apocalyptic material is found not within the world itself as an autonomous operation but in its relationship to God as the creative ground and reason for its existence and continuance. Nature therefore can never be conceived as the "ultimate."[22]

Second, the concern is raised whether it is possible to address nature apart from humankind in biblical thought. Further, does the unique interrelatedness of humanity and nature lessen the importance of the created order? It will become clear that from a biblical perspective the false dichotomy of some "nature theologies" between nature and humanity's existence and history cannot be maintained. Certainly, the motive for this distinction is commendable. It attempts to assuage the suffering of nature conceived in terms of the context and instrument of humankind which robs the world of its inherent significance.[23] The scriptures, however, present humanity as both a *part of* and *apart from* creation. Humanity, while clearly distinguished from the rest of creation as made in the image of God, is nevertheless indissolubly related to the created order. While *methodologically* the physical order may be addressed separately, it is *ontologically* impossible to extricate their relationship. This

---

[22]The absence of an OT equivalent to the modern concept of nature or the Greek idea of φύσις does not indicate a disinterest in the created order. It is, however, clear that the Hebrews' concept of "nature" in contrast to the Greek affirmed the creation as contingent and dependent upon the creator. As Robinson states, "The only way to render this idea [nature] into Hebrew would be to say 'God'." *Inspiration and Revelation*, 1. The difference lies in the way in which the Hebrews and moderns theorize about the natural world. See J. W. Rogerson "The Old Testament View of Nature: Some Preliminary Questions," in *Instruction and Interpretation: Studies in the Hebrew Language, Palestinian Archaeology and Biblical Exegesis* (Leiden: E. J. Brill, 1979), 73. However, cf. Gerhard von Rad, *Old Testament Theology*, trans. D. M. G. Stalker (New York: Harper & Bros., 1962) 1:152.

[23]John Macquarrie rejects this monarchial view of creation in favor of an "organic" model that affirms humanity's kinship with and responsibility for the created order. "Creation and Environment," *ExpTim* 83 (October 1971): 4-9.

understanding actually elevates the status of creation. The relation of humanity and nature derives not only from the original creative event in which humankind (אדם) was fashioned from the dust of the earth (אדמה), but as this study contends, the importance of the created order arises also from the concept of redemption. Both are the objects of God's concern and both are responsive to his redeeming activity. Moreover, the history of humanity and nature not only moves toward the same salvific end, but that goal is interrelated. This relationship therefore makes it appropriate to speak of nature's redemption as well as that of humankind. Cross avers:

> Nature is no more an "it" than is God or Adam. Nature, while dethroned from divine rank, is still "Thou." The creation, created "good," falls into decay, sterility, wilderness, cursed by God. The earth is cursed for the sake of one of its natural creatures. The human spirit corrupts nature, and man is one with nature. Humankind belongs wholly to the realm of nature, mortal. His attempt to become a god, to transcend the insecurity of mortal flesh, is his primal sin. He is not half-god, half-animal. His soul contains no spark of the divine. He is an animal, a stately animal, theomorphic indeed, but he cannot free himself now or in the Beyond from nature. In him nature is an actor in the drama of salvation, and also apart from him nature is an actor, fleeing the divine wrath, transfigured by the divine . . . glory, redeemed insofar as man is redeemed, damned insofar as humanity is damned.[24]

The environmental crisis often has been adduced as an incentive for the reconsideration of creation, and this is no doubt true in many instances. Additionally, it will be noted that the revival of apocalyptic also has contributed to this renewed interest in the natural order in biblical studies. At first glance one may not realize the relationship between creation and apocalyptic. However, besides sharing the same lackluster existence in theology, the two important themes are related. As the following

---

[24]Cross, "The Redemption of Nature," 94-95. See the comments of Richard Bauckham, "First Steps to a Theology of Nature," *EvQ* 58 (July 1986): 229-44.

chapter reveals, apocalyptic thought with its belief in God's *universal* redemptive scope has provided a much needed opportunity for creation to escape the shadow of the anthropocentrism so evident in biblical studies.

CHAPTER I
SURVEYING THE TERRAIN:
CREATION AND APOCALYPTIC

Introduction

The created order often has been relegated to a subsidiary role in biblical interpretation. This in turn has precipitated a neglect of the eschatological aspects of creation and therefore fostered an imbalance of soteriological and cosmic concerns. A review of the traditional approach in OT and NT studies will permit a better conceptualization of the matters pertinent to this inquiry. In addition, two issues require attention before embarking upon the study proper: the meaning of "apocalyptic" and the interpretation of language and imagery in apocalyptic literature.

Creation and Redemption in Retrospect[1]

Creation in Old Testament Studies

Although most OT theologies include a discussion of creation, interest in the created order has been overshadowed in OT studies primarily due to an overemphasis upon history. The biblical theology movement with its insistence upon God's revelation in history left little room for God's action in the world or

---

[1]The division of the following discussion is arbitrary and does not intend to suggest a strict compartmentalization. The writers in both the OT and NT fields were mutually affective with regard to the concept of creation.

cosmos. This perspective further entrenched biblical faith in the past and effectively ignored the future.[2] In addition, the relative silence concerning creation in the earliest biblical traditions and the late dating of the Genesis 1 account of creation contributed to the understanding that "creation faith"[3] or a clearly professed belief in God as creator was an historically late and a theologically subsidiary doctrine to that of salvation faith.

This *soteriological* understanding of creation in the OT received its primary impetus from Gerhard von Rad's 1936 epoch-making article, and subsequent theologies were written in the shadow of his contentions. Von Rad argued that the doctrine of creation was secondary in Israel's faith both in sequence and significance. When a clearly articulated confession of God as creator fully emerged during the period of Second Isaiah it served the interests of soteriological matters rather than as an independent doctrine.[4] The divine redemptive event of the Exodus was therefore the pivotal touchstone by which Israel *deductively* regarded God as the sovereign creator of all. Israel worshipped the *God who acts* while creation served only as a handmaiden to history.[5] Even the creation accounts of Genesis played a sup-

---

[2] See *IDBSup*, s.v. "Revelation in History," by James Barr, 746-49.

[3] The term "creation faith" is an unfortunate and moreover a theologically loaded term suggesting a well defined and articulated doctrine. The OT *and* NT "doctrine" of creation was more assumed than argued.

[4] Gerhard von Rad, "The Theological Problem of the Old Testament Doctrine of Creation," in *The Problem of the Hexateuch and Other Essays*, trans. E. W. Trueman Dicken (New York: McGraw Hill, 1966), 131-43. [Originally published as "Das theologische Problem des alttestamentlichen Schöpfungsglaubens," in *Werden und Wesen des Alten Testaments*, BZAW, no. 66 (Berlin: Topelmann, 1936)]. Von Rad later acknowledged the existence of older passages reflecting a belief in God as creator but insisted that Israel's faith was exclusively a religion of salvation as evidenced in the earliest credal confessions (Deut. 6.20-24; 26.5b-9; Josh. 24.2b-13). *Theology*, 1:138-39. However, see Th. C. Vriezen who asserts that these credos may in reality be a product of a much later period. *An Outline of Old Testament Theology*, 2d ed. rev. (Newton, MA: Branford, 1970), 295-96.

[5] See G. Ernest Wright, *God Who Acts: Biblical Theology as Recital*, SBT (London: SCM, 1952), 42-43. "The movement in the OT is not from creation to history but *vice versa*. It is not that the Creator is Yahweh but rather Yahweh, the God of Israel, is Creator." *TDNT*, s.v. "Κτίζω," by Werner Foester, 3.1005.

porting role to history. Their place and purpose served merely to accentuate salvation history.[6] Such was and often is the understanding with regard to creation in OT theology.[7] Although it was an important theme, the creation of Israel rather than the creation and maintenance of the world was determinative in Israel's relationship with God.

It is not that this approach erred; rather, the "revelation in history" emphasis was too narrow and thus presented an imbalanced view of the OT concept of creation. It is well known that OT theologies have been notoriously deficient in providing an inclusive approach which adequately addresses the diversity of OT traditions.[8] In fact, the inability of any particular leitmotif in OT theology to embrace the variety and richness of the OT has led to the neglect of many important themes especially wisdom which in biblical thought lies in close connection to creation.[9]

Although some of the OT theologians from the "salvation history" school appeared to recognize that creation had been unjustly overshadowed,[10] the environmental crisis particularly

---

[6]von Rad, *Theology*, 1:138-39; Walther Eichrodt, *Theology of the Old Testament*, trans. J. A. Baker, OTL (London: SCM, 1961-67), 1:41-43, 2:100-101.

[7]Walther Zimmerli, *Old Testament Theology in Outline*, trans. David E. Green (Atlanta: John Knox, 1978), 32-33.

[8]Gerhard F. Hasel, *Old Testament Theology: Basic Issues in the Current Debate*, rev. ed. (Grand Rapids: Eerdmans, 1975), 41-96. The diversity of traditions in OT thought is reflected in the prominent role given to history in the Mosaic covenant tradition while creation receives primary emphasis from the Davidic royal theologians. Bernhard W. Anderson, "Mythopoeic and Theological Dimensions of Biblical Creation Faith," in *Creation in the Old Testament*, ed. Bernhard W. Anderson, IRT, no. 6 (Philadelphia: Fortress, 1984), 3-11. Cf. von Rad, *Theology*, 1:139.

[9]Wisdom and creation often have been treated as the proverbial stepchildren of OT theology. Cf. von Rad, *Theology*, 1:139. However, see Hans-Jürgen Hermission, "Observations on the Creation Theology in Wisdom," in *Creation in the Old Testament*, ed. Bernhard W. Anderson, IRT, no. 6 (Philadelphia: Fortress, 1984), 118-34.

[10]Edmond Jacob reacted against Barth's view that creation is secondary to the covenant. He boldly announced that "the first covenant is possible only within a cosmic framework." *Theology of the Old Testament*, trans. Arthur W. Heathcote and Philip J. Allcock (New York: Harper & Bros., 1958), 136-38. Cf. Bernhard W. Anderson, *Creation Versus Chaos: The Reinterpretation of Mythical Symbolism in the Bible* (New York: Association, 1967), 51-52.

encouraged a re-evaluation of the imbalance of this emphasis. Accordingly, von Rad in a 1964 article observed that the OT concept of nature actually had never been addressed. He further admitted, "if I am right, we are nowadays in serious danger of looking at the theological problem of the Old Testament far too much from the one sided standpoint of an historically conditioned theology."[11] Still others attempted to *redeem* creation in OT theology by asserting that redemption and creation belong together "as the obverse and reverse of the same theological coin."[12] This perspective, which is undeniable in some texts and far more desirable than the alternative, still lessens the importance of the created order in its own right since it implies a necessary connection with Israel's history for its ultimate value. The relevance of the creation will continue to be ignored and considered as possessing little inherent value as long as it is esteemed primarily as the realm of Israel's existence and salvation.

The recent writings of Goldingay, Steck, Knierim, Hayes, and others have made significant advances in stressing the importance of creation in the faith of Israel.[13] Knierim in particular views God's relationship to and presence in the cosmic order as a more inclusive approach to Israel's apprehension of God in history and creation. A re-reading of the OT texts reveals that history was not the only mode of God's revelation to Israel nor was it the only manner in which Israel comprehended the world.

---

[11]Gerhard von Rad, "Some Aspects of the Old Testament World-View," in *The Problem of the Hexateuch and Other Essays*, trans. E. W. Trueman Dicken (New York: McGraw Hill, 1966), 144-45. See the comments of John Goldingay, *Theological Diversity and the Authority of the Old Testament* (Grand Rapids: Eerdmans, 1987), 202-4.

[12]Anderson, "Creation Faith," 6. Cf. Claus Westermann, *Blessing: In the Bible and the Life of the Church*, trans. Keith Crim (Philadelphia: Fortress, 1978), 4.

[13]Goldingay, *Theological Diversity*, 200-239; Odil H. Steck, *World and Environment*, BES (Nashville: Abingdon, 1980); idem, *Der Schöpfungsbericht der Priesterschrift*, FRLANT, no. 15 (Göttingen: Vandenhoeck und Ruprecht, 1975); Rolf Knierim, "Cosmos and History in Israel's Theology," *BT* 3 (June 1981): 59-123; John H. Hayes and Frederick Prussner, *Old Testament Theology: Its History and Development* (Atlanta: John Knox, 1985), 273-76. Note also the earlier contributions of H. H. Schmid, George M. Landes, and Hermission in *Creation in the Old Testament*, ed. Bernhard W. Anderson, IRT, no. 6 (Philadelphia: Fortress, 1984).

Knierim asserts that the creation is the presupposition and ground of history.

> Indeed, the cosmic cyclic structure of the earth and of human existence associated with it, existed before the unfolding of human history. And insofar as it does exist with human history it is the indispensable presupposition and the basis for human history. It can continue to exist without human history, but human history cannot exist without it. . . .[14]

While some may regard this as an overstatement, this approach nevertheless represents an advance over the previous understanding of the created order in OT studies and encourages a re-evaluation of the theological function of creation in its various literary contexts. It is evident that creation is not always subordinated to soteriological interests.[15] Even in the primeval material where generally it is accepted that creation is linked with history one must wonder whether the detailed description of the origin and maintenance of the world is merely for ornamental purposes.

The increasing recognition of an overemphasis on history has provided an opportunity to address other long neglected OT traditions particularly as they relate to the natural world. Brueggemann, for example, sees the land as a central if not *the* central theme in the OT. He observes that the "preoccupation with existentialist *decisions* and transforming *events* has distracted us from seeing that this God is committed to this land and that his promise for his people is always his land."[16] One must also note the revival of interest in apocalyptic which, no doubt due to von Rad's negative assessment. previously was hindered from bringing to OT studies important motifs especially its cosmic scope.[17] This renewed emphasis upon creation also has

---

[14]Knierim, "Cosmos and History," 60, 83.

[15]See H. H. Schmid, "Creation, Righteousness, and Salvation: 'Creation Theology' as the Broad Horizon of Biblical Theology," in *Creation in the Old Testament*, ed. Bernhard W. Anderson, IRT, no. 6 (Philadelphia: Fortress, 1984), 112-17.

[16]Walter Brueggemann, *The Land: Place as Gift, Promise, and Challenge in Biblical Faith*, OBT (Philadelphia: Fortress, 1977), 6.

[17]von Rad, *Theology*, 2:301-15.

provided a consideration of the eschatological aspects of the material order. Those passages especially in the message of Isaiah which affirm the transformation of nature concomitantly with the new Exodus traditionally have been interpreted as metaphors serving only to heighten the significance of Israel's *historical* restoration. Once again creation stands in the shadow of history. Eschatology in the OT has tended to focus almost exclusively upon the nationalistic interests of Israel.[18] Yet the OT understanding of creation is directly related to eschatology. Passages, such as Isaiah 65, while still nationalistic in orientation nevertheless demonstrate a concern and hope for the created order.

Creation in New Testament Studies

NT studies have not completely disregarded the theme of creation, but the anthropocentric-soteriological preoccupation all but eclipsed any interest in the created order in itself. Barth's massive work on the doctrine of creation had far reaching implications for Protestant theology in further entrenching an already prevailing anthropocentrism. Barth's aversion to natural theology and his insistence that creation is known only through the word, Jesus Christ,[19] relegated the natural world to the "theatre of the history of the covenant of grace."[20] God's work in the world has significance only as it exists for the redemptive relation between God, Jesus Christ, and his people.[21] The Christian doctrine of creation therefore, according to Barth, "means anthropology--the doctrine of man." In fact, scripture has absolutely no interest in the "cosmos" since it is concerned only

---

[18]A notable exception is Donald E. Gowan, *Eschatology in the Old Testament* (Philadelphia: Fortress, 1986). Gowan observes that while some interest has been rekindled with regard to creation theology little has been done with the eschatological aspects of the biblical theology of nature (108).

[19]Karl Barth, *Church Dogmatics*, trans. G. W. Bromiley, ed. G. W. Bromiley and T. F. Torrance (Edinburgh: T. & T. Clark, 1975), 3:1,28. Barth's doctrine of creation and his influence in theology is discussed by Santmire, *Travail of Nature*, 145-55.

[20]Barth, *Church Dogmatics*, 3:1,44.

[21]Ibid., 2:2,7-8.

with God and humanity.[22] Paul's remarks about the longing of creation in Rom. 8.18-21 are incidental to the main theme of the redemption of humanity.[23]

Interestingly, Barth found an unwitting ally in the otherwise diametrically opposed view of Bultmann--at least as his view impacted the importance of creation.[24] The hermeneutic of Bultmann (and his "school") in reducing faith's affirmation about Christ to purely existential categories as Barth had reduced them to anthropology summarily excluded the creation from consideration. What is important to Bultmann is that in the *kerygma* God "acts on me, speaks to me, here and now" and initiates a new self-realization.[25] Any statement concerning God must therefore relate to the existential relation between God and humanity. All other comments about God's action in the cosmos are illegitimate.[26] Furthermore, NT eschatology is not concerned about the future of the world. It is interested only in God's future, that is, an openness and preparedness for what the future may bring. Therefore, for Bultmann the future is *now*. The world has already passed away for the one who has been made new in Christ.[27]

Biblical theology affirmed that the early church did not espouse a doctrine of creation. The NT conception of creation like that of the OT faith was historically oriented and incorporated only at a later period into an already basic and vital concept of historic redemption in Christ. Creation therefore received its value in its relation to redemption. According to Cullmann, the

---

[22]Ibid., 3:2,4-19.

[23]Karl Barth, *The Epistle to the Romans*, trans. Edwyn C. Hoskyns (London: Oxford University, 1957), 306-10.

[24]H. Paul Santmire, "Toward a New Theology of Nature," *Dialog* 25 (Winter 1986): 44.

[25]Rudolf Bultmann, *Jesus Christ and Mythology* (New York: Scribner, 1958), 64.

[26]Ibid., 69, 83-85. Of course Bultmann did not share the mythological view of the eschatological cosmic drama of redemption as depicted in the NT. Such references were to be demythologized into existential meaning (14-21). See also, idem, "The New Testament and Mythology," in *Kerygma and Myth: A Theological Debate*, ed. Hans Werner Bartsch (New York: Harper & Bros., 1961), 1:1-15.

[27]Bultmann, *Mythology*, 31-32; idem, "NT and Mythology," 31-33.

early confessions of the church

> Teach us quite clearly that the first Christians did not derive their faith in Christ from their faith in God the Father, the Creator, but that on the contrary they also regarded their faith in the Creator entirely in the light of the Christocentric line of salvation. They teach us that the first Christians fitted even their faith in divine creation into the entire process of redemptive history.[28]

Cullmann, unlike Bultmann, did not discount the entire eschatological future especially with regards to the creation. He viewed redemptive history as unfolding progressively from creation to consummation. The movement is twofold: the many to the one, that is, Jesus Christ, and from the one to the many, the people of God and ultimately to the redeemed new heavens and new earth.[29] The redemptive work of Christ is yet to be fully realized, and moreover it includes the created order. "Just as the decision in Jesus Christ has already occurred upon the earth, so even more must the completion take place precisely upon earth."[30] This approach brings the concept of cosmic renewal into close connection with redemptive history. However, while Cullmann was aware of the importance of creation as it relates to the cosmic lordship of Christ, future interests are diminished as eschatology gives way to Christology since the most significant happening in history already has occurred--Christ as the *Mitte* or decisive event of history.[31]

In a small work (the title is suggestive), Moule reflects what has been the general consensus of NT scholarship regarding the

---

[28]Oscar Cullmann, *Christ and Time: The Primitive Christian Conception of Time and History*, rev. ed., trans. Floyd V. Filson (Philadelphia: Westminster, 1964), 113. Aware of the danger of such an imbalance, Cullmann observes that the "confession 'Kyrios Christos,' or 'Christ rules as Lord,' confirms the view that, paradoxical as it may seem, the concentration upon redemptive history signifies the very opposite of indifference toward the world process." (178).

[29]Ibid., 116-17.

[30]Ibid., 139-42.

[31]Ibid. "The norm is no longer that which is to come; it is He who has already come. Eschatology is not put aside, but is dethroned. . . ."

created order. Although Moule urges environmental consciousness upon Christians as God's responsible stewards or vice-
regents within this world, he states unequivocally that the "nonhuman nature has no independent rights." Its significance lies
only in its relation to humankind.[32] Once again as in the OT
discussion historical and anthropological concerns have prevailed
serving to assign the created order to a secondary position. Even
when this injustice has been observed and confronted it has been
addressed with an anthropocentric focus. Lampe, for example,
argues that Paul's statement about the groan of the creation is incidental to the main theme of God's work in humanity's salvation.
The subject is introduced merely as a "cosmic extension or pro-
jection of the conscious expectation of humanity."[33] Notably, John
Gibbs has attempted to address the imbalance of the twin motifs
of creation and redemption throughout Paul's writings although
his intention was not to explicate the cosmic dimensions of God's
redemptive purpose.[34]

The renewed appreciation for apocalyptic has provided a
promising avenue for adequately addressing the individual and
universal aspects of God's redemptive work. Apocalyptic, long
neglected because of its primitive, bizarre, and enigmatic worldview, was all but abandoned by the church and scholarship and
left to the aberrant heretical sects and in recent times to extrem-
ists who revel in the apocalyptists' speculations about the end
times. In theology existential categories became preeminent as
apocalyptic myth was regarded as merely a husk to be stripped
away or demythologized. Eschatological interests yielded to
Christology as the promise of the new heavens and new earth

---

[32]C. F. D. Moule, *Man and Nature in the New Testament* (London:
Athlone, 1964), 4-5.

[33]G. W. H. Lampe, "The New Testament Doctrine of 'Ktisis,'" *SJTh* 17
(December 1964): 456-57; W. Dantine, "Creation and Redemption: An
Attempt at a Theological Interpretation in the Light of the Contemporary
Understanding of the World," *SJTh* 18 (June 1965): 129-47.

[34]John G. Gibbs, *Creation and Redemption: A Study in Pauline Theology* (Leiden: E. J. Brill, 1971), 2. However, see his discussion of "The Cosmic Scope of Redemption According to Paul," *Biblica* 56/1 (1975): 13-29.
Gibbs comments that "Christ's cosmic work was no less essential to Paul's
christology than Christ's redemptive work." Idem, "Pauline Cosmic Christology and Ecological Crisis," *JBL* 90 (December 1971): 476.

were spiritualized.[35]   The pivotal essay of Käsemann with his contention that "apocalyptic was the mother of all Christian theology" helped rescue the writings from their shadowy existence and once again brought them to bear on the interpretation of the NT.[36]   This renaissance also has encouraged interest in the long neglected subject of creation since cosmic renewal is an important theme in apocalyptic writings.

In theology, Moltmann's apocalyptic emphasis has stressed the importance of creation from the perspective of eschatology. According to Moltmann, not only does this approach affirm the importance of the present created order, but apocalyptic rescues theological eschatology from an exclusively individual focus.[37] "Ecological theology" has likewise noted the contribution of apocalyptic.   Santmire observes that the implications of the motif of the new heavens and new earth or cosmic renewal offers great promise in preserving the importance of the created order.   Further, he suggests that this motif may even have the same kind of centrality in NT theology as the land has in OT theology.[38]

Moreover, in biblical studies Beker contends that apocalyptic is not a "peripheral curiosity" in Paul.   It is rather the "central climate and focus of his thought" like that of other early Christian writers.   While the apocalyptic motifs were modified by Paul's understanding of the Christ event, the intensity of future expectation remains.   Indeed, the resurrection for Paul is

---

[35]See Berkouwer, *Return of Christ*, 295-96.   Zachary Hayes, e.g., sees the language about the new heavens and new earth as symbolic of the believer's presence with Christ in eternity.   *What Are They Saying About Creation?* (New York: Paulist, 1980), 29-30.   Cf. the comments of J. Christiaan Beker. *Paul the Apostle: The Triumph of God in Life and Thought* (Philadelphia: Fortress, 1984), 145-47; idem, *Paul's Apocalyptic Gospel: The Coming Triumph of God* (Philadelphia: Fortress, 1982).

[36]Ernst Käsemann, "The Beginnings of Christian Theology," in *New Testament Questions of Today* trans. W. J. Montague, SBT, no. 41 (Philadelphia: Fortress, 1969), 82-107.   Klaus Koch chronicles the renaissance of apocalyptic in *The Rediscovery of Apocalyptic*, trans. Margaret Kohl (Naperville. IL: Allenson, 1970).

[37]Jürgen Moltmann, "Creation and Redemption," in *Creation, Christ and Culture*, ed. Richard W. A. Mckinney (Edinburgh: T. & T. Clark, 1976), 120; idem, *Theology of Hope* (New York: Harper & Row, 1965), 137-38.

[38]Santmire. "New Theology of Nature," 48.   Santmire also notes the contribution of Beker.

both promise and token of the ultimate apocalyptic triumph of God over his creation. This perspective balances individual and cosmic concerns.

> Anthropology becomes disoriented if it is not viewed within the coordinates of the "objective" categories of the Christ event and the created order. The resurrection of Christ and the final resurrection of the dead are crucial events, not because they are the guarantee of eternal personal survival but because they express the inner connection of the salvation of the created order with the final triumph of God. For the resurrection of the dead signals the liberation of the created order "to the freedom of the glory of the children of God" (Rom. 8:21).[39]

The full realization of the believer's new life in Christ is not limited to personal salvation in heaven. It also includes the universal perspective so much a part of apocalyptic. In fact, it can be asserted confidently that without the worldview of apocalyptic redemption collapses into anthropology and effectively nullifies the created order. The esoteric character and grotesque imagery of apocalyptic writings must not obscure the central theme so applicable to the present era, namely, the cosmic reach of God's redemptive purpose. Any other approach seriously truncates the salvific work of Christ.

Defining "Apocalyptic"

The present study endeavors to examine the worldview of apocalyptic with regard to creation and redemption or cosmic hope. The problem immediately arises concerning the meaning of the term "apocalyptic." The Hebrew and Christian canon contains only two apocalyptic writings: Daniel and the Revelation of John.[40] The term "apocalyptic" is derived from the first

---

[39]Beker, *Paul the Apostle*, 144, 55. Cf. the comments of George S. Hendry, "Faith and the Cosmos," *PSB*, n.s. 10 (July 1989): 90.

[40]While the dating and unity of Daniel remains unsettled, the apocalyptic nature of Daniel 7-12 is evident. John E. Goldingay, *Daniel*, WBC (Dallas: Word, 1989), 320-22. Cf. the discussion of J. C. Whitcomb, *NBD*, s.v. "Daniel," 263-64.

word in the opening verse of the NT book of Revelation (Ἀποκάλυψις Ἰησοῦ Χριστοῦ). Lücke's work in the early nineteenth century extended the term to classify other writings which shared the same features with the NT apocalypse, that is, those purporting to be secret divine disclosures about the future salvation and judgment of humanity and the world.[41]

The variety of definitions that have been offered for this group of writings reflects the diversity of views as to what actually constitutes an apocalyptic text.[42] The problem is compounded since with the exception of Revelation the ancient writers did not define or otherwise characterize the writings presently considered as apocalypses. At issue is whether to define apocalyptic writings according to literary characteristics or content. Russell, following Lindblom, suggests certain features which distinguish apocalyptic: transcendentalism, mythology, a cosmological survey, historical pessimism, dualism, division of time into periods, the two ages, numerology, pseudoecstasy, false claims to inspiration, pseudonymous authorship, and esoterism. He also adds the concepts of the unity of history, a view of cosmic history which treats heaven and earth, primordiality with its revelation concerning creation and the fall of men and angels, angelic powers as the source of evil in the world, conflict of light and darkness, good and evil, God and Satan, the Son of Man, life after death, and an emphasis on individual eschatology.[43] Although Russell recognizes the composite nature of apocalypses, his approach confuses the issue of concept and form. Koch, more sensitive to this, delineates six literary features to which he

---

[41]Friedrich Lücke, *Versuch einer vollständingen Einleitung in die Offenbarung Johannis und in die gesamte apokalyptische Literatur* (Bonn: Weber, 1832). The term "Apocalypse" appears in the Muratorian Canon ca. AD 200 and in the title of 2 Baruch although its antiquity in the latter is questionable. Philip Vielhauer, "Apocalypses and Related Subjects," in *New Testament Apocrypha*, ed. E. Hennecke and W. Schneemelcher (Philadelphia: Westminster, 1965), 2:581-600. Cf. Morton Smith, "On the History of ΑΠΟΚΑΛΥΠΤΩ and ΑΠΟΚΑΛΥΨΙΣ," in *Apocalypticism in the Mediterranean World and the Near East*, ed. David Helholm (Tübingen: Mohr, 1983), 9-20

[42]See Margaret Barker, "Slippery Words: Apocalyptic," *ExpTim* 89 (July 1978): 324-29.

[43]Russell, *Jewish Apocalyptic*, 105.

adds eight conceptual and eschatological motifs.[44]

In an attempt to clarify the discussion, Hanson suggests that the term "apocalyptic" should be avoided altogether in favor of the more specific terminology of "apocalypse," "apocalyptic eschatology," and "apocalypticism." He distinguishes an apocalypse as a literary genre from apocalyptic eschatology which is a particular form of eschatological belief that may or may not appear in various literary forms. Additionally, apocalypticism is a form of religious faith or idealogy that arises in certain social settings in which apocalyptic eschatology plays a prominent role. Hanson endeavors to point out that these three do not always coincide exactly. One writing may reflect revelatory visions and not envision a particular apocalyptic eschatology. He does appropriately permit the use of the term "apocalyptic" to denote the general phenomenon and perspective characteristic of apocalypses.[45]

A systematic analysis of the form and content of all the literature typically regarded as "apocalyptic" persuaded the participants of the Society of Biblical Literature Genres Project to formulate the following working definition:

---

[44]Koch, *The Rediscovery of Apocalyptic*, 28-32. See also the discussions of Paul D. Hanson, "Apocalyptic Literature," in *The Hebrew Bible and Its Modern Interpreters*, SBLBMI, ed. Douglas M. Knight and Gene M. Tucker (Philadelphia: Fortress, 1985), 465-88 and E. P. Sanders, "The Genre of Palestinian Jewish Apocalypses," in *Apocalypticism in the Mediterranean World and the Near East*, ed. David Helholm (Tübingen: Mohr, 1983), 447-59.

[45]*IDBSup*, s.v. "Apocalypticism," by Paul D. Hanson, 29-30; idem, *Dawn of Apocalyptic*, 10-12. Also noteworthy is Hanson's distinction between prophetic and apocalyptic eschatology. Apocalyptic eschatology like that of the prophets is a religious perspective which views the future as the context of God's saving and judging activity. Apocalyptic eschatology, however, is distinguished in its view of God's future salvific works outside the political structures and historical events and a deliverance out of the present age into a new transformed order. However, it must not be assumed that the apocalypses present a consistent eschatology. One may reflect an emphasis on the judgment of individuals without reference to the end of history. All expect some kind of retribution beyond the bounds of this history. See John J. Collins, "Apocalyptic Eschatology as the Transcendence of Death," in *Visionaries and Their Apocalypses*, ed. Paul D. Hanson (Philadelphia: Fortress, 1983), 61-84; idem, *The Apocalyptic Imagination: An Introduction to the Jewish Matrix of Christianity* (New York: Crossroad, 1984), 9.

"Apocalypse" is a genre of revelatory literature with a narrative framework, in which a revelation is mediated by an otherworldly being to a human recipient, disclosing a transcendent reality which is both temporal, insofar as it envisages eschatological salvation, and spatial insofar as it involves another, supernatural world.[46]

This view takes into consideration both the manner of the revelation as well as the content of what is revealed. It does not, however, address the sociological aspects of apocalyptic. The narrative framework provides the manner of revelation and is usually mediated through visions and other-worldly journeys supplemented by discourse or dialogue. This revelatory element includes a spatial axis that involves other-worldly journeys in which the supernatural world and the activities of supernatural beings are disclosed. The temporal aspect envisages history and individual and cosmic eschatological salvation. The identification of a common core of elements provides an adequate basis of understanding without ignoring those works which are apocalyptic in perspective or "tone" but cannot be designated as apocalypses.[47] This study thus uses the term "apocalypse" to designate a distinct literary genre and "apocalyptic" to denote those

---

[46]John J. Collins, "Introduction: Towards the Morphology of a Genre," in *Apocalypse: The Morphology of a Genre*, ed. John J. Collins, Semeia, no. 14 (Missoula, MT: Scholars, 1979), 9. Collins identifies fifteen Jewish apocalypses dating from 250 BC to AD 150: Daniel 7-12; 1 Enoch consisting of the Book of the Watchers (chs. 1-36), the Similitudes (chs. 37-71), the Heavenly Luminaries or Astronomical Book (chs. 72-82), the Animal Apocalypse (chs. 83-90), and the Apocalypse of Weeks (chs. 91-108); Apocalypse of Abraham; 2 Enoch; Jubilees 23; 2 and 3 Baruch; 4 Ezra; Testament of Levi 2-5; Testament of Abraham 10-15, and the Apocalypse of Zephaniah (28).

[47]Ibid., 5-10. James H. Charlesworth believes that Collins goes too far in his attempt to define a common core of constant features. Since apocalyptic writings reflect a varied character, he insists that it is the "tone" that designates a writing as an apocalypse. "The Apocalypse of John--Its Theological Impact on Subsequent Apocalypses," in *The New Testament and Pseudepigrapha: A Guide to Publications with Excurses on Apocalypses*, ed. James H. Charlesworth and James R. Mueller (Metuchen, NJ: American Theological Library and Scarecrow, 1987), 23. Cf. Christopher Rowland who sees the "the disclosure of the divine secrets through direct revelation" as the fundamental quality of apocalyptic. *The Open Heaven: A Study of Apocalyptic in Judaism*

features and ideas inherent to such literature.

This understanding provides the most useful working definition and classification of apocalyptic works for the purpose of this study. It also identifies important theological and literary aspects which help determine the presence of apocalyptic motifs in other types of writings not designated as an apocalypse. Further, it is important to keep these "features" in mind in approaching the NT since the NT as a whole reflects a general apocalyptic orientation in its revelatory character as well as in its anticipation of the ultimate intervention of God through his supernatural agent to accomplish eschatological salvation on behalf of humanity and creation.

Language and Imagery in Apocalyptic

Bultmann believed that the mythical concept of the world had passed away for modern humanity. Yet he suggested perceptively that the NT biblical eschatology with its vision of the cataclysmic collapse of human and worldly structures could very well return in a new form. This was especially so in light of the advances of modern technology which had opened the way for atomic destruction and the abuse of the environment.[48] If this prospect threatened Bultmann's day, then it looms even larger in the current setting. Koch has attributed the resurgence of interest in apocalyptic to a fresh re-reading of the texts and more directly to the renewed inquiry of NT scholarship especially systematic theology.[49] While this is no doubt true particularly with the discovery of the Qumran documents, this renaissance is also due to the relevance of the language and imagery of those writings to our modern apocalyptic era.[50] The present doomsday mentality is brought into close connection with the apocalyptists

and Early Christianity (New York: Crossroad, 1982), 20. Sanders prefers the motif of reversal and restoration. "Jewish Apocalypses," 458.

[48]Bultmann, *Jesus Christ and Mythology*, 25.

[49]Koch dates the renaissance of apocalyptic in postwar systematic theology to Wolfhart Pannenberg. *Rediscovery of Apocalyptic*, 13, 101.

[50]This was the focal point made by H. H. Rowley, *The Relevance of Apocalyptic: A Study of Jewish and Christian Apocalypses from Daniel to the*

of the ancient world. People disenfranchised, persecuted, and faced with the threat of nuclear and ecological ruin are like their ancient counterparts engaged in a fierce struggle for survival. Modern humankind is indeed kindred spirits with those who are depicted by John the seer as they cry out, "How long O Lord, holy and true, until you judge the inhabitants of the earth and avenge our blood?" (Rev. 6.10). Approaching apocalyptic from an interpretive viewpoint, then, demands the goal of *relevance*.

In this regard, Bultmann's program of demythologizing was appropriate in intent. Whatever criticisms may be marshalled against his approach--and there have been many--his purpose was to communicate the language and religious values of the scriptures to the modern reader. He therefore attempted to translate the so-called mythical language of the NT into existential categories because the ancient and esoteric worldview had become incredible.[51] Certainly, Bultmann's approach erred in part due to his failure to realize that one cannot always divorce the mythological language or vehicle of meaning from the reality it represents. Myth is not the opposite of *kerygma*.[52] Bultmann was correct, however, that the language of apocalyptic must become relevant to the present experience. Two issues must be considered which will make apocalyptic intelligible and therefore better able to speak to the modern reader.

First, one must recognize the nature of apocalyptic language. This perhaps may best be illustrated by comparison. Paul's epistles are well known for their variety of expression.

Revelation, 2d ed, (New York: Association, 1963), 166-93. See also the insightful comments of D. S. Russell, *Apocalyptic: Ancient and Modern* (Philadelphia: Fortress, 1978) and Paul D. Hanson, "The Apocalyptic Consciousness," *QRev* 4 (Fall 1984): 23-39. Although there is certainly common ground between ancient and modern apocalyptic perspectives, Stephen H. Travis correctly notes that the decisive distinction is that "most modern 'apocalyptic' (so-called) is Godless, and therefore pessimistic about any possibility of 'salvation' or a new beginning." "The Value of Apocalyptic," *TynBul* 30 (1979): 56.

[51]Bultmann, "NT and Mythology," 3.

[52]James D. G. Dunn, "Demythologizing--The Problem of Myth in the New Testament," in *New Testament Interpretation: Essays on Principles and Methods*, ed. I. H. Marshall (Grand Rapids: Eerdmans, 1977), 298-300.

Each reflects carefully arranged argumentation from the volatile Galatian correspondence and the reflective Roman epistle to the poetic quality of 1 Corinthians 13. Paul's words evoke powerful and even humorous images, such as his sarcastic suggestion that the subversives who wished to circumcise the Galatian Christians might "let the knife slip" and emasculate themselves (Gal. 5.12). Apocalyptic language, as seen most notably in the canonical Apocalypse, requires a reversed hermeneutic, as it were. Certainly one is immediately aware of Paul's incisive metaphors and imagery.[53] However, the difference is not only in degree but in the manner of presentation. Generally speaking, Paul's words give rise to images. John's mental images *to a greater extent* evoke powerful words and emotions. Thus, one reads Paul's rather lengthy and careful *explanation* regarding the resurrection of the dead in 1 Cor. 15.20-58 while John *portrays* the future resurrection and God's ultimate victory with graphic kaleidoscopic images which not only inform but also involve the readers.

Apocalyptic is characterized by a mythopoeic worldview expressed through pictorial language. The language of prose proves incapable of conveying the full meaning intended by the writers. As in poetry the visionaries use picture language to reveal a depth of reality which eludes discovery by scientific inquiry.[54] The writers evince an unrestrained imagination in contrast to the OT prophets in their depiction of other-worldly journeys, heavenly warfare, ultimate judgment, the imminent defeat of chaos, and cosmic transformation. The apocalyptists' vivid symbols and images no doubt may be attributed in part to a fertile imagination. However, they had at their disposal stereotyped language and symbols much of which is traceable to the

---

[53]See especially Robert W. Funk's remarks on Paul's figurative language. *Parables and Presence: Forms of the New Testament Tradition* (Philadelphia: Fortress, 1982), 119-24.

[54]Paul Tillich observes that ultimates can be adequately expressed only in symbolic language. Like a picture or a poem figurative language functions primarily to open levels of reality which are otherwise inaccessible. "The Nature of Religious Language," in *Theology of Culture*, ed. Robert C. Kimball (New York: Oxford University, 1959), 54-67.

OT.[55] A notable characteristic is the allusions to the OT phrases or motifs which often provide depth to the meaning of the text. Moreover, the reinterpretation of earlier traditions not only adds richness but also furnishes different levels of meaning which often evades explanation by a single referent.

Central is the use of mythological language and allusions. The diverse terminology and understanding of myth has led not only to confusion concerning definition, but it has tended to equate the use of myth with that which is prescientific and therefore false.[56] Apocalyptic literature as well as the Hebrew and Christian scriptures, which are also full of imagery, metaphor, and mythical allusions, are thus often dismissed as flights of fancy and poetic embroidery having little if anything to do with reality. The present scientific mind-set accepts only the literal as value laden since it avoids all ambiguities. This empiricist posture in biblical studies is in fact the historical critical method gone to seed! Only symbols which can be decoded or reduced to objective propositions are approved as meaningful expressions of truth; all others are false. In this regard Funk is correct that the study of theology should begin with poetry because "theology seems to have gone a-whoring after the scientific flesh pots of Egypt."[57]

This leads to the second consideration regarding the function and meaningfulness of the language. Scholarship has exhibited a divided approach to interpreting apocalyptic lan-

---

[55]Russell, *Jewish Apocalyptic*, 122-27.

[56]Bultmann regarded myth in this manner, but correctly recognized its function in the language. "Myths give to the transcendent reality an immanent, this worldly objectivity. Myths give worldly objectivity to that which is unworldly." *Jesus Christ and Mythology*, 19-20. J. W. Rogerson isolates twelve different senses in which the term "myth" is used. *Myth in Old Testament Interpretation*, BZAW, no. 134 (Berlin: De Gruyter, 1974), 174-78. The understanding of Collins is appropriate for our purposes. Mythological allusions and language refer to motifs and patterns ultimately derived from the religious stories of the ancient Near East and the Greco-Roman world. *Apocalyptic Imagination,* 15.

[57]Funk, *Parables and Presence*, 111. Hence, his objection to the position that "myth that does not have literal sense has no sense" (115). See also the comments of Philip Wheelwright, *Metaphor and Reality* (Bloomington, IN: Indiana University, 1962), 38-40.

guage. On the one hand, the language has been regarded as referential or objective referring to real persons or concepts in the writers' time and in the future. Especially in Daniel and Revelation, the symbols are approached as cryptograms which may be deciphered in order to forecast the future. On the other hand, it has been argued that while the language has an informational aspect, it primarily functions to express a certain view of reality which then seeks to involve the reader in that view. Rather than serving the interests of "futurology," the purpose of the language is to influence life in the present through the values expressed in the symbolic and narrative forms.[58] Accordingly, modern interpretation of prophetic and apocalyptic language has suffered from the "either/or" mentality. One must interpret a certain passage either literally or figuratively.[59] There is no middle ground. Is there an acceptable alternative? How can one acknowledge the mythological language and imagery in such a way that affirms its meaning without slipping into pedantry? That the language of apocalyptic is not to be interpreted literally or pedantically is evident from the wide use of symbols. The writ-

---

[58]Adela Yarbro Collins, "'What the Spirit Says to the Churches': Preaching the Apocalypse," *QRev* 4 (Fall 1984): 78.

[59]Most interpreters intend the term "literal" to mean the customary or usual sense of the words or passage as intended by the author. In actual practice, however, it has often become a synonym for "letterism." Perhaps a more useful expression is the term *Peshat* which for Jewish exegetes denotes the "simple, plain sense" of the text. Three criteria are utilized which avoid the intimation of wooden literalism. One must determine whether the explanation and what follows it is logically coherent, whether it fits the context, and whether it is compatible with the grammar of the language. Yeshayahu Maori, "The Approach of Classical Jewish Exegetes to *Peshat* and *Derash* and Its Implication for the Teaching of the Bible," *Tradition* 21 (Fall 1984): 40-41. Thus one employs the rules of setting and grammar as well as that of critical reasoning and logic. One is not a slave to the word or passage but is in *dialogical communion* with the text. Note especially Uriel Simon's remark that just "labeling an interpretation *Peshat* does not determine its correctness." "The Religious Significance of *Peshat*," *Tradition* 23 (Winter 1988): 43. This is offered as a semantic convention although this writer is aware that some early Jewish exegetes often used the term in reference to the traditional and authoritative teaching of the text. See Raphael Loewe, "The 'Plain' Meaning of Scripture in Early Jewish Exegesis," in *Papers of the Institute of Jewish Studies*, ed. J. G. Weiss (Jerusalem: Magnes, 1964), 1:140-85.

ers were creative and imaginative artists acutely aware of their linguistic tools.[60] Moreover, it is difficult to believe that the readers of these writings who had constantly heard the OT read in their assemblies and who were also familiar with other apocalyptic works would fail to interpret the language in keeping with generally accepted practices of their own generation. Otherwise, the writings would have been unintelligible and their role in the community would have offered little meaning or hope. The use of figurative and metaphorical statements enabled the apocalyptists and biblical writers to open new dimensions of meaning not otherwise attainable. Figurative language has more than an ornamental or emotional value. Particularly, the use of metaphor with its semantic impertinence often provides a rich resource for the authors as they attempt to convey the transcendent. It effects a tension between the commonly understood context and the figurative and incongruous which gives rise to new information. A new level of meaning is disclosed which the literal cannot expose.[61]

    This therefore raises the issue of the meaningfulness of such picturesque statements. As mentioned previously, there are often attempts especially with regard to apocalyptic to contrast "block" or literal language with "fluid" or figurative language. The literal is regarded as factual and is contrasted with poetic. The distinction between the two types of language, however, is semantic not ontological. It concerns the *way* in which language operates and not the ontological issue of whether the object referred to has *real* existence.[62] For example, Boring argues that

---

[60]G. B. Caird presents guidelines for determining whether the author intended his statements as figurative or literal. *The Language and Imagery of the Bible* (Philadelphia: Westminster, 1980), 183-97.

[61]Paul Ricoeur, "Biblical Hermeneutics," in *Paul Ricoeur on Biblical Hermeneutics*, ed. John D. Crossan, Semeia, no. 4 (Missoula, MT: Scholars, 1975), 75-82. New meaning is achieved by the stress between the literal and metaphorical creating an absurdity which is transformed into a meaningful contradiction. This "twist" or "semantic impertinence" forces a new meaning on the word; an extension of meaning which permits it to make sense when a literal interpretation would not.

[62]Philip Wheelwright, "Semantics and Ontology," in *Essays on Metaphor*, ed. Warren Shibles (Whitewater, WI: Language, 1972), 64-65. Wheelwright distinguishes between "steno-symbols" (sometimes called "block") or those that

John's apocalyptic language is neither propositional nor pure description. His literary style stands between word and picture and functions to evoke images in the imagination.[63] The mythical language is robbed of its power if merely reduced to logical propositions. In like manner, its meaning is violated if one fails to recognize its referential value. The antithesis between literal and figurative must not become the basis of denying the reality to which it refers. Farrer declares, "there is a current and exceedingly stupid doctrine that symbol evokes emotion, and exact prose states reality. Nothing could be further from the truth: *exact prose abstracts from reality, symbol presents it*" (emphasis mine).[64] Boring comments with reference to the book of Revelation that

> The language of Revelation is not only expressive poetry, it is also referential language. It is glad to abandon any claim to describe this reality in an objectifying manner, for the reality to which it points transcends anything that can be objectively described by finite minds and language. But the content of Revelation is not just the subjective poetic outpourings of John's own religious experience. What John has to say does indeed refer to something: God's transcendent world and the ultimate goal of creation. It points to these transcendent realities in language which knows the limitation of language itself to express them. . . . It cannot fully describe or communicate them. It points--but it points to something.[65]

Therefore, John like the other apocalyptists often utilizes pictures rather than objective language. Further, the pictures themselves are not for illustrative purposes which can then be reduced to discursive or logical language. Indeed, they can stand

---

have a one to one correspondence with the object they represent and "tensive" or fluid symbols which cannot be exhausted by a single referent.

[63]M. Eugene Boring, *Revelation*, IBC (Louisville: John Knox, 1989), 54.

[64]Austin Farrer, *A Rebirth of Images: The Making of St. John's Apocalypse* (Boston: Beacon, 1963), 19-20.

[65]Boring, *Revelation*, 53. The abundance of imagery in Revelation is actually atypical of apocalyptic writings. Apocalyptic literature represents a "mixed bag" of literary and conceptual content.

alone as meaningful statements. That to which they immediately refer somtimes may be determined by historical critical analysis which then becomes the basis for interpretation; yet even this must be done with care. As noted, the multifarious nature of the language and imagery often refuses to allow one to extract a single meaning from the text in a univocal way.[66] A careful reading of apocalyptic literature reveals that the writers were not engaging in fanciful literary acrobatics. One can see fertile and imaginative minds at work wrestling with the issues at hand and attempting to give meaning to the present calamitous situation. As noted, one is often prevented from positing a chronological or logical expression of the material. Systematic presentation often yields to an apocalyptist's desire to address the immediate crisis. Logical expression is not always the primary goal of the melange of images. Indeed, the cumulative effect is often the more powerful conveyor of reality.[67] One must therefore tread carefully in apocalyptic. The nature of the language is intimately related to its function. Its function is to provide meaning for a meaningless situation. It portrays above all else the sovereignty of God in his ultimate triumph over evil and the establishment of *shalom* for his people and creation. The failure to recognize the pictorial nature of the language in apocalyptic and prophetic literature has produced some unfortunate and even humorous results.

---

[66]Collins has warned that critical methodology with its penchant for identifying the references in an unambiguous manner has failed to appreciate fully the symbolic character of apocalyptic writings. *Apocalyptic Imagination*, 11-13. This is not to suggest that one should "just enjoy the view" without any guidelines for interpretation. In addition to Caird cited above (note 60), cf. Helge S. Kvanvig, "The Relevance of the Biblical Visions of the End Times: Hermeneutical Guidelines to Apocalyptical Literature," *HBT* 11 (January 1989): 35-58 and Gordon D. Fee, *New Testament Exegesis* (Philadelphia: Westminster, 1983), 42-44. Two excellent, brief surveys regarding the nature and interpretation of apocalyptic language are found in Boring, *Revelation*, 35-62 (to whom this writer is particularly indebted) and John P. Newport, *The Lion and the Lamb* (Nashville, Broadman, 1989), 38-58.

[67]The lack of logical consistency has been one of the chief canons of literary critics for discerning the various sources and arrangement of apocalyptic documents. See the approach of R. H. Charles, *The Revelation of St. John*, 2 vols., ICC (New York: Scribner, 1920); G. H. Box, *The Ezra-Apocalypse* (London: Pitman, 1912). See above note 66.

The depiction of the new Jerusalem of Revelation 21.9-22.5 as a cubic crystal cathedral suspended above the earth during the so-called millennium diminishes the impact of John's stress on God's presence among his people (vv. 3, 22). Further, that it is temporarily withdrawn at the end of the millennium when the earth is destroyed clearly depreciates the created order.[68] Such an *ultraliteral* interpretation suggests a Gnostic dualism which affirms the heavens and denigrates the material world. The opposite extreme is just as damaging. The promise of a new creation is more than a message of the restoration of harmony between God and humanity. This imagery should not be relegated to the realm of archaic mythology to be spiritualized or demythologized. The significance of this theme for the OT and NT conception of the creation is so fundamental that it must be taken seriously. The imagery regarding the hope for the new heavens and new earth reflects God's intention to reaffirm the inherent goodness of the creation.

In addition, Enoch's tour of the heavens and the ends of the earth cannot be easily dismissed as merely cosmological speculation (1 Enoch 17-36). Certainly, the revelation of a prison prepared for the wicked attests to the sovereign power of God to vindicate his people. More importantly, Enoch's journey reflects an interest in a just and orderly creation much like that found in Hebrew wisdom literature. The affirmation of a just arrangement established in the created order provides assurance for Enoch that the wicked will be punished and the righteous will experience blessing. Such justice is in fact determined by the order embedded in the universe.[69]

Likewise, reducing to objective language Isaiah's magnificent vision of the messianic kingdom in which the wolf and lamb and cow and bear graze together and the lion eats straw like the ox destroys the significance of the image (11.6, 7; 65.25). As Moule retorts, "what blasphemous injury would be done to great poetry and true mythology by laying such solemnly prosaic

---

[68]This fanciful view is presented by John F. Walvoord, *The Revelation of Jesus Christ* (Chicago: Moody, 1966), 323-24. See also Hal Lindsey, *There's a New World Coming* (Santa Ana, CA: Vision, 1973), 288-89.

[69]See discussion below, pp. 88-90.

hands upon it!"[70]   Isaiah envisions the messianic age as a world in which all relationships--human and animal--are restored. To require the transformation of the digestive system of the carnivore to that of a herbivore is senseless. It violates the image of a reality in which even the worst of enemies--even those physically designed to oppose one another--reside in peace. To press too literally Isaiah's vision is thus to destroy its impact upon the imagination. This reality will exist. Its description, however, far surpasses the meaning of a literal interpretation.

The preeminent function of poetic or picture language is to define the indefinable.[71] Whether one may describe apocalyptic language as figurative, symbolic, or merely as highly dramatic in form and presentation, the prevalence for vivid imagery and mythological allusions witnesses to the value of its language which often eludes the pedantic mind, namely, the ability to grasp and communicate the transcendent. Understanding the language of these writers from this perspective perhaps will permit the apocalyptists to communicate more effectively to the present apocalyptic age.

---

[70]Moule, *Man and Nature*, 12.
[71]Cf. John Middleton Murry, "Metaphor," in *Essays on Metaphor*, ed. Warren Shibles (Whitewater, WI: Language, 1972), 33.

CHAPTER II
CREATION AND REDEMPTION IN
THE OLD TESTAMENT

Introduction

The biblical hope for cosmic redemption presupposes that humanity, including the created order, has gone awry and is in need of deliverance. Nevertheless, it has been argued that the idea of a sinful and fallen creation entered the Western Christian tradition from extrabiblical sources especially from platonic speculation as adopted by Origen.[1]

---

[1]Santmire, *Brother Earth*, 162-73; 192-200. Santmire discusses Origen's ideas in *Travail of Nature*, 49-53. While it is not the purpose of this section to address thoroughly Santmire's view, his contentions merit a response. First, the concept of new creation, according to Santmire, does not presuppose a cosmic fall. This is merely the biblical concept of linear time in contrast to pagan cyclical thought. It was predetermined in this type of thought that Adam, Eve, and Paradise would have a history and would experience transformation even if Adam had never sinned. In Santmire's words, "Paradise is not the eternal now of mythological thinking; it is the created beginning of a real history whose goal is something *new*, the final re-creation." However, the biblical concept (especially as espoused by the Salvation-History School following Cullmann) sees the movement of history toward the incisive point (*Mitte*) of Christ as redeemer and the consummation as the ultimate remedy for sinful humanity including a fallen creation. Second, Santmire's rejection of a "cosmic fall" may appear to be semantic on the surface. He agrees that due to a solidarity of relationship humanity's sin affected nature. Nature, however, is not directly judged but is implicated in humanity's judgment. Nature is therefore not intrinsically corrupt. Sin is fundamentally a spiritual issue and humanity is in need of *spiritual* salvation. The redemptive act of Christ remedies the spiritual alienation

Others have noted competing traditions in the OT regarding the created order. One tradition views creation as corrupt due to humanity's rebellion and sin. Another presents God's creation as good and free from the perversion of humankind.[2] What is the authentic picture? That both views are presented in the OT is evident. However, the two contrasting traditions are not mutually exclusive. The OT writers as well as the later apocalyptists are at one in their view of the created order as good yet perverted. Each affirms that God created the world perfect but something indeed has gone wrong. While the source and extent of this dilemma is answered differently in the various writings, the prospect is the same. This dialectic of a good yet marred creation exhibited in the Bible is resolved in the apocalyptic motif of the new heavens and new earth.

The Old Testament View of Creation

The Genesis Traditions

The subordination of creation to redemptive history in OT theology has been previously noted.[3] Contrary to von Rad's view, the location of the creation accounts at the beginning of Israel's history is not misleading. His perspective assumes that the so-called Priestly and Yahwistic accounts of creation were

---

from God and frees humankind from its exploitative endeavors toward nature. This writer agrees that the created world is not *intrinsically* corrupt. Santmire's affirmation of the inherent dignity of creation apart from humanity is admirable and appropriate. However, his argument pivots on the radical discontinuity of humanity and nature although he has previously affirmed their interrelation in his discussion of God's judgment of creation. Perhaps it is more fitting to use the terminology of a "marred" or "perverted" creation in the sense that human sin has prevented nature from fulfilling its *telos*. Nevertheless, the solidarity of humanity and the natural world is such that one cannot deny that both are the aim of God's judgment and salvific activity.

[2]Bruce V. Malchow, "Contrasting Views of Nature in the Hebrew Bible," *Dialog* 26 (Winter 1987): 40-43. Those passages Malchow adduces as reflecting "corruption by guilt" appear more often in the prophets and later apocalyptic writings. The traditions affirming creation are found primarily in wisdom. See also Goldingay, *Theological Diversity*, 225.

[3]See discussion above pp. 14-20.

placed at the beginning not to affirm creation for its own sake but to reinforce God's work of redemption.[4] The final form of the biblical record, however, points to a different conclusion. While commentators continue to stress the disparate material utilized to produce Genesis, this study affirms a canonical approach. This methodology identifies the final literary work as the actual context for interpreting the primeval record rather than the prehistory of traditions. This is especially appropriate since only the final product was recognized as authoritative by both Jewish and Christian communities--past and present. In relation to this discussion, the canonical view rejects the ancillary role for creation and in fact urges upon the reader its importance as the presupposition and foundation of redemption.[5] Beginning the Hebrew canon with the theme of creation therefore has significant theological implications for understanding the created order and its relation to history; it is given priority.

While this may seem to ignore the time honored findings of the traditio-historical method, recent source critical analysis actually appears to enhance the theological implications provided by the canonical approach. Previously, the Yahwistic account of creation in Genesis 2 with its clear anthropocentric emphasis was given the preeminent place as the oldest of the two stories. An understanding of creation must begin with humanity. However, the reevaluation of the sources with the possibility of the Priestly source (Gen. 1.1-2.3) as earlier invites a different assumption regarding the Hebrews' interest in the created order as concerned primarily with humanity and its domain.[6] In any event, the

---

[4]Gerhard von Rad, *Genesis: A Commentary*, rev. ed., trans. John Marks, OTL (Philadelphia: Fortress, 1972), 45-46.

[5]Brevard S. Childs, *Introduction to the Old Testament as Scripture* (Philadelphia: Fortress, 1979), 145-49.

[6]Critical scholarship has identified two creation stories in the opening chapters of Genesis: Gen. 1.1-2.4a or the Priestly account ("P") dating from the postexilic period (ca. 538-450 BC) and that of the Yahwist ("J") found in Gen. 2.4b-25 which dates to ca. 950 BC. See von Rad, *Genesis*, 24-25. However, the old consensus of the documentary hypothesis has been challenged by critical scholarship. A recent appraisal and summary is presented by R. N. Whybray, *The Making of the Pentateuch: A Methodological Study*, JSOTSup, no. 53 (Sheffield: JSOT, 1987). Gordon J. Wenham has dispensed altogether with the "E" source and regards J as the main redactor of Genesis who revised

canonical perspective leaves little doubt as to the axiological priority of creation for the OT. God's relationship to the world derives not from Israel alone but from his initial creative purpose for the creation.[7] Moreover, Goldingay appropriately observes that

> Even if traditio-historically the primeval history is secondary to salvation history, and even if it is added to aid an understanding of Israel's significance, this does not establish that the object of the creation of the world is the existence of Israel rather than that the object of Israel's existence is to stand in service of God's creation of the world.[8]

This perspective, in addition to the fact that Genesis 1 has been considered by many as the locus for the environmentally disastrous doctrine of *dominium terrae*, makes it fitting for this study to begin with the Priestly account and its contribution toward an understanding of creation in the OT.

The history of interpretation of Genesis 1 generally does not betray an emphasis upon the importance of the created order apart from humankind. Von Rad's exposition reflects the majority view that finds the creation of humanity in the image of God as the apex of creation "toward which all God's creativity from v. 1 on was directed." The sequence of acts is thus given ontological significance. The successive orders of creation are presented as rapidly moving vignettes toward the goal of God's preeminent creative work--humankind.[9] Is it possible to read the passage another way? This is not to suggest that one

accurately the traditions transmitted through oral and written means. Significant for this study is Wenham's reversal of the dating for P and J--a pre-Wellhausen position. *Genesis 1-15*, WBC (Waco: Word, 1987), xxv-xlv.

[7]Childs, *Old Testament as Scripture*, 155.

[8]*Theological Diversity*, 232. Wenham recognizes the "methodological blindspot" inherit in reading the text as a compilation of J and P without first dealing with the final literary composition. He appropriately avers that "it is the commentator's first duty to understand the present form of the text, what Genesis meant to its final editor or author. Then the commentator may embark on the task of defining the pre-existing sources used by the final editor and what they meant." *Genesis 1-15*, xxxvi.

[9]von Rad, *Genesis*, 57. However, cf. Steck, *Schöpfungsbericht*, 15.

ignore or discount the importance of humanity made in the image of God. However, the author's detailed and orderly, even pedantic narration of God's creative activity reveals a studied reflection on the world. Furthermore, the passage places humanity within rather than above the created order. That is to say, its focus is not so much upon humanity's supremacy over creation as it is with humankind's relation within the creation itself. Genesis 1, then, is neither cosmological nor anthropological but rather ecological.[10]

The writer's concern for the created order especially for the earth is apparent from the beginning. The statement regarding God's creation of the universe or the heavens and earth is quickly narrowed to center attention upon the earth (v. 2).[11] This concern, however, does not suggest that the narrator is interested in the earth only as the realm or future habitation and activity of

---

[10]Bernhard W. Anderson, "Creation and Ecology," in *Creation in the Old Testament*, ed. Bernhard W. Anderson, IRT, no. 6 (Philadelphia: Fortress, 1984), 152-71.

[11]Note the disjunctive use of 1 (cf. 3.1; 4.1, 4). Thus ארץ receives the emphasis and narrows the topic of discussion. This observation regards v. 1 as an independent clause serving as an introduction and summary of the following account. בראשית is taken as referring to the absolute beginning of creation. Claus Westermann, *Genesis 1-11: A Commentary*, trans. John J. Scullion (Minneapolis, MN: Augsburg, 1984), 93-101; von Rad, *Genesis*, 48-49; Walther Eichrodt, "In the Beginning: A Contribution to the Interpretation of the First Word of the Bible," in *Creation in the Old Testament*, ed. Bernhard W. Anderson, IRT, no. 6 (Philadelphia: Fortress, 1984), 65-73. The debate surrounding the translation of v. 1 is far from resolved. The issue concerns whether v. 1 should be translated as a main independent clause (Aquila: ἐν κεφαλαίῳ; cf. LXX, John 1.1; NASB, NIV, RSV) or as a dependent temporal clause (NEB, JPSV, NRSV). Grammatical, syntactical, stylistic, and theological arguments have been adduced as support for both readings. See Gerhard F. Hasel, "Recent Translations of Genesis 1.1: A Critical Look," *BT* 22 (October 1971): 154-67. Von Rad observes that accepting the verse as a dependent clause would permit the word about chaos to stand logically and temporally prior to the word about creation. While the idea of a created chaos may appear to be a contradiction, von Rad warns about pressing too far into areas that lie beyond human imagination (48). However, that God should create chaos should be no more problematic than that he took six days to complete creation rather than instantaneously creating the world. Nahum M. Sarna, *Genesis*, JPSTC (Philadelphia: Jewish Publication Society, 1989), 6.

humanity. Indeed the importance of the created order as an orderly whole has left its mark on the very structure of the text.

Anderson's literary analysis has revealed that the creation drama is presented as two movements in two triads of days which are clearly earth centered. The structure of the account highlights the third and sixth days of creation that concern the land and its inhabitants. This is also stressed by the double declarative ("and God said"; vv. 9, 11, 24, 26) and approbation formulas ("it was good"; vv. 10, 12, 25, 31) which occur at the climax of the two parallel days.[12]

Day 1: Light   Day 4: Luminaries
Day 2: Waters above   Day 5: Waters below
Day 3: Land & produce   Day 6: Land and inhabitants
              Day 7: God's Rest

Attention to the contents as well as the structure of the account reveals further interest in the creation. While this passage cannot be considered a "scientific" account, the writer displays a "scientific" inclination in the meticulous narration of God's creative activity.[13] The passage discloses the writer's sense of awe at God's cosmic order. Each part of creation has its proper place and function. The details are not for decorative purposes; they actually inform the reader. For example, the creation of vegetation is classified as two types: seed bearing plants and trees that bear fruit (vv. 11-12). Further, that the plants and animals are to reproduce "according to their own kind" reveals that God has given them the ability for self-replication. The permanence and conservation of the plant and animal world can hardly be ignored in this passage.[14] The creation

---

[12]Bernhard W. Anderson, "A Stylistic Study of the Priestly Creation Story," in *Canon and Authority: Essays on Old Testament Religion and Theology*, ed. George W. Coats and Burke O. Long (Philadelphia: Fortress, 1977), 154-59. Noteworthy is Anderson's argument that the *toledot* formula of Gen. 2.4a belongs essentially to the following account rather than as the conclusion to ch. 1. As a preface to the primeval history it therefore provides the theological foundation and presupposition for Israel's redemptive history.

[13]See Bernhard W. Anderson, "Cosmic Dimensions of the Genesis Account," *DG* 56 (Spring 1986): 1-13.

[14]Cf. Steck, *World and Environment*, 101.

story of Genesis 1 therefore should not be read in such a manner that regards the writer's references to the created order as merely brief detours on the way to the main theme of humanity. Certainly, humankind's significance is important not only due to the distinctive as made in the image of God. It is evidenced as well by the fecundity blessing which in the second movement of the passage is reserved only for the supreme land animal--humankind (v. 28).[15] Nevertheless, while it is true that humanity was created at the climax of creation, it must also be observed that both humanity and the land animals were created on the same auspicious day. It is clear that there exists between humankind and the animals an interrelationship which underscores an ecological emphasis. In this relationship humanity has a unique and important role.

The nature of humanity's role in creation is illuminated by an understanding of the phrase "image and likeness of God" (v. 26). Although the exact meaning of this expression has occasioned lively debates, an important aspect of its significance is provided by the context.[16] The connection of verse 26 with the following verses admonishing humanity to "have dominion" establishes a clear relation between humankind made in the image of God and the responsibility within the created order. Whatever may be suggested by the phrase "image of God" regarding the spiritual nature or moral capacity of humanity, its close association with the instruction "to rule" stresses a functional role as God's vice-regent in creation. The idea finds a striking parallel in ancient Near Eastern texts reflecting the idea of the reigning monarch as the earthly image or representative of the gods. Humankind in the image of God thus offers the twofold dimension of royalty exalted above the creation with it at his disposal and more importantly the concept

---

[15]Anderson, "Ecology," 159.

[16]Westermann regards Gen. 1.26-30 as an originally independent narrative about the creation of mankind and therefore unrelated to a stewardship theme. The "image of God" connotes the meaning of "one corresponding to" and thus conveys the idea of creating one to whom God can relate. *Genesis*, 156-57. Von Rad is correct that the text does not define what the image of God is but denotes the consequence of being in God's image. In the present context a functional concept prevails. *Genesis*, 59.

of humanity as the symbol or visual representation of God on the earth.[17] Thus, created in God's image speaks not to the essence of humanity but to the role as God's representative. It involves the accomplishment of God's tasks in accordance with his original intentions. Human responsibility for the created order is therefore a visible manifestation of God's activity within his world. A solemn accountability is asserted rather than a *carte blanche* to ravage the resources which God has entrusted to one's care.

That the verbs כבש ("subdue") and רדה ("rule") are harsh words is a matter of lexical fact (v. 28).[18] That they encourage or present the opportunity for exploitation of the natural world, however, cannot be derived from their present context. In particular, the command "to subdue" is applied to the ground which could mean only that humanity is to take it under control for cultivation.[19] Further, any hint of violence or cruelty toward humanity's "partner" is altogether absent in the passage. One is called "as" God's image on the earth, that is, to *image* or behave in the same manner as the one who is represented. Being in the image of God therefore denotes not the power of abuse but of respect and responsibility.[20] This consideration for the whole of creation actually is intimated in humanity's relation to the animal world. The exercise of oversight or ruling is limited to the animals in verse 28b. Yet this does not exclude humanity's

---

[17]Egyptian and Assyrian texts describing the ruling monarch as the צלם ("image") or דמות ("likeness") of deities provides the background. Especially noteworthy are the Assyrian royal steles depicting the gods by their symbols: Ashur by winged disks; Shamash by the sun disk and so on. To be sure, the Hebrews democratized the concept. They believed every person not just the king was made in the image of God. Sarna, *Genesis*, 12; Wenham, *Genesis*, 30-31. See Bernhard W. Anderson, "Human Dominion Over Nature," in *Biblical Studies in Contemporary Thought*, ed. Miriam Ward (Somerville, MA: Greeno, Hadden, & Co., 1975), 27-45.

[18]Both verbs occur in contexts denoting enslavement: כבש (cf. Jer. 34.11, 16; Mic. 7.19); רדה (cf. Lev. 25.43, 46, 53; Isa. 14.2, 6).

[19]Donald A. Hay, "Christians in the Global Greenhouse," *TynBul* 41.1 (May 1990): 116-17.

[20]Anderson, "Human Dominion," 44-45. The preposition ב can also be translated "as" denoting the manner in which something manifests itself (36, n. 18).

obligation toward the nonliving or material order (cf. v. 26). Westermann observes that "a person's 'dominion over matter' is not excluded by Gen. 1:28b; P indicates in unmistakable terms that all human relationships with the rest of creation are to be determined by one's rule over the animal world."[21]

While it has been argued that the present environmental crisis is due to a greater extent to the Christian teaching of humanity's dominion over nature, the biblical account reflects a different perspective. This exercise of dominion, or "responsible oversight," occurs in a context where there is perfect harmony between humankind and the created order (cf. Gen. 2.15, 19, 20). Furthermore, it reflects a positive viewpoint. The blessing for humans to be fruitful and multiply and the call to subdue and rule the earth are intimately related. Humanity's role as a responsible steward ensures the continuance of the created order in accordance with God's original intentions which in turn guarantees the success and permanence of the human order. Thus, the summons is to responsible stewardship as one who is a part of creation and upon which humanity's success and destiny depends. Creation, then, can be understood as the foundation of humanity's history. Evidently, the narrator not only exhibits an interest in the importance of the created order in its own right but he also wishes to convey a moral perspective regarding its importance and preservation as God's good creation. This now leads to additional observations provided by the Genesis traditions regarding creation.

Significant for a general understanding of God's relationship to the natural world is the creation of the world by God's command or effective "word" (cf. Ps. 33.6-9). God both commands and brings the directive to fulfillment.[22] Precluding any idea of emanation or struggle, God is portrayed distinct and

---

[21]Westermann, *Genesis*, 159-60. This element of "humanness" with creatures is readily apparent when one considers the importance people often place on their favorite pet. This concern is to be extended to the entire creation.

[22]Genesis 1 evinces a formulaic pattern of 1) declarative formula, "then God said," 2) command, "Let there be," 3) fulfillment of command, "and it happened," and 4) an approval statement, "it was good." Anderson, "Stylistic Study," 151-52.

transcendent from his creation as its creator and lord.[23] The elements out of which God shapes the universe are no more than mere objects; hence, the appropriateness of the verb ברא which is used exclusively for God's unique creative work. Although ברא is partly synonymous with עשׂה, it has the specific shade of meaning connoting the idea of novel or extraordinary (Isa. 48.6; Exod. 34.10) and certainly implies the idea of effortless divine creation of something absolutely new.[24] Creation by the word clearly affirms that everything owes its existence to God's creative activity. The natural order is not viewed as a self-sustaining entity.

As God's creation, it is pronounced "very good" (v. 31). This exclamation reflects the idea of a creation which gives the creator pleasure because it conforms to his wishes and design and thus attests to its inherent value. To understand the import of the term "good" an appeal to the LXX is helpful. In the present context טוב, like its Greek counterpart καλός, embraces the dual concept of aesthetic beauty and purposefulness. Each part of creation thus corresponds to God's creative intentions. As such, it could be translated "completely perfect."[25] In this

---

[23]Foester argues that the translators of the LXX preferred the word group κτίζειν over δημιουργεῖν because of the strong emanative implications of the latter. Κτίζω was more appropriate to the OT concept since it was used in ancient literature to designate creative activity as a volitional process by a sovereign power. "Κτίζω," 3:1024-26. James Barr, however, contends that δημιουργεῖν was rejected primarily because it denoted the idea of a workman and therefore was not suitable as a solemn designation for God in the synagogue setting. *Semantics of Biblical Language* (London: SCM, 1961), 224-25. The theological significance of this phenomenon is therefore uncertain. What can be stated is that in Genesis 1 the LXX creation verb for ברא is ποιέω (1.1, 7, 16, 25, 27). Κτίζω does not appear in Genesis 1. The verb later acquired theological import as witnessed in the translations of the minor Greek versions which replaced ποιέω with κτίζω in vital verses (Gen. 1.1, 27; cf. Isa. 65.17, 18).

[24]God appears exclusively as the subject of ברא and it always takes as its object the resultant product rather than the creative material. See also Westermann, *Genesis*, 98-100; *TDOT*, s.v. "ברא," by K.-H. Bernhardt, G. Botterweck, and H. Ringgren, 2:242-49. Note the synonymy of עשׂה (1.11, 12, 16, 25, 26, 27, 31; 2.2, 3).

[25]Significantly, the approval formula occurs seven times in this passage. The following translation for the LXX has been suggested: ". . . and behold [it

regard, von Rad's observation is instructive.

> No evil was laid upon the world by God's hand, neither was his omnipotence limited by any kind of opposing power whatever. When faith speaks of creation, and in so doing directs its eye toward God, then it can only say that God created the world perfect.[26]

Evil is not ontological or a necessary part of being. It is historical as reflected in the writer's juxtaposition of the primeval creation with that of paradise and the fall. The belief in a "good" creation rejects all metaphysical dualism which suggests that the created world is inherently evil and one must somehow escape its grasp. This perspective therefore views life in this world as a blessing to be enjoyed "for everything created by God is good" (1 Tim. 4.4).[27]

Additionally prominent in these traditions is the portrayal of humanity in unique solidarity with creation. Genesis 2-3 establishes this relationship by affirming that all human beings are bound to the earth from which they are taken and to which they will return (2.7; 3.19). Furthermore, when humanity transgressed, it not only disrupted relationships within the human race but adversely affected the created world as well (3.18; cf. 9.2-3). While Genesis 2-3 do not present a *modus operandi* concerning the transmission of sin within the human race, the far reaching effects are unmistakable. One cannot help but notice that the writer of Genesis follows the "fall" account in chapter 3 with events that manifest an implicit involvement of following generations in the original sin. In like manner, the passage of note does not delineate how the earth incurred the pain of humanity's transgression; it merely establishes the fact. The creation is

---

was] completely successful." *NIDNTT*, s.v. "Καλός," by E. Beyreuther, 2:102-5. Cf. *Tg. Onq.* Gen. 1.31: "Then the Lord perceived that all that He had made was very proper." See also *TDNT*, s.v. "Καλός," by G. Bertram, 3:543-44; Westermann, *Genesis*, 166-67.

[26]von Rad, *Genesis*, 61. Cf. Eichrodt, *Theology*, 2:108.

[27]See especially the comments of Langdon Gilkey, *Maker of Heaven and Earth* (New York: Doubleday, 1959), 48-65.

cursed and at enmity with humanity.[28] The ground therefore
brings forth its fruit only with difficulty and in meager portion
(Gen. 3.17, 18). More importantly, however, evil is presented as
an intruder and not a constituent part of creation. It is portrayed
as an independent hostile power from without crouching at the
door awaiting to consume humanity and corrupt creation (cf.
Gen. 4.6, 7). Thus, humanity's rebellious act opens the door for
the evil that ultimately affects all creation.[29] That the effects of
humanity's sin extended beyond the human realm is also revealed
in the flood narrative. The pollution of the earth by evil is epi-
demic "for all flesh had corrupted their ways upon the earth"
(6.12). While evil cannot be traced to the natural world, the flood
account affirms a general corruption which pervades all of cre-
ation--human and nonhuman.[30] The Genesis narrative clearly
moves from creation to chaos and to a new creation after the
flood. But does the writer intend to suggest that the effects of the
fall have been wiped away with the renewal of creation? It must
be observed that even after the flood the ambiguous nature of creation continues to be manifested. Although an estrangement
between humanity and the animals persists (9.2), the importance
of both is demonstrated by God's establishment of a covenant
with "all living creatures" (9.9-17), and his intention to hold both

[28]The conception of a "cursed" earth or land, as the discussion below
reveals, does not detract from the teaching a good creation but refers to its
resultant condition due to humankind's rebellious activity.

[29]Regarding Gen. 1.1 as a temporal clause, Jon D. Levenson argues that
the author of Genesis intended to portray creation as a *chaoskampf* in which
God continually engages in a struggle with evil for domination. Evil thus has
primordial existence. It is not due to humankind or history but to a greater
suprahistorical struggle. Evil existed before creation and will continue beyond
it until the new world. *Creation and the Persistence of Evil: The Jewish
Drama of Divine Omnipotence* (San Francisco: Harper & Row, 1988), 47-53,
passim. Levenson contributes to the understanding of the use of the chaos
myth in the OT portrayal of the creation as fragile and thus in constant need of
God's supervision and maintenance--an *Urzeit-Endzeit* concept.

[30]Whether "all flesh" is intended to include all creatures, i.e., נפש חיה or
only humans is unclear. Note that the NIV translates בשר to refer to people
(1.12, 13) and creatures (6.17; 7.15, 16, 21; 8,17). However, that 7.21-22 refers
to judgment upon all living things save Noah and his cargo as well as the
prophetic tradition which anticipates a reconciliation within the animal kingdom suggests that its use is inclusive. See also Anderson, "Ecology," 161-63.

accountable for their actions (9.4-5).[31] Moreover, not only is God
concerned about sentient beings but his preservation of the
"times and seasons" as originally intended further accentuates the
value of all creation and reflects the continued obedience of the
created order to the creator (8.22). Thus, one finds an appreciation for creation but also a realization that something has gone
wrong. Whereas the notion of a marred creation due to human
sin is repugnant to the modern mind, the biblical writers suggest
that this fact arises from the unique kindred relationship of
humankind and the created order that reaches to the foundation
of the very being of humanity. It is undeniable that creation suffers the effects of humanity's fall. The most important issue yet
to be answered is whether one can say that the created order *itself*
is fallen.

Notably, the concept of a disrupted creation often recedes
into the background in the OT message as seen in the Psalms.
Contemplation of God's creation is an occasion for praise. The
Psalms that reflect the creation itself as offering praise to God
are particularly suggestive (cf. Ps. 98.7-9). Are these just poetic statements? Robinson comments that "nature is alive
through and through, and therefore the more capable of sympa-
thy with man, and of response to the role of its Creator and
Upholder, on whom it directly depends."[32] Such language suggests a relationship of God and his creation which transcends
human comprehension. Especially noteworthy is Psalm 104
which reflects the inherent dignity of the created order. God is
said to rejoice in all his works (v. 31). The Psalm even portrays
the Leviathan as created for the pleasure of the creator (v. 26).
One must note the unfortunate tone of verse 35: "Let the sinners
be consumed from the earth, and let the wicked be no more."
The joy of creation for its own sake is marred by the realization
of humanity's rebellion. Evil is thus perceived as a perversion
rather than a necessary part of the world existence and as such

---

[31]Both humankind and the animals are considered נפש חיה.

[32]Robinson, *Inspiration and Revelation*, 16. Genesis 1 and 2 constitute
only a small part of creation passages in the OT. Particularly important are the
praise of creation found in Pss. 8, 19, 104, and 148. The limits of space pre-
vent their consideration.

must and will be corrected. The hope of rectifying this wrong on both historical and cosmic levels is seen especially in the second half of Isaiah. Proto-apocalyptic statements in the OT concerning the return to primeval conditions and the renewal of creation were later developments linked to the concept of a degenerating world spoiled by the wickedness of humanity. The solidarity of humanity with creation clearly was an underlying presupposition.

Creation and World Order

The themes of creation and wisdom in the OT are intimately related. While ברא the central "creation" verb, יסד is also used to picture God as an architect who lays the foundation of a building and supervises its construction.[33] The verb establishes that indeed "the earth is the Lord's" (Ps. 24.2) and further that an ordered creation invites investigation and provides intelligibility. Creation theology performs a necessary function in the message of wisdom literature. While the sages do not appeal directly to creation as the reason for their council, it nevertheless forms the foundation for their thought. Crenshaw contends that the orderliness of the creation provides the basic premise in humanity's attempt to understand the nature of reality.[34] One's ability to comprehend and adapt to this world order is impossible without the design and regularity embedded in the creation. Proverbs 8 is the classic example of wisdom's search for the knowledge of regularity and meaning in the world. Wisdom personified represents a rational principle in the world which can be comprehended by humanity as the result of God's creative activity. When Proverbs 8 speaks about creation it therefore speaks of wisdom, that is, the intelligibility of the world predicated upon God's creation and maintenance of the natural order.[35] Moreover, one's ability to comprehend the world order is not innate; rather, it is founded upon God's creative activity in the

---

[33]Jacob, *Theology of the Old Testament*, 142.

[34]James L. Crenshaw, *Studies in Ancient Israelite Wisdom* (New York: KTAV, 1976), 33.

[35]Hermisson, "Creation Theology in Wisdom," 120.

world and humanity. It affirms that God has created both the world and the "organs of cognition" suitable for it. As the sage writes, "the hearing ear and the seeing eye, the Lord has made them both" (Prov. 20.12).[36] Creation theology serves to indicate that wisdom, as the rational guiding principle in the world, is dependent upon God's role as creator.

Furthermore, an interconnection is evident between ethical conduct and the permanence of the universe. To seek after the "good," that is, to live in accordance with God's designs evident in an orderly creation not only secures one's existence but even strengthens the world order itself. Disobedience, however, contributes to the forces ever waiting to return the world to its prechaotic state. Cosmic design as the basis for a just and stable society is therefore assumed. The cosmic, political, and social orders of life are governed by the concept of a harmonious, regulated, and hence a just creation.[37] Schmid contends that this perspective is the best explanation why an offense on the social level is understood as affecting nature and even the political environment. This "act-consequence" concept reveals that whoever transgresses the natural order inflicts damage that must be rectified. The transgressor must suffer or the act must be expiated.[38] Thus, orderliness in the social and political sphere is grounded firmly in the concept of the divine arrangement inherent in creation. The political and social orders are viewed as only aspects of one comprehensive system.[39] The principle of cosmic order therefore dominates the presuppositions underlying all aspects of life and this perspective plays an important role in the later apocalyptic understanding.

Israel and the Land

The value of creation in Israel's faith is also directly related to the concept of the land. It is unnecessary to argue for the

---

[36]Ibid., 122.

[37]James L. Crenshaw, *Old Testament Wisdom: An Introduction* (Atlanta: John Knox, 1981), 19-20, 66-67.

[38]H. H. Schmid, "Creation, Righteousness, and Salvation," 103-7; Knierim, "Cosmos and History," 100-101.

[39]Knierim, "Cosmos and History," 100-101.

centrality of the land in the life and faith of Israel. The idea of the land promised and granted by God is, according to von Rad, found in all the sources of the Hexateuch.[40] Brueggemann contends, moreover, that it is perhaps the central theme of biblical faith.[41] The land as token of God's faithfulness in fulfilling his covenant promise makes an important contribution to the OT understanding of the inherent worth of the material order. However, it is not the significance of the land as a geopolitical entity that is important for this study but the ecological interrelationship of God, the land, and Israel which has vital implications for God's people in a more contemporary setting.[42]

Two issues were determinative in Israel's understanding of and relationship to the land. First, the importance of the land derived from the realization that it was God's unique possession (Lev. 25.23; cf. Josh. 22.19). This affirmation formed the basis for the cultic statements regarding the sabbatic year, first fruits of the harvest, the tithe, and so forth. Since God was perceived as the landholder, the land--earth and soil--belonged not to any one tribe but was rented out, as it were (Deut. 14.22; 16.9-12; 26.9-15).[43] Particularly noteworthy is the provision of the seventh year fallow for the land characterized as a "sabbath to the Lord" (Lev. 25.1-7). The humanitarian focus is readily apparent in this legislation (cf. Exod. 23.11).[44] Furthermore, that a rest for the land ensured future productivity is likewise a consideration. However, to so limit the provision is to overlook the theological motivation. The weekly sabbath in Exod. 20.8-11 is justified on the ground of God's rest at creation which in turn can be appro-

---

[40]Gerhard von Rad, "The Promised Land and Yahweh's Land in the Hexateuch," in *The Problem of the Hexateuch and Other Essays*, trans. E. W. Trueman Dicken (New York: McGraw Hill, 1966), 79.

[41]Brueggemann, *The Land*, 3.

[42]See the general discussion of Patrick D. Miller, Jr., "The Gift of the Land: The Deuteronomic Theology of the Land," *Interp* 23 (October 1969): 451-65.

[43]von Rad, "The Promised Land," 85-86.

[44]Christopher J. H. Wright argues that the primarily humanitarian Jubilee year law of release in Lev. 25.8-55 "is best interpreted as an extension of the agrarian principle of the fallow year for the land, rather than a slave release law, . . ." "What Happened Every Seven Years in Israel?" *EvQ* 56 (April 1984): 132-34.

priated as the basis for the sabbath rest of the land and even to the jubilee year. While the ancient world recognized the necessity for "crop rotation" to ensure future productivity, Israel transferred this to a theological plane, to affirm the sole proprietorship of God. This observance reminded Israel of the direct relatedness of the land with God as well as deterred the farmer from exploitation. Indeed, in Lev. 25.2 the legislation not only encouraged Israel's respect for the land as having its own divine rights but, significantly, the "rest" reflected the land's responsiveness and devotion to God. Davies comments that

> It is not the people who are commanded to allow the land to rest: rather the land itself, personified, seems to be addressed. The land, too, owes worship to Yahweh, to signify that special relationship which it enjoys with him. The land's rest recalls the seventh-day rest of the Lord himself after the creation, and came to symbolize Yahweh's creation and ownership of the land.[45]

Closely related to this first consideration is Israel's recognition of the land as gift.[46] Clements notes that Deuteronomy teaches a "holy materialism" that affirms the right to enjoy the fruit of the land but recognizes that this right ultimately is traceable to the land as God's gift.[47] That the possession of the land was not by Israel's power or merit is made unequivocally clear: "Know, then, it is not because of your righteousness that the Lord your God is giving you this good land to possess, for you are a stubborn people" (Deut. 9.6). The land as God's possession and gift protected it from being regarded as a commodity to be owned and sold (Lev. 25.23). Israel viewed the land as a

---

[45]W. D. Davies, *The Gospel and the Land: Early Christianity and Jewish Territorial Doctrine* (Berkeley: University of California, 1974), 29; Martin Noth, *Leviticus: A Commentary*, rev. ed., OTL (Philadelphia: Westminster, 1977), 186.

[46]However, see Harry M. Orlinsky, "The Biblical Concept of the Land," in *The Land of Israel: Jewish Perspectives*, ed. Lawrence A. Hoffman (Notre Dame: University of Notre Dame, 1986), 42-45. Rather than gift, the idea of a contractual agreement predominates, i.e., a *quid pro quo*.

[47]Ronald E. Clements, *God's Chosen People: Theological Interpretation of the Book of Deuteronomy* (London: SCM, 1968), 52.

blessing to be cherished and preserved not because of its divine power but because of its derivative worth as God's possession. Deuteronomy especially reflects a remarkable balance in Israel's relationship with God and land. Brueggemann notes appropriately that

> Israel's involvement is always with the land and with Yahweh, never only with Yahweh as though to live only in intense obedience, never only with land, as though simply to possess and manage; always *with land* and *with Yahweh*, always receiving gifts from land, always being addressed by Yahweh . . . always being of the family of earth, but always . . . Yahweh's peculiar listening partner in historical covenant.[48]

The theological concept of the land like the Genesis accounts of creation reflects an ecological perspective. The writers see the land and all other living things as partners in the covenant that God established with Israel. Israel, indeed all people, have a responsibility toward the created world and their actions can have adverse consequences for all creation. Thus, in the Covenant and Holiness Codes there are provisions not only for the land but also for the animals. Regulations are given even for the harvesting of the birds (Exod. 23.4-5; Lev. 25.6; Deut 22.4, 6-7; 25.4). Significantly, in war when devastation is an accepted consequence, the preservation of trees is ensured (Deut. 20.19-20).[49] This ecological, covenantal relationship is particularly apparent in the passages concerning blessings and curses in which obedience or disobedience to God's commandments affect the land. Obedience yields regularity of seasons for plants and harvests. Even harmful animals will be eliminated (Lev. 26.4-6). Yet disobedience brings an unfruitful and unresponsive soil and animals and plagues will be unleashed against the people (Lev. 26.19-22). Further, the most horrifying repercussion is that disobedience will cause the land to dispossess Israel as it had its former inhabitants (Lev. 18.24-30). Inherent to the land and indeed all of creation, then, was a sacred order the violation of

---

[48]Brueggemann, *The Land*, 52.
[49]See Austin, *Hope for the Land*, 97-105.

which disrupted the natural world and threatened to return the world to chaos.[50]

These comments sufficiently underscore the interrelatedness between God, the land, and Israel. It may be observed also that while the importance of the land as a sacred geographic location diminished in later Judaism and in the NT period, its evocative power as an eschatological symbol of God's universal rule and the reestablishment of the order of creation persisted.[51] Local concerns yielded to cosmic speculations as the prophets, visionaries, and the NT writers announced the dawning of the new heavens and a new earth. In the OT Second Isaiah especially prepared for the cosmic dimensions of the eschatological hope for the created order.[52]

The Old Testament Hope for Creation

The "Suffering" of Creation

As noted, Israel's view of the covenant led to a realization of a moral and material connection with the land. Human

---

[50]See Davies, *Gospel and Land*, 31-35 and discussion below pp. 55-62.

[51]As election served as a symbol and instrument of God's plan for the salvation of all humankind, the sanctification of the promised land served as a symbol or token of God's universal triumph over the creation. Simon J. De Vries, *The Achievements of Biblical Religions: A Prolegomenon to Old Testament Theology* (New York: University Press of America, 1983), 234-35. See also von Rad, "The Promised Land," 92-93.

[52]Davies argues that the idea of the land as a geopolitical entity was rejected, spiritualized, treated historically, and sacramentalized. Primarily in the NT, life in the land gave way to life in Christ. *Gospel and Land*, 318, 366-76; idem, *The Territorial Dimensions of Judaism* (Berkeley: University of California, 1982). Brueggemann in response to Davies contends that the theme of the land is more prominent than assumed and is often presented in a dialectical way in the NT. In conflict with Gnosticism the motif was taken in a more physical, historical way while in political contexts it was regarded in a more symbolic manner. *The Land*, 170-84. The silence of the NT concerning the land, in this writer's opinion, owes essentially to a cosmic concern. Life in the land is indeed replaced by life in Christ, but the NT writers also anticipated that life would be enjoyed and set in the new creation. Davies acknowledges this factor (370). See also the comments of Richard C. Oudersluys, "Israel: The Land and the Scriptures," *RefR* 33 (Autumn 1979): 9-14.

behavior was therefore believed to affect the environment. This concept was based upon the land's value as ultimately derived from its relationship to God (Num. 35.34). The prophets' message of judgment, then, often revealed that the sins of the people had not only alienated God but also placed them at odds with the created order. Particularly intriguing are those passages which portray the earth as suffering or "mourning" under the weight of sin in the world. The term אבל important in this regard for it is frequently employed to denote the suffering of the land due to humanity's transgressions.[53] Our contemporary society tends to be concerned only with human affliction. This section concentrates upon the biblical view that reveals the presence of anguish in every realm of creation which demands reparation.

Some may suggest that the language representing creation as suffering is metaphorical and merely reflects the writers' concern for a land that has become unproductive and therefore is no longer beneficial to humanity. Yet one also cannot easily ignore the sensitivity of the prophets as they looked in horror upon the created order in a state of total disrepair not of its own making. Hosea, for example, employing the style drawn from Israelite court procedure, presents Israel with a subpoena regarding the case of God versus Israel in Hos. 4.1-3. God as prosecuting attorney, witness, and judge points to the widespread rebellion as indicative of the people's lack of faithfulness, kindness, and most importantly their lack of the knowledge of God (v. 1). Consequently all forms of wickedness prevail: swearing, deception, murder, stealing, and adultery (v. 2). So enormous and extensive is Israel's defiance against God's covenant that even the land itself is depicted as suffering.[54]

---

[53]When used of inanimate objects the reference is most often to the ארץ "land" of Israel. Note the exceptions: city gates (Isa. 3.26); wine (Isa. 24.7); Judah (Jer. 14.2); roads of Zion (Lam. 1.4); walls and ramparts (Lam. 2.8). All of these, however, refer to the nation and hence a landed concept. At times this was given universal significance as illustrated below in the discussion of Isaiah 24-27.

[54]The judgment referred to may be present or yet future in the mind of Hosea. Luther L. Mays argues that the description far exceeds the limits of a present drought or some other situation. *Hosea: A Commentary*, OTL (Philadelphia: Westminster, 1969), 65.

"Therefore the land mourns,[55] and everyone who lives in it lan-guishes along with the beasts of the field and the birds of the sky; and even the fish of the sea disappear" (v. 3). Israel's sin is so weighty that it affects land, inhabitants, and animals.

A solidarity between humanity and creation is revealed also in Hosea's eschatological oracle concerning the time when God will make a covenant with all creatures and the earth once again will become responsive (2.18-20). The importance of the animals is accentuated by their participation in the covenant with God that will be established in the end times (v. 18). It is also notable that renewal is occasioned by a return to a knowl-edge of God (v. 20). Disorder in every part of the creation abounds without the knowledge of God in the world. Hosea like the other OT prophets longed for a day when the earth would be filled with the knowledge of God (cf. Isa. 11.9).[56]

Jeremiah frequently projected the activity of mourning onto the land. In some cases the pain and desolation of the land takes on cosmic proportions such as described in Jer. 4.23-28. Judah's approaching ruin by Babylon is described in the vivid imagery of the chaos myth as if already experienced. The dev-astation is cosmic and earthly. The earth has returned to its primeval chaotic state (תהו ובהו; v. 23). Mountains quake and birds and humanity flee. The land mourns and becomes deso-late. All creation suffers under the weight of God's wrath. Note

---

[55]In this and the following texts where the verb אבל ("mourn") occurs, it is regarded by many commentators as properly translated "wither" parallel with אמל and in other contexts with יבש (II KB, not in BDB). Hans W. Wolff, *Hosea*, trans. Gary Stansell, Hermeneia (Philadelphia: Fortress, 1974), 65; Douglas Stuart *Hosea-Jonah*, WBC (Waco: Word, 1987), 72. Such is unnec-essary. Cf. the LXX: πενθήσει ἡ γῆ καὶ [σμικρυνθήσεται + Rahlfs]. Whether אבל is regarded as reflecting a condition of drought or as a figurative expression connoting the anguish of the created order, the latter half of v. 3 (and so in the other passages) reveals the OT conception of a corruption so extensive that the natural order "along with" (ב; GKC, §119h) the inhabitants of the land suffer under the judgment of a world marred by sin. Cf. *TDOT*, s.v. "אבל," by A. Baumann, 1:47.

[56]See Francis I. Anderson and David Noel Freedman, *Hosea*, AB (New York: Doubleday, 1980), 334-35. The writers observe that although the focus of judgment in 4.1-3 is Israel, the wording suggests also a universal emphasis.

Bright's translation of verse 28: "For this let the earth and the heavens above don mourning, . . ."[57] Thus, Jeremiah presents a total reversal of the "very good" of creation. While the immediate source of devastation is Babylon, the context of the oracle witnesses that the ultimate cause of Judah's plight is their own sin (v. 18; cf. 5.7-8.26). These verses therefore function to warn that the violation of God's covenant nullifies the world order on both historical and cosmic levels. Even more noticeable and equally severe is Jeremiah's insistence that the wickedness of the people had disrupted the natural order of the seasons. Although the verb אבל is absent in this text, the notion of a world diminished by human iniquity is evident. Jeremiah 5.23-25 celebrates the power of God in creation in conquering the chaotic sea (v. 23) and providing the rains and the seasons (v. 24). The nation, however, did not acknowledge God's sovereignty either in creation or in its own life. Interestingly, this passage offers a striking contrast of an obedient creation and a mutinous people. Jeremiah therefore declares, "your wrongdoing has upset nature's order, and your sins have kept from you her kindly gifts" (v. 25, NEB).[58]

The motif appears also in Jeremiah's lament (12.4, 11) and in Jer. 23.10 which indicates two reasons for the suffering of the land depending upon the reading of the text: widespread adultery, perhaps a figure of pagan cultic involvement, and "because of the curse."[59] The reason for Jeremiah's distress is not so much the rampant immorality--although this is sufficient cause--as the curse upon the land due to the immorality of the people. The condition of the land is therefore directly related to human behavior.

When one turns to the so-called "Isaianic Apocalypse"

---

[57]John Bright, *Jeremiah*, AB (New York: Doubleday, 1965), 31.

[58]Cf. *Frg. Tg. Jer.* 32.5: ". . . that crooked and twisted generation has changed its ways; and therefore, the orders of the world."

[59]The second, treated by the BHS as an addition and omitted in the LXX relates the state of the land to those whose behavior is described as evil and whose power is false. Robert P. Carroll, *Jeremiah*, OTL (Philadelphia: Westminster, 1986), 451-52.

(chs. 24-27) the same perspective prevails.[60] Isaiah like Jeremiah uses creation language to describe the national desolation which especially in these chapters widens to cosmic proportions as God's dealings with Israel are seen as paradigmatic for the entire world.[61] The earth is thus pictured as under a divine curse.

---

[60]These chapters have been the subject of great discussion. At issue is whether Isaiah 24-27 usually considered a unit should be regarded as apocalyptic or eschatological. When read through the literary lens of Daniel or 1 Enoch the unit is regarded as apocalyptic in character dating anywhere from the sixth to the second century BC later inserted into the present context. The themes of worldwide destruction, a return to chaos, inauguration of the new age, imprisonment of the heavenly host, and resurrection of the dead have been adduced primarily as evidence. Cf. William R. Millar, *Isaiah 24-27 and the Origin of Apocalyptic*, HSM, no. 11 (Missoula, MT: Scholars, 1976); Hanson, *Dawn of Apocalyptic*, 313-14; Otto Plöger, *Theocracy and Eschatology*, trans. S. Rudman (Richmond: John Knox, 1968). The apocalyptic nature of this section is less than certain. See G. W. Anderson, "Isaiah XXIV-XXVII Reconsidered," in the *Congress Volume*, VTSup, no. 9 (Leiden: Brill, 1963), 118-26. Note also the recent analysis of Dan G. Johnson, *From Chaos to Restoration: An Integrative Reading of Isaiah 24-27*, JSOTSup, no. 61 (Sheffield: University of Sheffield, 1988). Johnson dates the chapters to the time of the exile (24.1-20, 587 BC; 24.21-27, exilic period) and regards them as eschatological in perspective (16-17). It appears unlikely that the ties to the historical and political realms have been entirely severed in chs. 24-27. At most one may regard them with Millar as proto-apocalyptic (114). Hanson, cited above, designates these chapters as early apocalyptic (313-14). Others tend to date the chapters during the Assyrian crisis. See, e.g., John N. Oswalt, *The Book of Isaiah: Chapters 1-39*, NICOT (Grand Rapids: Eerdmans, 1986), 440-46. Whatever the specific historical setting, an eschatological perspective is evident. The prophet, like Jeremiah and Ezekiel, believed that the ultimate reign of God would commence only with the restoration of the nation.

[61]The term אֶרֶץ receives the emphasis in vv. 1-20 occurring some sixteen times. Note that although הָאָרֶץ is translated elsewhere in Isaiah as "the land," here it is given universal connotations by most translators as "the earth" (RSV, NIV, NASB, NEB). This is due to its parallel with תֵּבֵל ("world") and perhaps to presuppositions regarding the apocalyptic nature of these chapters. See John D. W. Watts, *Isaiah 1-33*, WBC (Waco: Word, 1985), 315-17. Cf. the LXX: ἡ γῆ, καὶ . . . ἡ οἰκουμένη ("inhabited world," v. 4). Further, the prophet's announcement of a coming destruction in cosmic terms conceivably could be based on the OT concept of Israel as the center of the earth. It could then accurately be described as the desolation of the known world and creation's return to chaos. For this concept see Luis I. J. Stadelmann, *The Hebrew Conception of the World*, AnBib, no. 39 (Rome: Pontifical Biblical Institute,

The words of Isaiah 24 are unsurpassed in portraying the reality of creation marred by humanity's sin.

> [1] Behold, the Lord lays the earth waste, devastates it, distorts its surface, and scatters its inhabitants. . . . [3] The earth will be completely laid waste and completely despoiled for the Lord has spoken this word. [4] The earth mourns and withers, the world fades and withers, the exalted of the people of the earth fades away. [5] The earth is also polluted by [under] its inhabitants, for they transgressed laws, violated statutes, broke the everlasting covenant. [6] Therefore, a curse devours the earth, and those who live in it are held guilty. Therefore, the inhabitants of the earth are burned, and few men are left. [7] The new wine mourns, the vine decays, all the merry-hearted sigh.

In the opening section of the passage the prophet presents the creation in disarray (vv. 1-20). As in the account of Genesis 3 the inhabitants have sinned but the earth also experiences the consequences. Especially vivid is the picturesque use of the perfects in verse 4 to depict the judgment of the world as if already complete. The land or earth is represented as donning mourning apparel as if grieving over the dead. The withering earth acutely reflects the exhausted, impotent state of the land due to the weight of humanity's sin and thus it lies languishing (v. 4).[62] Verse 5 specifies the reason for the judgment. The inhabitants have violated God's everlasting covenant. The wide sweeping perspective of the passage brings to mind the Noachic covenant and refers to the universal laws or principles that govern the relationship of humanity with the created order.[63] The curse upon

---

1970), 147-54. Most accurate and to the point is Oswalt's observation that the universal outlook is rooted in the prophet's understanding of Israel as typical of God's treatment of the entire world. *Isaiah*, 444. See comments below on Isa. 65.17-25.

[62]E. J. Young, *The Book of Isaiah*, NICOT (Grand Rapids: Eerdmans, 1969), 2:154-55. Cf. *Tg. Isa.*: "And the earth has sinned under its inhabitants."

[63]Oswalt, *Isaiah*, 27-29. Commentators are in general agreement that the reference is to God's covenant with Noah. That humanity was able to break an everlasting and unconditional covenant is nevertheless problematic. Johnson dissents and contends for a Mosaic reference although he admits that the

the earth is given life by the prophet as it devours the earth and its inhabitants (v. 6).[64] Moreover, the land is in such a state that the grapes and the vine that bears them lament their inability to produce a fruitful harvest. The entire natural order participates in the sorrow of the earth spoiled by sin.[65] Perhaps the strongest language regarding the suffering of creation under God's wrath is verses 19-20.

> [19] The earth is broken asunder, the earth is split through, the earth is shaken violently. [20] The earth reels to and fro like a drunkard, and it totters like a shack, for its transgression is heavy upon it, and it will fall, never to rise again.

Like a drunken person or a frail straw hut against a vigorous wind, the earth is unstable and therefore unable to bear its load of sin. Contrary to Oswalt's suggestion that this implies the inevitable and ultimate demise of the world, this imagery is best taken as reflecting the burdensome consequences of human sin upon creation.[66]

One may demur that in view of the theophanic character of these passages such violent language is naturally ubiquitous. However, a more sensitive reading reveals that these passages reflect the reality of a world run amok due to the sin of humanity. This actuality notwithstanding, these texts do not suggest that God is in anyway displeased with his creation. It still remains essentially his good creation even when implicated in humanity's judgment. In fact, the announcement of the earth's collapse may well be a message of hope for both the nation and creation. The prophet believed that the plight of Israel was so deplorable that it

---

Sinaitic covenant is never elsewhere referred to as ברית עולם. *Chaos*, 27-28. Otto Kaiser notes that the Noachic covenant includes the legal ordination of Num. 35.33 regarding bloodguilt (cf. Gen. 9.6). *Isaiah 13-39*, trans. R. A. Wilson, OTL (Philadelphia: Westminster, 1974), 183. In any case, the covenant of Gen. 9.8-16 subjected humanity to certain moral laws to be observed within the created order the violation of which would pollute the creation.

[64]The curse then becomes synonymous with the power of God's anger released upon all of humanity. Ronald E. Clements, *Isaiah 1-39*, NICOT (Grand Rapids: Eerdmans, 1980), 202.

[65]Young, *Isaiah*, 2:161.

[66]Oswalt, *Isaiah*, 446.

could be rectified only by a divine act of transformation universal in scope.[67]

Creation and Eschatology

It is perhaps appropriate at this juncture to consider the eschatological aspect of creation. As the message of creation affirms a time of absolute beginning, so it looks forward to the end and ultimate consummation when the creator will restore humanity and creation according to his original purpose. The Bible from both a canonical and theological perspective links decisively the concepts of creation and its ultimate redemption in a dynamic unity, and as such points from the "first things" to a vision of the new heavens and earth in the Apocalypse of John. It is no mere coincidence that these concepts are brought together by the seer of the Apocalypse in the climactic statement, "I am the Alpha and the Omega, the first and the last, the beginning and the end" (Rev. 22.13). Anderson observes that creation and consummation like Siamese twins are indissolubly related. "The first words of the Bible, 'in the beginning,' have as their counterpart the prophetic expectation, 'in the end.'"[68]

God is the creator and "re-creator"[69] and thus both beginning and end belong to his creative activity. Accordingly, the relationship of the two concepts is evidenced in the placement of salvation history within the framework of beginning and consummation (Isa. 44.6).[70] By placing the account of creation at the

---

[67]Anderson, "Isaiah XXIV-XXVII Reconsidered," 124.

[68]Anderson, *Creation Versus Chaos,* 110; Eichrodt, *Theology,* 2:110. This discussion is indebted particularly to the writings of Anderson.

[69]The terms "re-creation" and "consummation" are used synonymously since the prophets viewed the new creation as the fulfillment of God's original creative intentions and in continuity with the present order. See Eichrodt, *Theology,* 2:107.

[70]Cullmann's view of salvation history as interrelated units stretching from creation to ultimate consummation places the primal and end times myths on the same interpretive level as salvation historical events. *Christ and Time,* 100-102; idem, "The Connection of Primal Events and End Events with the New Testament Redemptive History," in *The Old Testament and Christian Faith,* ed. Bernhard W. Anderson (New York: Harper & Row, 1963), 115- 23. Claus Westermann distinguishes primal and end events from salvation history

base of the salvation history scheme, it acquires the character of an "initial act" and thus the inevitability of the accomplishment of God's plan of salvation.[71] Even the primeval account displays an eschatological intention. The motif of rest in the scheme of a week serves to give creation the historical character as an event that moves through time toward a goal. This linear quality reflects that the ultimate goal of God's creation is not humanity, but ultimately what is suggested in the description of the seventh day.[72] The seventh day is significant not in itself but as a symbol of the potential rest for which all creation longs to experience under the lordship of God as in the beginning.[73]

The motif of the *chaoskampf* also points forward in eschatological hope. While there is only a faint echo of this myth in the word תהום ("deep," v. 2) in Genesis 1, the Hebrews believed that the forces of chaos were ever threatening to return and devour their world.[74] An important element of this concept was the struggle against chaos often personified as a dragon or Leviathan of the primordial sea. Thus, the sea became a menacing foe in Israel's writings. Once subject to God's lordship, the waters could be viewed as a source of blessing. God, however, merely subjugates rather than eradicates the primordial chaos. Psalm 104.5-9 and Genesis 1 presents God as confining the watery chaos to its boundaries which implies the possibility of

---

and thus the primeval event is not the beginning of history. *Beginning and End in the Bible*, trans. Keith Crim (Philadelphia: Fortress, 1972), 28-29.

[71]As stated above, Gen. 1.1 as a main clause denotes a temporal beginning and attests to an absolute beginning of creation. See also Eichrodt, "In the Beginning," 71; Jacob, *Theology*, 138-39.

[72]Westermann, *Genesis*, 90. See also Steck, *Der Schöpfungsbericht*, 15-16.

[73]Anderson points to the writer's concern for the creation and ordering of time which looks toward the fulfillment of God's purposes. *Creation Versus Chaos*, 112.

[74]John Day argues that the OT imagery derives essentially from the Canaanite myth of Baal's conflict with the sea god Yam and his dragon associates Leviathan or Rahab rather than from the Babylonian myth of Marduk's conflict with Tiamat in the *Enuma elish*. *God's Conflict with the Dragon and the Sea* (Cambridge: University, 1985), 1-18. According to Day, Genesis 1 is dependent upon Psalm 104 which more clearly reflects the *chaoskampf* theme (51-53).

its return and creation's subsequent plunge into chaos.[75] The water thus is portrayed as longing to return to its original place. This prospect occurs momentarily in the flood event although the waters are clearly the instrument of God and not his foe.[76] The potentiality of destruction, then, is inherent in the creation process itself. The use of the creation myth to underscore the contingency of creation displays a dynamic tension between beginning and end, creation and consummation.

It is in the apocalyptic passages that the forces of evil ultimately are destroyed as creation is renewed and once again becomes wholly subject to its creator. The seer John affirms that with the coming of the new heavens and earth the sea will be no more (Rev. 21.1). The motifs and language of the *chaoskampf* became useful to the prophets and apocalyptists for conveying the sovereignty of God in restoring order whether moral, political, or natural since in the OT there is a clear continuity between the primal event and salvation history.[77] In the face of hostile forces of every kind, creation theology, as in other religions of the ancient Near East, functioned as liberation theology.[78] While the myth often served historical purposes, one must not disregard the import of such language for an understanding of the freeing of the cosmos.

The prophecies of Isaiah, especially as found in chapters 40-66, played a prominent role in preparing for an understand-

---

[75]Day, *God's Conflict with the Dragon*, 5-9.

[76]Jacob, *Theology*, 140. Von Rad asserts that there is no hint of a dualistic struggle between chaos and God in the priestly account. Chaos does not have any power of its own, but exists only in submission to the creator's will. *Genesis*, 65. The mythological allusions perhaps reflect a polemical intention. Gerhard F. Hasel, "The Polemic Nature of the Genesis Cosmology," *EvQ* 46 (April-June 1974): 82-102.

[77]Dennis McCarthy observes that the *chaoskampf* became for the writers of the Old Testament merely a source for figures of speech without accepting its reality. "'Creation' Motifs in Ancient Hebrew Poetry," in *Creation in the Old Testament*, ed. Bernhard W. Anderson, IRT, no. 6 (Philadelphia: Fortress, 1984), 80. One must, however, acknowledge the *reality* reflected in the figures of speech or motifs.

[78]George Landes, "Creation as Liberation Theology," in *Creation in the Old Testament*, ed. Bernhard W. Anderson, IRT, no. 6 (Philadelphia: Fortress Press, 1984), 136.

ing of cosmic redemption.[79] Second Isaiah, more than any other prophet, recognized the relation between creation and redemption. Utilizing the mythological language of creation and the Exodus tradition, the prophet joined the concepts into a dynamic unity. The creator *is* the redeemer.[80] Isa. 51.9-11 combined the motifs of God's victory over chaos personified by the mythological Rahab--representing both the monster created at creation and Egypt at the Exodus--to stress that the new beginning for Israel hovering just above the horizon would be an entirely new redemptive event--a new creation.[81] The cosmic language enhanced the historical events and revealed that while the new events were analogous to the great redemptive works of the past, they would reach far beyond in significance, purpose, and quality of existence.[82] Such was the magnificence of the new event that cosmic change was evident in his message of hope as the natural world is transformed and renewed in anticipation of the new Exodus (Isa. 40.1-5; cf. 43.19, 20; 44.3).

The excitement of the new beginning is evidenced also in Isa. 43.15- 21. Second Isaiah sees himself standing at the threshold of the renewal of creation. In this passage the prophet reminded Israel that her existence rested entirely upon God's act of redemption. He uses language that recalled the experience of the Exodus. However, God's original creative act of deliverance pales in comparison to what God is going to do. "Do not call to

---

[79]Isaiah was a major contributor to the concept of the transformation of the natural world: 11.6-9; 29.17; 30.23-26; 32.15; 35.1-7; 40.17-20; 43.16-21; 51.3-6; etc.

[80]Bernhard W. Anderson, "Exodus Typology in Second Isaiah," in *Israel's Prophetic Heritage*, ed. Bernhard W. Anderson and Walter Harrelson (New York: Harper & Bros., 1962), 181-85.

[81]Claus Westermann, *Isaiah 40-66: A Commentary*, OTL, trans. D. M. G. Stalker (Philadelphia: Westminster, 1969), 33; idem, "God and His Creation," *USQR* 18 (March 1963): 197-209; Day, *God's Conflict with the Dragon*, 92.

[82]Regarding typological interpretation of biblical history in the OT see Gerhard von Rad, "Typological Interpretation of the Old Testament," in *Essays on Old Testament Hermeneutics*, ed. Claus Westermann, trans. James Luther Mays (Richmond: John Knox, 1964), 17-39 and Leonhard Goppelt, *Typos: The Typological Interpretation of the Old Testament in the New*, trans. Donald H. Madvig (Grand Rapids: Eerdmans, 1982), 32-41.

mind the former things, or ponder things of the past. Behold, I will do something new, . . ." (v. 19). God as creator of Israel was prepared to perform a mythological act of "re-creation."[83] Once again God will bring order out of chaos. Although the creation language stresses the historical drama of Israel's new redemption from Exile, it nevertheless broadens to cosmic proportions reflecting the intense expectation of universal redemption. God will "make a roadway in the wilderness, rivers in the desert"(v. 19). The new Exodus will be the climax of God's work and hence something totally new and unprecedented with cosmic consequences.[84]

While it is true that Second Isaiah anticipated a local change and national renewal, in light of the present plight of Israel, the restoration could only be accomplished as a part of a transformation universal in extent. Such a universal view led the prophet to propose two periods of history: the past that was to be forgotten and the new which was about to spring forth. Hanson finds here the embryonic thought for the apocalyptic concept of two ages.[85] As lord over history God would accomplish his intentions in this new event. It therefore has eschatological significance. Koehler attests that this concept is implicit in the understanding of the beginning. "To the beginning corresponds an end, to creation there corresponds a consummation, to the very good, here, a 'perfectly glorious' there. They belong together. *Creation in the OT is an eschatological concept.*"[86] Since the beginning must have an end, creation must be followed by redemption or renewal. Furthermore, this motif of renewal in the new Exodus pointed forward in hope toward the end when God's creative intentions would be fully realized in a new creation. This soon found expression in later passages of Isaiah and apocalyptic.

Despite Second Isaiah's use of mythological language, he

---

[83]See Anderson, *Creation Versus Chaos*, 130-31.

[84]That the new Exodus would be a new and unique work is stressed by the use of the creation verb ברא to denote eschatological deeds (cf. Isa. 41.20; 45.7, 8; 48.7; 57.18; 65.17, 18). Anderson, *Creation Versus Chaos*, 125-26.

[85]Hanson, *Dawn of Apocalyptic*, 121.

[86]Ludwig Koehler, *Old Testament Theology*, trans. A. S. Todd (Philadelphia: Westminster, 1957), 88.

never allowed his message to leave its firm rootage in history. As will be seen in apocalyptic passages, the writers tend to literalize poetic language. By contrast, Second Isaiah stated the coming redemption in terms of secular world history, as for example, through the person of Cyrus (cf. 44.28; 45.1). In later passages of Isaiah's prophecies Hanson contends that this dialectic between the mythological and historical is not so closely guarded. When the mythological embellishment serves the prophet not as an historical enhancement but as a new vehicle for interpretation in view of their present plight, then prophetic eschatology begins to yield to apocalyptic eschatology.[87] The stress was no longer centered on past or even immediate events but on the end times. One must keep in mind, however, that there is a distinction between the eschatology of postexilic prophecy and that of later apocalyptic. The transformation of life in Isaiah 65, for example, is still very much this-worldly and historically oriented.

The NT writing of 2 Peter likewise affirms an eschatological concept of creation.[88] The entire argument of 2 Pet. 3.5-13 presupposes a correspondence between beginning and end. In response to those who falsely asserted that the Lord was not returning, the writer argues that just as the creation experienced destruction and judgment in the beginning so will it in the end. In fact, the one promises the other--a typological hermeneutic as in Second Isaiah. The flood points to a future destruction of the world by fire and the creation of the new heavens and earth in which righteousness will reign. Although the focus upon the flood is a type of future destruction, the beginning and end are nevertheless cemented together.[89] The end is therefore in some manner analogous to the beginning. Moreover, in the typological understanding of the biblical writers the end not only corresponds to the beginning, the beginning actually calls the fulfillment into existence. That is to say, the events of the beginning are both symbols and promises of God's future "re-creative" work. In the

---

[87]Hanson, *Dawn of Apocalyptic*, 127-31.

[88]For additional examples in the NT see Nils A. Dahl, "Christ, Creation, and the Church," in *The Background of the New Testament and Its Eschatology*, ed. W. D. Davies and David Daube (Cambridge: University, 1954), 422-43.

[89]Goppelt, *Typos*, 33, 158. Cf. 1 Enoch 10.2; 83.3-5; Matt. 24.37.

last times, God who is the first and the last (Isa. 44.6; Rev. 1.8) will right all wrongs, reward the righteous, and restore the world to its primordial state of perfection.

This perspective, however, rejects all connotations of a cyclical view of history. In his classic work, Gunkel noted that the speculation concerning the relation of *Urzeit* and *Endzeit* was based on the recognition that the last things are derived essentially from the beginning. This concept is represented in the apocryphal writing of Barnabas: "Behold I make the last things as the first" (Barn. 6.13). Gunkel noted several recurring elements of the first things: new creation of heaven and earth, second Adam, paradise with its life giving tree, new Exodus, with its attending plagues, and a new Moses. If one desires to know how the end will be then one must consider the beginning. This conviction, according to Gunkel, was the basis of a greater part of the NT speculation concerning Christology, predestination, and end times which expressed the form of equating the first and last.[90] His phrase, "Urzeit gleich Endzeit," is misleading. The writers of the OT and NT did not expect merely a return to the former things--a restoration of the original. As noted above, the new while typical of the old would supersede the first things. There is no *myth of the eternal return*.[91] The destiny for humanity and the universe always is directed toward *newness*.

Although we do not wish to anticipate prematurely the results of our investigation, an additional comment may be stated regarding the eschatological hope of creation. As noted above, the correspondence between creation and consummation, first and last things, is prominent in the Bible and especially in apocalyptic literature.[92] This focus is not simply a romantic spec-

---

[90]Hermann Gunkel. *Schöpfung und Chaos in Urzeit und Endzeit: Eine religionsgeschichtliche Untersuchung über Gen. 1 und Ap. Joh. 12* (Göttingen: Vandenhoeck & Ruprecht, 1895), 367-69. See also Gösta Lindeskog, *Studien zum Neutestamentlichen Schöpfungsdanken* (Uppsala: Lundequistika, 1953), 1:107-8. Lindeskog observes that "Eschatologie ist futurale ktisiologie" (119).

[91]See the comments of Eliade, *Eternal Return*, 112-37.

[92]A study of early Jewish and Christian sources by Dahl reveals several main types of correlation of first and last things which were often combined in various ways: analogy or parallelism, e.g., ideas of new creation, new heavens and earth, new earth as transformation of the first creation; identical corre-

ulation longing for a return to paradise; rather, it is rooted in the recognition of God as creator. The writers were convinced that as God first created the world in perfect harmony so he would ultimately restore it to its original divine purpose and state. God's work in the world and history is therefore meaningful and teleological. The end will manifest the faithfulness of God in bringing to fulfillment his creative intentions. However, even this statement should not be understood as only reflecting the religious or psychological motivation for the phenomena which then can be spiritualized into a universal maxim. It is far more than this. The prominence of the reestablishment or renewal of creation and its constituent elements rather than a spectral existence in a heavenly domain attests unequivocally that in the minds of the apocalyptists and biblical writers the consummation would never be regarded as a blessing apart from the restoration of the physical creation. This teaching thus does not evince any spiritual-material dualism which depreciates this world.

The New Heavens and New Earth

It has been observed that the OT reflects more of an interest in the created order than usually assumed. This is especially evident when viewed from the theological perspective of creation as an eschatological concept. The theme of the restoration of creation is thus prominent in texts regarding the last days. For example, Ezekiel's message of the restoration of Israel in chapters 34-36 promises the transformation of the natural world. The prophet anticipates the installment of a Davidic king whose reign of righteousness pervades all inhabitants of the kingdom including the animals. Significantly, the alienation between humanity and the earth is removed due to the implanting of a new heart and new spirit (36.25-30). Thus, the restoration of a proper relationship between God and his people will affect even

---

spondence between the first and last things, e.g., paradise, tree of life, first and second Adam; reservation of first things for the end of the world; perfection of the old creation abolishing the powers of darkness, etc.; preexistence of the things appearing in the end times which have existed from the beginning as "heavenly" realities in the mind and purpose of God. "Christ, Creation, and the Church," 425-29.

the created order.[93]

It would, however, be misleading and inaccurate to suggest that the eschatological passages depicting a return to a paradisal condition are entirely "nature" oriented. To be sure, the prophets responding to the needs of ancient humanity envisioned an era of *shalom* where even the natural world would no longer constitute a threat to life. Therefore, the righteous are promised a life of peace in a transformed Jerusalem in a renewed world where the blessings of salvation may be enjoyed. Gladness and everlasting joy will be the order of the day. The land that previously was decimated due to the judgment of God upon sinful humanity once again will be so fruitful that it will look like a forest and hunger will be a thing of the past.[94] Wild animals will be banished from the land and offer humanity no further threat. Therefore the scriptures state that people can sleep even in the woods without fear and domestic animals can roam freely (Ezek. 34.25; cf. Isa. 35.9, 20). Indeed, peace will reign even in the animal kingdom (Isa. 11.6-9; 65.25).[95] Prosperity in God's land will ultimately arrive so that each one can sit under his luxurious fig tree in security (Mic. 4.4).

Gowan in his discussion of the natural world in Hebrew eschatology argues that the theme of "nature" is thus primarily anthropocentric and at times theocentric as the natural elements are often used as symbols of the power and presence of God.[96] In many texts regarding the reestablishment of Zion, references to the creation serve only to glorify God's power. Gowan's observations notwithstanding, the eschatological passages neverthe-

---

[93]Cf. Gowan's discussion, *Eschatology*, 101-3.

[94]The motif of a revitalized land is prominent: Isa. 29.17; 32.15; 34-35; 51.3; Ezek. 34-36; Zech. 14.9-11. This theme, as expected, is intertwined with that of increased or re-population, a major tenet of Hebrew eschatology: Isa. 54.1-3; Jer. 3.16; Ezek. 36.10-11, 37; Hos. 1.10; Zech. 8.5; 10.8.

[95]The prospect of peace in the animal kingdom, according to Gowan, is due largely to the Hebrews' reticence to the taking of life either human or animal. Wildlife management without predatory instincts are of little concern to the prophet. The prophet pictures a time in which violence of any kind will be eradicated. *Eschatology*, 104.

[96]Ibid., 113-18. The power and holiness of God is especially magnified in the passages which speak of the response of creation at the theophany of the Lord in judgment (Isa. 24.23; Joel 2.30, 31).

less reveal a concern for the redemption of creation itself as well as humanity. For example, although the theme of a return to paradise in Ezek. 47.1-12 reveals a concern primarily for humanity, the creation is not totally overshadowed. Ezekiel's temple vision, like Gen. 2.10, depicts a life giving river flowing forth so broad and swift that it revitalizes the barren desert and sweetens the waters of the Dead Sea (vv. 1-8). The supernatural fertility of the water that issues forth from the temple is illustrated by the swarming life in the river and the abundance of the monthly yield of the fruit bearing trees. Only the marshes and swamps are left untouched; yet they now serve to supply the salt previously provided by the Dead Sea (vv. 9-12). The passage portrays the return of creation to its former glory. Moreover, the interrelatedness of the creation and humanity is evident. The abundance of fish and the fruit of the trees are said to furnish food, the leaves provide healing, and the salt marshes supply the precious commodity necessary for human life.

This writer would agree with Gowan that one cannot manipulate the biblical material to prove an overwhelming interest in the created order that prevails over the well-being of humanity.[97] The primary concern is that of life without the limitations imposed by sin. It is nevertheless evident that the creation is important in God's plan of salvation. The vision of Ezekiel clearly affirms above all that the ultimate source of all spiritual and material blessings are derived from God. God's presence gives life, and that life relates not only to the spiritual dimension but to the physical. God not only transforms one inwardly but also transforms one's world. Notably, in support of the contentions in this study, Gowan acknowledges that an interest in the natural order in eschatological passages cannot be ignored without serious harm to the doctrine of creation in the present or in the future. They attest that the created order also has its rights.[98]

A final consideration must be given to the passage regard-

---

[97]Ibid., 109.

[98]Ibid. He states correctly that if one takes seriously the scripture's vision of the future "as the key to what God wants, then any arbitrary or irresponsible hurting or destroying of anything in this world must surely be judged as contrary to what God is doing."

ed as the *locus classicus* for the OT concept of eschatological renewal. The motif of the new heavens and a new earth is nowhere more clearly and decisively described than in Isa. 65.17-25.[99] While the writer describes the conditions of prosperity in the new Jerusalem, the imagery also reveals a bal-

---

[99]The issues regarding the authorship of Isaiah 65 and indeed all of Isaiah are complex. Since the development of the historical critical method a general consensus has prevailed among scholars that the entire book does not derive from Isaiah of Jerusalem and that the document gives evidence of passages which originate from a later period. Consequently chs. 40-55 and 56-66 (as well as individual passages, e.g., 13.1-14.23; chs. 24-27; chs. 35-36, etc.) find their setting in the Babylonian and postexilic era respectively. R. E. Clements has called the shape of the book "one of the most complex literary structures of the entire Old Testament." "Beyond Tradition-History: Deutero-Isaianic Development of First Isaiah's Themes," *JSOT* 31 (February 1985): 98; idem, "The Unity of the Book of Isaiah," *Interp* 36 (April 1982): 117-29. The issues surrounding the nomenclature "Second" or "Third" Isaiah while important should not disturb or otherwise obstruct this study. It would be sheer hypercriticism to deny Isaiah any part in the composition of chs. 40-66. However, even those who contend for full Isaianic authorship to the entire work must admit that some of the book contains parts which are not from Isaiah. Thus, Ridderbos asserts that the book contains "an Isaianic core, upon which the prophet's disciples (men who felt themselves closely bound to him) later worked in the spirit of the original author." One may affirm the participation of Isaiah while at the same time recognize later additions attributed to those who, like Isaiah, worked under the guidance of the Spirit and hence are unnamed prophets. *NBD*, 2d ed., s.v. "Isaiah, Book of," by H. N. Ridderbos, 522-24. See also the comments of William S. LaSor, David A. Hubbard and Frederic Wm. Bush, *Old Testament Survey* (Grand Rapids: Eerdmans, 1983). To the point is the authors' comment that "it is no more difficult to accept the concept of 'an unknown prophet of the Exile' than that of an unknown author of the epistle to the Hebrews" (372). Other scholars contend that Isaiah may be regarded as an anthology which was arranged in its present form by Isaiah's disciples after his death. Thus, in chs. 40-66 Isaiah of Jerusalem presupposed the Exile and return in his utterances. See *ISBE*, s.v. "Isaiah," by R. K. Harrison and G. L. Robinson, 2:885-904. Cf. also Oswalt, *Isaiah*, 23-29; Young, *Isaiah*, 3:547-48.

The date and historical background of this particular chapter is likewise problematic. Commentators who posit multiple authorship contend that the issue of worship in the new temple and the division within the community help place the text within the historical setting of the restoration of Jerusalem (520-515 BC). The function of the oracle served to keep hope alive in God's salvific plan for Israel and the world during the dismal days of the restoration. Watts, *Isaiah*, 352-53; Westermann, *Isaiah*, 307-8; R. N. Whybray, *Isaiah 40-66*, NCB (Greenwood, SC: Attic, 1975), 267.

anced concern for humanity and the creation.[100] This text therefore underscores the basic presupposition of the OT regarding
the universal character of God's work of redemption; namely,
that a redeemed humanity is not envisioned apart from a corre-
spondingly redeemed world.[101] The nature of Isa. 65.17-25 has
occasioned much debate particularly regarding its unique mixture of cosmic and historical or nationalistic elements.   The
bracketing of verses 18-24 by texts containing cosmic references
has led some to consider them as mere figurative expressions or
more likely late apocalyptic additions.[102] This is not a problem
for Hanson since the chapter exhibits the essential characteristics of apocalyptic. The mention of the new heavens and a new
earth is not surprising or intrusive in this context. The previous
verses in the chapter reflecting the inauguration of a new world
era prepares for the climatic expression of this concept in verse
17. The unified passage therefore reflects the radical dualism of
apocalyptic with the present world permeated by evil extending
even to the natural order so that only the replacement of the old
era with the new provides hope for the prophet.[103]

A radical rearrangement of the passage or the excision of
the offending verses is neither helpful nor necessary.[104] Moreover,
the apocalyptic nature of this section is doubtful since it lacks

---

[100]Isa. 66.22, a gloss taken from 65.17, does not impact the present topic
since it serves only as an illustration for the promise of the permanence of the
Jewish community. It shall endure as long as the new heavens and a new earth.
Westermann, *Isaiah*, 428.

[101]Gowan, *Eschatology*, 118.

[102]Some have argued that vv. 17 and 25 are out of place in this text even
though textual evidence is lacking. That v. 17 is foreign to the text is supported, according to Whybray, since the intervening vv. 18-23 have no cosmic
reference and much of v. 17 is duplicated in vv. 16b and 18. *Isaiah*, 266-67,
275. Westermann opines that either 17a is to be regarded as a figurative hyper-
bole along with v. 25--the only two verses which do not fit--or they are later
additions to the text. He suggests a transfer of v. 18a and the summons to
rejoice to precede v. 16b with v. 18b following v. 17. *Isaiah*, 407-11.

[103]Hanson, *Dawn of Apocalyptic*, 142-61.

[104]Whybray admits that the removal of v. 17 does not restore the inter-
nal unity to the text. *Isaiah*, 225. Verses 16b-19 present an especially striking
thematic unity. See Eberhard Sehmsdorf, "Studien zur Redaktionsgeschichte
von Jesaja 56-66 (I): (Jes. 65.16b-25; 66.1-4; 56.1-8)," *ZAW* 84 (1972): 519-
21.

many of the usual characteristics and interests associated with that literature or thought. The attempt to delineate the intrusive elements according to their apocalyptic traits also fails to consider the total evocative impact of the imagery presented by the prophet. Such language was part and parcel of the prophets' oracular repertoire. More decisive, however, is that the transformation is still very much this-worldly and finite even though an historic agent of salvation has been replaced by God himself.[105] It also may be noted that the combination of universal and local elements is not at all unique to this passage as noted above in previous passages of Isaiah. While the language suggests that the focus is primarily nationalistic, the prophets' perception of the nation as "a part that stands for the whole" affirmed that what happens to Israel has universal implications but it must first happen to Israel.[106] This explains why the writer can speak of local and universal changes almost with one breath.

The promise of the new heavens and a new earth arises in a context of contrasts. Verses 1-16a contrast the faithless and God's servants and their respective destinies. Verses 16b-25 likewise offer a contrast of the past troubles and future salvation. Salvation is announced in verses 17-19a while 19b-25 gives its description.[107] The prophet draws upon familiar motifs introduced in earlier prophecies but united in a powerful and evocative melange of images and expressions to portray the ultimate salvific act of God in history and creation.[108] The influence of Isa. 51.1-6 is especially noteworthy in view of the promise of a new creation. Previously in that passage the transitory nature of the world was stressed. Isaiah asserts in fact that the old world will be dissolved, "for the sky will vanish like smoke, and the

---

[105]Collins, *Apocalyptic Imagination*, 19-20; Westermann, *Isaiah*, 408. A comparison with Revelation, which utilizes many of these themes, reveals a far more radical break with history. See Ulrich Mauser, "Isaiah 65.17-25," *Interp* 36 (April 1982): 182-83.

[106]Walther Eichrodt, *Ezekiel: A Commentary*, OTL (London: SCM, 1966), 586-87. In this passage the movement narrows to center upon Jerusalem and life in the redeemed community. See also the comments above n. 60.

[107]Westermann, *Isaiah*, 407.

[108]Observe the previous motifs: v. 17a, cf. 51.1-5; v. 17b, cf. 43.18, 19; v. 18, cf. 62.4; v. 25, cf. 11.6-9.

earth will wear out like a garment" (v. 6). However, the context suggests that complete annihilation is not in mind. The language serves to remind the nations that the most permanent of all substantial realities of life is fleeting in comparison to God's saving act.[109]

The announcement of the new heavens and a new earth in Isa. 65.17-25 represents in the most comprehensive terms the work of salvation embracing both the faithful servants and their world.[110] The terminology recalling Genesis 1 is not coincidental. God intends to restore his creation and his people to their former and proper relationship.[111] The use of the creation verb ברא emphasizes the radical new quality of this eschatological event. As previously, the active participle points to God's continual work of salvation in the deliverance and restoration of Israel as a creative act which serves as a token of God's intention for the ultimate redemption of the entire creation. The word "new" while evocative does not contend for a new creation *ex nihilo* but as in previous prophecies it points to a miraculous transformation in history (v. 17a).[112] Like the message of Isa. 43.18, so absolute will be the new beginning that the former things are to be forgotten. The earlier passage points to the Exodus which will pale in comparison to the new Exodus. The prophet reinterprets the theme in reference to the entire creation

---

[109]See John L. McKenzie, *Second Isaiah*, AB (Garden City, NY: Doubleday, 1968), 180-81. Cf. Ps. 102.26; Isa. 40.6-8.

[110]The antithetical formula "heavens and earth" as in Gen. 1.1 is a widespread phenomenon in the ancient Near East denoting the totality of the universe. *TDOT*, s.v. "ארץ," by J. Bergman and M. Ottosson, 1:388-97. Cf. the comments of Knierim regarding the implications of this bipolar designation. "Cosmos and History," 76-80.

[111]The entire chapter resonates with the quality of newness. The faithful will be given a new name (vv. 15, 16), the new heavens and a new earth will be their abode with the central focus the new Jerusalem (vv. 17, 18), and there will be a new intimate relationship with God (vv. 24,).

[112]Westermann, *Isaiah*, 408 (cf. Isa. 42.9; 43.19; 48.6). North notes that in Second Isaiah renewal serves as a synonym for creation "but emphasizes the dynamic movement of continuity rather than replacement." Isa. 65.17 likewise is to be understood as continuous transformation. *TDOT*, s.v. "חדש," by C. R. North, 4:240-41. Note that חדש denotes the idea of renovation (2 Chron. 24.4, 12) or "restore" (Lam. 5.21; Ps. 51.12; 104.30).

with its troubles and pain that will be replaced by the new (v. 17b).[113]

A regard for both humanity and the creation is revealed in the following description of life in the transformed world. The imagery depicts in many ways an ordinary life in God's redeemed community and creation. The prophet thus envisions a rather this-worldly experience in which one may live a full and meaningful existence.[114] Jerusalem as the center of the world in Hebrew thought naturally receives the focus as it will be reestablished. Distress and pain will be replaced by rejoicing (vv. 18, 19). Death remains but premature death is a thing of the past. Longevity of life will return as in the era prior to the flood. Life will be settled, productive, and secure (cf. Hos. 5.11). Further, alienation no longer will reign between the farmer and the land for the curse has been lifted. He shall cultivate successfully and enjoy the fruits of his labor (vv. 21-23). Clearly this era of salvation does not exist beyond space and time. Unlike many today who look forward to an early retirement and a life of leisure, the prophet depicts life in the renewed community as one of activity, challenge, and growth. Moreover, all will experience intimate communion with God for they will enjoy "a free access to the wellspring of life."[115] What initiates this new transformed existence? The powerful presence of the creator effecting a new relationship with humanity and creation (v. 24).

Verse 25 is clearly a summary of Isa. 11.6-9.[116] The apocalyptic nature of this text and v. 17 has been previously discussed.[117] Central to this study is that this verse and indeed the entire passage

---

[113]Whybray, *Isaiah*, 276. The reference is properly to the old heavens and earth but as the setting for the former troubles.

[114]Cf. *Tg. Isa.* 65.18a: "But they will be glad in the age of the ages which I create."

[115]Westermann, *Isaiah*, 409-12.

[116]The statement about the snake is intrusive. C. C. Torrey notes the sly humor in the reference. While peace reigns in the animal world, there will be no change for the evil serpent. Dust will still be his main course and his curse will not be lifted. *The Second Isaiah*, (New York: Scribner, 1928), 470-71. This statement perhaps suggests that for the prophet sin and death have not been totally abolished.

[117]See also the discussion of Sehmsdorf, "Redaktionsgeschichte von Jesaja 56-66," 522-24.

under consideration reflects not merely an existence in an idyllic environment beyond history, but God's intention to meet the needs and longings of humanity and creation in a holistic manner. Political victory, security, prosperity, and gaiety are inadequate for the prophet. The earth and its inhabitants also must experience restored fruitfulness and felicity. The hope for the new heavens and new earth underscores for Israel as well as for the modern interpreter that the creation has not become superfluous in view of spiritual or national deliverance. A concern and love for the good earth and its constituent elements remains. This is the import of the "motif of the new heavens and new earth" in the OT and especially in later apocalyptic thought.[118]

Summary and Conclusions

This chapter has discussed the importance of the created order in OT thought from various perspectives. Significantly, the centrality of the creation throughout the OT whether assumed or expressly stated is such that it refuses to be relegated to a secondary status in God's redemptive plan. This study also observed that the OT reveals an intense concern for the plight of the creation. In this regard, the question posed previously whether the creation itself is sinful or fallen may now be addressed. The notion of an *intrinsically* fallen creation is rejected. Yet one is reminded of Bauckham's observation that one need only observe the "gratuitous cruelty" of a cat playing with its catch to realize that the created order is not as God originally intended. Even the recognition that death, decay, and to some extent disease, are good does not solve the problem of excessive pain and brutality in the natural world.[119] The terminology of a good yet perverted creation therefore adequately reflects the dialectic view of the OT which reveals a world spoiled by the sin of humanity.[120] The zealous environmentalist may

---

[118]Cf. the comments of Mauser, "Isaiah 65," 181-86.

[119]Bauckham, "Theology of Nature," 241 and n. 18.

[120]Cf. Goldingay: "There is nothing wrong with the realm of creation in itself. The cosmos was created whole . . . and remains so (Gen. 1) even if humanity and history have put themselves out of joint in relation to it, . . . If

tend to attribute all of the ecological ills to a society which with impunity has polluted and thus brought suffering upon its world. This is only partially true. Karl Heim poignantly observes that there exists in every realm of creation an endless state of warfare betraying a more complex reality of disruption.

> Among the animals there are no criminal types, no asocial elements to be blamed for the frightfulness which prevails everywhere in the animal world. . . . But wherever there live together different kinds of animals which are dependent on one another for their food, for example in a wood or in a marshy pool of water swarming with living creatures, or in the sea, a constant state of war prevails. No creature's life is safe even for a moment. It is in constant danger, and murder may lurk everywhere. Clandestine assaults are the order of the day. . . .
>
> . . . .
>
> This continuous state of war, this constant threat of impending danger, is not confined to the animal world, although it is only the sufferings of the animal world with which we human beings can to some extent sympathize, because the animals are "our unknown brothers." . . . If even the plants have sensation, then the fierce battles in which they must struggle for their lives when set upon by their deadly foes, must also be accompanied by pains which are probably no less than the sufferings which we experience when our life is at stake. . . .
>
> . . . .
>
> But so much at any rate we must say, that the whole creation, not only the world of mankind, but also the world of animals and plants and inorganic nature, is subject to one common, fundamental law. Everywhere the principle of polarity prevails, although in the most diverse variations. Everywhere there reigns an unremitting warfare. Creatures, which need each other for their life, obstruct and destroy each other. The whole of nature is pervaded by an unsatisfied need. Paul can therefore speak in ch. VIII of his Epistle to the Romans of a groaning of the whole cre-

---

the OT comes to promise a new creation it is because humanity's rebellion makes human beings experience the present cosmos as a locus of disorder." *Theological Diversity*, 225.

ation crying out for deliverance from the bondage of corruption.[121]

These words reflect what is strongly suggested in biblical thought, that is, that something indeed has gone wrong with the creation which goes much deeper than can be remedied by any environmental program.   The prophets recognized that correction demanded more than human repentance and the restoration of healthful relationships between humanity and the created order. To remedy creation's plight required the redemption of the created order--the arrival of the new heavens and new earth.

---

[121]Karl Heim, *The World: Its Creation and Consummation*, trans. Robert Smith (London: Oliver & Boyd, 1962), 105-9.

CHAPTER III
CREATION AND REDEMPTION IN
JEWISH APOCALYPTIC

Introduction

Although the phrase "new heavens and new earth" is rare, the motif of a new creation evoked intense speculation in apocalyptic literature as many of the writers envisioned the dissolution of the old world order and the arrival of the new. The prevailing optimism of the OT prophets and sages toward history and creation gave way to apocalyptic eschatology. As such, the general consensus of apocalyptic specialists has been that these writings have little or no interest in the created order. The apocalyptists believed that evil had so permeated the present world order that nothing had been left untainted including the realm of nature. This pessimistic perspective, observes Hanson, was "the cradle of the growing speculation regarding a new creation, . . . a radical re-ordering of the earth and heavens."[1] Gowan's response to this *communis opinio* has been previously noted.[2] The focus of this investigation will be to reassess the writers' view toward God's creation, particularly whether each work projects a negative, positive, or indifferent attitude toward the creation itself.

Cosmological concerns have not gone unnoticed in previous studies in Second Temple literature. The major weakness of these has been the tendency to systematize evidence from

---

[1]Hanson, *Dawn of Apocalyptic*, 376.
[2]See above p. 6.

material of disparate traditions and provenance.[3]   While a summation is appropriate once the evidence is weighed, the nature of the material requires that each work be studied for its own view.   This caution is especially appropriate since the attempt to study a particular theme is inherently difficult and tends toward inaccurate generalizations.   Moreover, the works consulted, for example 1 Enoch, may span several hundred years. Therefore, care is taken to study each of the Jewish apocalyptic writings in consideration of their individual literary formulations. Obviously, the entire corpus generally listed as "apocalypses" cannot be discussed in this presentation. However, we believe that those works which have been chosen are sufficient to accommodate the aims of this thesis. Thus, the investigation is limited to the following selected sources dating prior to and contemporaneous with the NT: 1 Enoch, Jubilees, the QL, 4 Ezra, and two writings from diaspora Judaism, the Sibylline Oracles and 2 Enoch. These represent important works in the body of apocalyptic literature and therefore should yield vital information.[4]

The analysis in this section proceeds inductively. Each writing in part and as a whole is examined in order to further inform this inquiry regarding the view of creation and cosmic hope expressed in Jewish apocalyptic literature. This is done with careful attention toward relevant content and with particular issues in mind. What is the author's view of the created order and how does it compare with that of the OT? Does the writing reflect the idea of a fallen creation? If so, what is the primary reason for the creation's present dilemma? Is the apocalypse gen-

---

[3]This was mentioned by Donald E. Gowan in a personal letter to this writer dated April 1989. See also his comments, "Fall and Redemption of the Material Order," 88. Cf. the following studies which Gowan also cites. Lindeskog, *Schöpfungsdanken*, 93-121 and Hans-Friedrich Weiss, *Untersuchungen zur Kosmologie des hellenistischen und palästinischen Judentums*, TU, no. 97 (Berlin: Akademie, 1966).

[4]The problematic relation of 2 Baruch to 4 Ezra as well as the complex issue of Christian interpolation in the Testaments of the Twelve Patriarchs requires that these writings be omitted from consideration. See the introductions to each writing in James H. Charlesworth, ed., *OTP*, 2 vols. (New York: Doubleday, 1983-85). All citations of the Pseudepigrapha unless otherwise noted are taken from the *OTP*.

uinely other-worldly in perspective to the neglect of the present natural order? Is the writer interested in the salvation of the individual, nation, or the entire world? Does the author intend to depreciate the material order even in the new age? While the study is not ordered according to these questions, they help focus the issues of this chapter as each work is examined.

The Book of 1 Enoch

The composite nature of 1 Enoch is well known. Further, within the varying traditions of five accepted works one is faced with still other sources.[5] Black comments that there are a "bizarre variety of often disparate and overlapping traditions . . . side by side with redactional supplements etc. . . . each and all of them traceable to 'authors' of different periods and persuasions." The book therefore can be described as "an intricately devised jig-saw puzzle" or more accurately a collection of puzzles.[6] Some have attempted to set aside such considerations arguing for a unified perspective perhaps accomplished by the work of a final redactor.[7] However, the various traditions, which

---

[5]1 Enoch consists of five distinct works: The Book of the Watchers (chs. 1-36), Similitudes (chs. 37-71), The Astronomical Book (chs. 72-82), The Book of Dreams (chs. 83-90), and The Epistle of Enoch (chs. 91-108).

[6]Matthew Black, *The Book of Enoch or 1 Enoch: A New English Edition,* SVTP, no. 7 (Leiden: Brill, 1985), 8, 12. See the general introduction by Ephraim Isaac, "1 Enoch," in *OTP* (New York: Doubleday, 1983), 1:5-12. See also his descriptions and dating for the various manuscripts referred to in this discussion (6). A thorough analysis of the various manuscripts available for 1 Enoch is presented by Siegbert Uhlig, *Das äthiopische Henochbuch,* JSHRZ, no. 5 (Gütersloh: Mohn, 1984), 470-83.

[7]Robert A. Coughenour believes that a unified view was accomplished through the wisdom perspective of the final editor. 1 Enoch 1-5 evince wisdom phraseology and elements later elaborated in the rest of the book. These were composed as an introduction to the entire work by a sage steeped in wisdom tradition who presented the work to a Jewish eschatological wisdom group perhaps in Galilee during the first century (94-64 BC). "Enoch and Wisdom: A Study of the Wisdom Elements in the Book of Enoch" (Ph.D. diss., Case Western University, 1972), 34-39; idem, "The Wisdom Stance of Enoch's Redactor," *JSJ* 13 (December 1982): 48-55. Coughenour has only affirmed what R. H. Charles suggested earlier that these chapters serve as an introduction and have themes in common with the rest of the book. *The Book of Enoch or 1 Enoch,*

likely had an extended period of independent circulation before the book assumed its final form, makes it more appropriate to approach 1 Enoch as five individual works with only loosely related themes.[8]

A particularly thorny issue in this regard relates to the portion of the writing designated as the "Similitudes" or "Parables" of Enoch (chs. 37-71). Since the publication of the Qumran Aramaic fragments of 1 Enoch by Milik the controversy over the dating of this writing has reached new heights especially in view of his attempt to identify this section as a post-Christian writing of the third century AD (ca. 270). According to Milik, the absence of any fragment of this work at Qumran and the lack of any quotations among the Christian writings of the first to the fourth century AD suggest that it was not an early pre-Christian work.[9] Milik's late date for the Similitudes has potentially the most influential impact upon the interpretive relationship of Jewish Second Temple literature and the NT. Especially significant is the direction of influence for the "Elect One" or "Son of Man" figure prominent in both the Similitudes and the Gospels. Few scholars, however, have followed Milik in his conclusions.[10] Scholarship is generally divided between a pre- or post AD 70 date with most maintaining a mid first century date.[11]

2d ed. (Oxford: Clarendon, 1912), 2-3. See the rebuttal of Michael E. Stone, "Apocalyptic Literature," in *Jewish Writings of the Second Temple Period*, Vol. 1, *Apocrypha, Pseudepigrapha, Qumran, Sectarian Writings, Philo, Josephus*, CRINT, ed. Michael E. Stone (Philadelphia: Fortress, 1984), 400-401.

[8]Russell, *Jewish Apocalyptic*, 53.

[9]J. T. Milik, ed., Matthew Black, collaborator, *The Books of Enoch: Aramaic Fragments of Qumran Cave 4* (Oxford: Clarendon, 1976), 89-98.

[10]But note E. P. Sanders, *Paul and Palestinian Judaism: A Comparison of Patterns of Religion* (Philadelphia: Fortress, 1977), 346-47.

[11]The earliest date proposed is that of Charles who dated the Similitudes between 98-64 BC. *Book of Enoch*, 12-15. Milik's views have been subjected to rigorous analysis. For a discussion and further suggested dates see especially Jonas C. Greenfield and Michael E. Stone, "The Enochic Pentateuch and the Date of the Similitudes," *HTR* 70 (January-April 1977): 51-65 (AD 40); Michael A. Knibb, "The Date of the Parables of Enoch: A Critical Review," *NTS* 25 (April 1979): 345-59 (AD 100); David W. Suter, "Weighed in the Balance: The Similitudes of Enoch in Recent Discussion," *RelSRev* 7 (July 1981): 217-21 (AD 39-49); Collins, *Apocalyptic Imagination*, 142-54 (mid first century AD); Black, *1 Enoch*, 181-88 (pre-AD 70).

Moreover, the "Son of Man" figure and concept was part of the conceptual furniture of early Judaism due to the import of Daniel 7 and does not necessarily demand interpretive influence in either direction.[12] Consequently, while the Similitudes are clearly much later than the other parts of 1 Enoch, their value is such that they cannot be neglected in the present investigation.

The Book of the Watchers (chs. 1-36)

The opening section of 1 Enoch is an appropriate place to begin since it is one of the oldest parts of the book and more importantly it indicates the author's positive interest in the created order especially in chapters 2-5.[13] 1 Enoch 1-5 constitute an introduction to the entire work.[14] Particularly, the opening theophany of verses 3b-9 serve to set the tone for chapters 1-36. It effectively summarizes the concern of the entire book, namely, the origins, consequences, and judgment of sin.[15] The appearance of God in judgment is presented in typical OT theophanic language.[16] Important for consideration is the author's statement concerning the future judgment which affects not only the wicked but the created order as well. The presence of God terrifies the watchers (v. 5) and likewise creates a cosmic upheaval: "Mountains and high places will fall down and be

---

[12]Collins, *Apocalyptic Imagination*, 154.

[13]While 1 Enoch 1-36 represent several hands, Charles dates this section to the first third of the second century BC. *Book of Enoch*, 1-2. The Aramaic fragments recovered at Qumran indicate that the Book of the Watchers existed in the same form known in the Greek and Ethiopic versions since the first half of the second century BC. Milik, *Books of Enoch*, 25, 140. Milik suggests that the author was Judean and engaged in the aromatic trade (26).

[14]See the analysis of Lars Hartman, *Asking for a Meaning: A Study of 1 Enoch 1-5*, ConBNT, no. 12 (Lund: Gleerup, 1979), 16-21 and the comment above n. 7.

[15]James C. VanderKam, "The Theophany of Enoch 1.3b-7, 9," *VT* 23 (April 1973): 131.

[16]The arrival of God and the consequent effects upon the natural world comprise the formal and essential elements of an OT theophany. See Jörg Jeremias, *Theophanie: Die Geschichte einer Alttestamentlichen Gattung*, WMAT (Neukirchen-Vluyn: Neukirchener, 1965), 1, 15, 52-53; VanderKam, "Theophany," 131.

frightened[17] . . . and made low;[18] and they shall melt like a honeycomb before the flame" (vv. 6-7).   The vividness of the imagery gives the impression of a violent and fiery end for the creation at the advent of God.

The image is changed somewhat with an alternate reading of the Ethiopic text of verse 7.   Language reminiscent of the flood narrative of Genesis reflects the earth's plight due to humanity's wickedness as it returns to a chaotic state in the wake of God's judgment: "And the earth will sink [be submerged] and everything that is on the earth will be destroyed" (cf. Gen. 6.7, 13).[19]   The flood event thus serves as a type of God's judgment in the last days.   Although there is no expressed statement of a fallen creation, one cannot escape the conclusion that the sinful condition of the world as in the days of the flood demands God's judgment.   In light of these remarks, one may ask whether the apocalyptic writer has taken the language of the OT to another level and asserts the complete destruction of the creation at God's arrival.[20]   While the total dissolution of the world especially by fire may be intimated, it is better with Charles to observe that the passage does not go beyond OT theophanic texts where such language denoting the authority of God over his creation is common.[21]

---

[17]The Greek text (hereafter G) reads: "καὶ σεισθήσονται καὶ πεσοῦνται καὶ διαλυθήσονται (cf. the LXX of Nah. 1.5). Cf. 4QEnᵃ: And] the heights [shall be shaken . . . and be dissolved." Milik, *Books of Enoch*, 142. Two major portions of the Greek text have survived (chs. 1-32, 6th c. AD; chs. 97-107, 4th c.) and have been compiled along with the fragments of citations from Georgius Syncellus by Matthew Black, *Apocalypsis Henochi Graece: Fragmenta Pseudepigraphorum quae supersunt Graeca*, PVTG, no. 3 (Leiden: Brill, 1970).

[18]To stress the results G adds τοῦ διαρυῆναι ὄρη.

[19]The reading of ms B. Cf. the translation of Michael A. Knibb, *The Ethiopic Book of Enoch: A New Edition in Light of the Aramaic Dead Sea Fragments*, vol. 2, *Introduction, Translation, and Commentary* (Oxford: Clarendon, 1978), 59. See also the comments of VanderKam, "Theophany," 146-47.

[20]VanderKam, "Theophany," 146.

[21]Charles, *Books of Enoch*, 6-7. For the OT concept cf. Mic. 1.4; Nah. 1.5; Hab. 3.6. Jeremias notes the importance of the OT theophanic tradition for the apocalyptic writers. *Theophanie*, 22-24 (cf. 4 Ezra 3.18, 8.23; As. Mos. 103-6; T. Levi 3.9).

The apocalyptic interest in the wonders and secrets of the universe has been associated with the wisdom perspective of the Hellenistic world in recent studies.[22] Significant is the wisdom outlook which affirms that the world still has worth and even plays an important role in the message of the apocalyptists. The theme of eschatological judgment for the sinners and righteous in 1 Enoch 2.1-5.3 reveals the centrality of the created order. This passage, which reflects the concerns and style of wisdom traditions, contrasts the obedience of the natural order with the disobedience of the wicked and forms the basis for an ethical appeal.[23] The regularity and stability of the creation is a basic premise of OT wisdom. The realization of a fundamental order embedded within the creation to which one must conform is integral in order to experience life to the fullest.[24] However, it is noteworthy that an appeal to natural phenomena as a basis for exhortation in ethical behavior is unprecedented in the OT.[25] Hartman nevertheless suggests that the use of the natural realm for ethical admonition has its roots in the OT. He finds similar language in texts invoking heaven and earth as witnesses to the covenant obligations--a theme already introduced in the opening theophany--and divine lawsuit or *rib* patterned texts which were widely used in postbiblical Judaism as a foundation for council in righteous living.[26]

A series of imperatives draw attention to the elements of nature for parenesis in chapters 2-5.[27] The readers are enjoined to observe various natural phenomena as examples of order and

---

[22]Michael E. Stone, "Lists of Revealed Things in Apocalyptic Literature," in *Magnalia Dei: The Mighty Acts of God*, ed. Frank Moore Cross et al. (New York: Doubleday, 1976), 414-52. Cf. von Rad, *Theology*, 2:306-8.

[23]Black designates this passage as a "nature homily." *1 Enoch*, 13, 109.

[24]See the comments above pp. 50-51 and Crenshaw, *Old Testament Wisdom*, 19-20, 66-67.

[25]James C. VanderKam, *Enoch and the Growth of an Apocalyptic Tradition* (Washington, DC: Catholic Biblical Association of America, 1984), 120-21.

[26]Cf. Deut. 32.1. Hartman provides a chart of postbiblical texts and the relevant elements. *Asking for a Meaning*, 49-95. The OT sages noted the importance of the creation for instruction but explicit parenesis is lacking (Prov. 6.6-7; Job. 12.7-8; chs. 38-40).

[27]See Knibb, *Ethiopic Enoch*, 2.60, n. 2.

obedience to the commands of God.[28]

> [1] Examine all the activities which take place in the sky and how they do not alter their ways, and examine the luminaries of heaven . . . and they do not divert from their appointed order. [2] And look at the earth and turn in your mind [understand] concerning the action taking place in her . . . how all the work of God as being manifested does not change.[29] [3] And behold the summer and the winter, how the whole earth is filled with water and clouds and dew, and he causes rain to rest upon her (2.1-3).

The sage continues to describe several additional aspects of creation which conform to the laws of God: seasons (4.1), trees (3.1; 5.1), and even the seas and rivers (5.3).[30] These verses function primarily to contrast the idea of the obedient, immutable quality of God's works with the disobedience and rebelliousness of the sinners. The readers are therefore to observe and regard how readily the creation fulfills God's word whereas the sinners have disobeyed: "But as for you, you have not been long suffering[31] and you have not done the commandments of the lord, . . ." (5.4). The mention of God's commandments brings into close association the concepts of wisdom, creation, and law.[32] Luck argues that this relationship is implicit in wisdom since the law

---

[28] The use of the natural elements as exemplars of obedience becomes more pronounced in postbiblical literature as they are more often described as independent personalities (cf. Sir. 16.26-28). Michael E. Stone, "The Parabolic Use of Natural Order in Judaism of the Second Temple Age," in *Gilgul: Essays on Transformation, Revolution and Permanence in the History of Religions*, ed. S. Shaked, D. Shulman, and G. G. Stroumsa (Leiden: Brill, 1987), 298-308.

[29] G reads ὧ εἰσιν φθαρτά. Charles finds this reading intolerable in this context and regards it as corrupt. He adopts the reading "steadfast." *Book of Enoch*, 9. But cf. Coughenour, "Enoch and Wisdom," 9, 104-5.

[30] See the detailed analysis of Hartman, *Asking for a Meaning*, 16-17. G adds οἱ ποταμοί.

[31] The contrast while more striking in G (ὑμεῖς δὲ οὐκ ἐνεμείνατε οὐδὲ ἐποιήσατε κ.τ.λ.) is still weak in cf. to 4QEnᵃ: "But ye, ye changed your works." Milik, *Books of Enoch*, 147.

[32] Charles identifies this reference with the "eternal law" of 1 Enoch 99.2, i.e., the Mosaic law. "1 Enoch," in *APOT*, ed. R. H. Charles (Oxford: Clarendon, 1913), 2:190, 270-71. Collins posits the "law of nature."

gives a concrete or tangible dimension to the universal law present in a just arrangement of the world. To obey God's revealed will is therefore to act in accordance with the divine will evident in creation.[33] The relationship of law and wisdom is even suggested in the Pentateuch (Deut. 4.5-6). The argument of the writer is rooted in the conviction that to transgress the law is to rebel against the very order of creation designed and maintained by God. The failure to observe and respond in obedience marks the sinners for the judgment described in 1 Enoch 1.3-9 and 5.4-6.

It is interesting to observe that the blessings for the righteous in 1 Enoch 5.7-10 are depicted in a very this-worldly manner similar to that portrayed in Isa. 65.17-25. The righteous will gain wisdom and sin will thus no longer be a part of their conduct. Joy and peace will characterize their lives. It is also said that they will *inherit the earth*.[34] The righteous will not suffer death due to plagues or wrath but "they shall complete the designated number of days of their life."

Furthermore, the apocalyptist's interest in the phenomena of the universe functions not only to accentuate the disobedience of sinners but the wisdom perspective in the Book of the Watchers also shows that individual eschatology and history are related to the cosmic order. Collins observes that the basic nexus between the apocalyptic and Hellenistic wisdom traditions is the conviction that "the experience of God and even eschatology" is

---

Apocalyptic Imagination, 38. Coughenour opines that this "means the creative word which has established the general order of the created world and by which it operates, as well as the substantial word that orders the societal life of mankind . . . ordered by the Torah." "Enoch and Wisdom," 117.

[33]Wisdom and law are virtually identified in Sirach 24. Ulrich Luck, "Das Weltverständis in der Jüdischen Apocalyptic: Dargestellt am Äthiopishen Henoch und am 4 Esra." *ZTK* 73 (September 1976): 288-92. Luck also contends that law and wisdom are disconnected in apocalyptic literature. The law is present but wisdom has receded to the heavens with God. He cites especially 1 Enoch 42 as an example. Such generalizations, however, need modification in light of the diverse traditions of 1 Enoch (292-94).

[34]Among the blessings promised the righteous, the importance of the land is accentuated in G by the threefold repetition of the phrase: αὐτοὶ κληρονομήσουσιν τὴν γῆν (5.6, 7, 8; cf. Ps. 37.11; Matt. 5.5).

mediated via the cosmic order.[35] The two heavenly journeys of Enoch in chapters 17-36 reveal not only astronomical mysteries but also the place of judgment for the fallen angels (18.11-19.3) and the underworld with the souls of the dead (ch. 22).[36] The information conveyed in this journey assures Enoch of the certainty of judgment for the wicked. More importantly, it witnesses to the justice imminent in the created order. This revelatory journey therefore establishes that one's destiny--judgment or blessings alike--belongs to the very order of the universe itself. The cosmic and ethical dimensions of life are interrelated.[37] This presupposition asserts the importance and necessity of a good creation. Collins notes an important distinction between wisdom in the Jewish and apocalyptic traditions. Jewish wisdom tradition affirms that wisdom may be found in all creation. By contrast, in the apocalyptic traditions wisdom has retreated into the heavens and is available only through special revelations. The earth is devoid of order and therefore stands in sharp discontinuity with the world above and the world to come.[38] Collins' observations are astute and appropriate but in need of qualification. His assertions apply to sections such as the wisdom poem of 1 Enoch 42 which he cites as an example. However, regarding 1 Enoch 2-5, the admonitions are predicated upon humanity's ability to observe, comprehend, and adapt to the basic principles by which the universe operates. Otherwise, parenesis would be useless.[39]

In addition, this focus upon the universe reveals more than a religious intent. The attention of the apocalyptist to the geographical and cosmological elements of the created order witnesses to an intense and positive interest in the wonders of the natural

---

[35]John J. Collins, "Cosmos and Salvation: Jewish Wisdom and Apocalyptic in the Hellenistic Age," *HR* 17 (November 1977): 135-36.

[36]Two sets of traditions constitute the tour of Enoch: chs. 17-19 and 20-36. The second presumes and builds upon the first. George W. E. Nickelsburg, *Jewish Literature Between the Bible and the Mishnah* (Philadelphia: Fortress, 1981), 54-55.

[37]Collins, "Cosmos and History," 135-38; Luck, "Weltverständnis in der jüdischen Apokalyptik," 296.

[38]Collins, "Cosmos and History," 137-41.

[39]VanderKam, *Enoch*, 121-22.

world. God is even portrayed as an architect who has designed and provided for the erection of the entire universe (18.1-3). The recurring refrain of praise, "at that moment, I blessed the Lord of Glory," is intoned following each site that Enoch visits (22.14; 25.7; 27.5), and the Book of the Watchers concludes with a praise to the creator (36.4).

Himmelfarb contends that the social impetus for an interest in the world such as reflected in this apocalyptic writing represents a reaction to the disappointment of the Exile and its aftermath. The writers looked not to the realm of history as evidence for the activity of God but to the creation as the repository of God's ways now accessible only to a chosen few. Only creation adequately disclosed the work and glory of God.[40] In any event, the interest in the natural phenomena and the traveler's panoramic view of the world exhibits an attitude of reverence for God's good creation. As in the OT tradition, the elements of the creation are not worshipped but reflect the majesty of the creator who alone is worthy of praise. Therefore, following the final journey to the South, Enoch erupts with praise for God's creation:

> And when I saw (this) I blessed--and I shall always bless--the Lord of Glory, who performed great and blessed miracles in order that he may manifest his great deeds to his angels, the winds, and to the people so that they might praise the effect of all his creation--so that they might see the effect of his power and praise him in respect to the great work of his hands and bless him forever (36.4).

The Book of the Watchers is thus bracketed by an introduction and a blessing formula both of which affirm the importance of the created order.

The central section of the Book of the Watchers in chap-

---

[40]Martha Himmelfarb, "From Prophecy to Apocalypse: The Book of the Watchers and Tours of Heaven," in *Jewish Spirituality: From the Bible Through the Middle Ages*, ed. Arthur Green (New York: Crossroad, 1986), 158-60. She further intimates that the absence of the theme of an imminent cataclysmic end to the world in the tour apocalypses allowed a positive view of creation to be maintained (147, 161).

ters 6-19 continues the theme of the origin of sin and its consequences introduced in 1 Enoch 1.3.[41] Containing a conflation of
two separate traditions based upon Gen. 6.1-4, the present
dilemma of evil in the world is attributed to the fall of angels.
The theme of "rebellion in heaven" is presented in four movements: rebellion, devastation, punishment, and restoration.[42]
Two chief angels, Semyaz and Azazel are identified as the leaders of the rebellious horde. The traditions give two different
bases for the presence of evil in the world. Semyaz and his band
consort with women and beget giants whose violence bring
destruction on both humankind and the creatures throughout the
earth (chs. 6-7). Azazel's crime was teaching the skills of metal-
lurgy from which humanity learned to make instruments of war
and women, adornments. This consequently lead to widespread
violence and immorality. Humanity thus cooperated with the
demonic angels and must bear a measure of responsibility for
evil (8.1-4). The presence of sin and evil in the world is then
more than wicked actions; it is of supernatural origin. While in
Gen. 6.1-4 the act is portrayed as a neutral event, 1 Enoch presents it as a direct rebellion against God and his entire creation.[43]
The ruinous effects of the angels' sin upon the creation is
demonstrated in the defilement that affects even the animals and
evokes a response from the earth.

---

[41]1 Enoch 6-19 form the core of the Book of the Watchers. Milik, *Books
of Enoch*, 25. Source critical analysis has argued that chapters 6-11 form a separate unit later integrated into the book. See George W. E. Nickelsburg,
"Apocalyptic and Myth in 1 Enoch 6-11," *JBL* 96 (June 1977): 384-86; Paul
D. Hanson, "Rebellion in Heaven: Azazel, and Euhemeristic Heroes in 1
Enoch 6- 11," *JBL* 96 (June 1977): 195-233. Collins disputes that these chapters ever circulated independently and are appropriate to their literary setting.
1 Enoch 12-16 continue the theme of the judgment of the watchers while chs.
17-36 resume the heavenly journey of Enoch begun in ch. 14. "Methodological Issues in the Study of 1 Enoch: Reflections on the Articles of P. D. Hanson and G. W. Nickelsburg," in *SBLSP*, ed. Paul J. Achtemeier, vol. 1 (Missoula, MT: Scholars, 1978), 315.

[42]Hanson, "Rebellion in Heaven," 196-97. Black suggests that both
Genesis 6 and 1 Enoch 6 "are descended from a common literary ancestor." *1
Enoch*, 124-25.

[43]Nickelsburg, "Apocalyptic and Myth," 386.

> ⁵ They [Giants] began to do violence to and to attack all
> the birds and the beasts of the earth and reptiles . . . ⁶ and
> they began to devour their flesh, and they were drinking
> the blood. Thereupon the earth made accusation against
> the lawless ones (7.5-6).⁴⁴

The reference is clearly to Gen. 9.4 and reflects the total disregard for the life of God's creatures and hence his mandate for a
harmonious and orderly creation. Hanson remarks that "this, in
biblical metaphor, is a description of the collapse of the order of
creation, with pugnacious forces unleashed in a vicious process
of degeneration and decay."⁴⁵

In chapter 10 the author utilizes an *Urzeit-Endzeit* typology to stress the expectation of final judgment and a new age
analogous to the judgment and new beginning in the time of
Noah. He sees demonic angels as the source of violence in the
world. Humanity and creation can only hope for divine intervention defeating the powers and renewing the earth.⁴⁶ The
archangel Raphael is dispatched to the scene, binds Azazel, and
casts him into darkness where he will remain until judgment
when he will be cast into the fire (vv. 4-6). The archangel
Michael is to bind Semyaz and his associates for seventy generations in the belly of the earth until judgment where they also
will be confined for all time to the fiery abyss in torment (vv. 12-
13). Raphael is instructed to "restore the earth which the angels
have ruined" (v. 7).⁴⁷ This action will involve the destruction of
all iniquity and then "the plant of righteousness and truth will

---

⁴⁴Black's translation, *1 Enoch*, 28. The Greek translator also accuses
the Giants of cannibalism and drinking their own blood: καὶ ἤρξαντο
ἁμαρτάνειν ἐν τοῖς πετεινοῖς καὶ τοῖς θηρίοις καὶ ἑρθετοῖ καὶ . .
. ἀλλήλων τὰς σάρκας κατεσθίειν, καὶ τὸ αἷμα ἔπινον. Cf.
Knibb's translation, *Ethiopic Enoch*, 79. Uhlig notes that it is unclear whether
"they" refers to the "Giants" or people. *Henochbuch*, 520. The context fits the
former.

⁴⁵Hanson, "Rebellion in Heaven," 200

⁴⁶Nickelsburg, "Apocalyptic and Myth," 387-89. The primordial drama
is extended to include all of time from the rebellion to the *eschaton*. Hanson,
"Rebellion in Heaven," 201.

⁴⁷Cf. G: καὶ ἰαθήσεται ἡ γῆ, . . . καὶ τὴν ἴασιν τῆς γῆς
δήλωσον, ἵνα ἰάσονται τὴν πληγήν, κ.τ.λ. Cf v. 7a in G Syncellus: καὶ
ἴασαι τὴν γῆν.

appear forever and he will plant joy" (v. 16). Chaos will give way to order and a restored primordial state of blessing. Life in the restored or healed world resembles that depicted in the OT. Note particularly the earth's renewed fruitfulness:

> [18] Then shall the whole earth be tilled in righteousness, and it shall be planted with trees, and filled with blessing. [19] And luxuriant trees will be planted in it and they will plant vines in it, . . . [which] will produce a thousand measures of wine, . . . [20] And as for you, cleanse the earth from all uncleanness. . . . [21] And all the children of men are to become righteous and all nations shall serve and bless me, and all shall worship me . . . . (10.18-21).[48]

Collins disputes the eschatological character of these chapters and contends that the healing of the earth in chapter 10 refers not to renewal in the end times but to the restoration following the flood of Genesis. He does recognize that the renovation after the deluge could serve as an eschatological pro-totype.[49] At any rate, the healing of the earth at the *eschaton* or an earlier period indicates the author's concern for the restoration of the created order to its original form and purpose. Moreover, the language of healing and cleansing does not suggest a total dissolution of creation but rather a renovation--in reality, a purging.

The Astronomical Book (chs. 72-82)

This work, also called the "Book of Heavenly Luminaries," constitutes the oldest of the five books attributed to Enoch. Milik observes that these chapters which are "essentially astro-

---

[48]Black's translation, *1 Enoch*, 31. See Charles, *Book of Enoch*, 25. Note the vivid imagery of v. 19 reflected in G: καὶ πάντα τά δένδρα τῆς γῆς ἀγαλλιάσονται· φυτευθήσεται, κ.τ.λ. For the OT concept Charles lists the following: Amos 9.13-14; Hos. 2.22-23; Jer. 31.5; Isa. 25.6; Ezek. 28.26; 34.26-27. Cf. the grandiose picture of 2 Baruch 29.5.

[49]"Methodological Issues in 1 Enoch," 317-19. Cf. Charles, *APOT*, 2:194-95. The language of the previous citation resembling the OT concept suggests an eschatological intention.

nomical and calendrical content was enriched by cosmographic information and moral considerations."[50] The introductory verse describes the purpose:

> The Book of the Itinerary of the Luminaries of Heaven: the position of each and everyone, in respect to their ranks, in respect to their authorities, and in respect to their season; each one according to their names and their places of origin and according to their months, which Uriel, the holy angel who was with me, and who (also) is their guide, showed me--just as he showed me all their treatises and the nature of the years of the world unto eternity, till the new creation which abides forever is created (72.1).

The following chapters, which present the author's lengthy and often redundant description of the movements of the luminaries and the blowing of the winds and their gates, reflect a reverential attitude toward an orderly, harmonious, and unchanging universe untouched by human sin.[51] In fact, a view similar to that of chapters 2-5 is demonstrated. Here, however, there is no attempt to use empirical observations for ethical purposes. The immediate purpose of 1 Enoch 72-79 appears to support a 364-day solar calendar like that advocated in Jubilees and in the Qumran community. These chapters, however, do not seem to polemicize against any known calendar in force at the time. Thus, the exact function of 1 Enoch 72-79 in this book is uncertain.[52] One implication may be surmised. Like 1 Enoch 2-5, right conduct is determined by understanding and adapting to

---

[50]The Qumran fragments date from the third century BC. Milik, *Books of Enoch*, 7-8. The present book in 1 Enoch represents a radical abbreviation of its original form (19). Nickelsburg suggests that 1 Enoch 81-82 are additions. *Jewish Literature*, 151. VanderKam argues that while ch. 81 may be set apart, ch. 82 is a fitting conclusion to the book. *Enoch*, 79.

[51]Collins, *Apocalyptic Imagination*, 47.

[52]The precise function of these chapters regarding the calendar has been the subject of great debate. It is generally acknowledged that unlike Jubilees and the QL these chapters do not aggressively advocate the use the calendar and therefore cannot be used to support a sectarian bias. See James C. VanderKam, "The 364-Day Calendar in the Enochic Literature," in *SBLSP*, ed. Kent Harold Richards (Chico, CA: Scholars, 1983), 157-65. See below n. 96 for the calendar of Jubilees.

the order of the universe.   Specifically, this is governed by adherence to the 364-day calendar.   One can thus learn about God and his directions for proper behavior by observing the cosmos and adapting to its laws as reflected in the calendar.

The eschatological perspective is introduced in verse 1 with the assurance that the heavenly order will hold "till the new creation."   This statement seems to focus more on the permanence of the created order than its demise and subsequent renewal.   It therefore offers little information regarding the arrival of a new creation other than to affirm it as a part of the general belief system of Judaism.   It does suggest the importance of the concept in the earliest of the postbiblical apocalypses. Cosmic transformation, if implied, is hardly the primary purpose of the verse.[53] Notably, the material in chapters 76-77 reflects more of a geographical than cosmological concern.   Whether the author's observations reflect a real or a mythological geography is uncertain.[54] In either case, this clearly reveals an interest in attaining knowledge of the universe as it is rather than an urgent desire for the end of the world where such would be unimportant.[55]

1 Enoch 80 stands apart from the previous chapters due to the ethical and eschatological emphasis.   Further, verses 2-8 state that sometime prior to the end of the present creation the natural laws will go awry while the author in 72.1 argues that they will remain intact as long as the creation endures.   This incongruity leaves VanderKam at a loss as to when and why these verses were ever inserted into the present section.[56] This may be pressing the language too closely.   The impact of the

---

[53]Matthew Black believes that in every case in 1 Enoch where the idea of new creation is mentioned or implied the writer is "always thinking" of a second Genesis, a new creation which embraces both the world and humankind. "The New Creation in 1 Enoch," in *Creation, Christ and Culture*, ed. Richard W. A. McKinney (London: T. & T. Clark, 1976), 14.

[54]Milik identifies three of the seven rivers mentioned in 77.5-7: Nile, Tigris, and Euphrates. *Books of Enoch*, 16-18.

[55]Rowland, *The Open Heaven*, 126.

[56]VanderKam, *Enoch*, 106-7. Accordingly, that chs. 80-81 are additions make it unlikely that the original Book of Dreams could be designated an apocalypse (107-9). See also Charles, *Book of Enoch*, 147-49. Note that ch. 80 is not attested at Qumran. Milik, *Books of Enoch*, 274.

imagery is often the focus of apocalyptic language rather than logical consistency.[57] This passage is clearly in accord with the OT tradition which affirms a moral and material relation between humanity and the creation. In its present adapted context 1 Enoch 80.2-8 reveals that the natural realm depicted so secure and harmonious in the previous chapters (and in chs. 2-5) will be perverted "in the days of sinners." The effects of sin upon the world reach catastrophic proportions: the heavenly luminaries will alter course, seasons will be shortened, crops will not appear at the proper time, "and plagues shall come upon them, so as to destroy all" (v. 8). This text asserts that sinfulness of both human and superhuman origin perverts the creation designed to act in obedience to God's design.[58]

The Book of Dreams (chs. 83-90)

The Book of Dreams comprises two visions: one recounted by Enoch to Methuselah regarding the deluge (chs. 83-84) and a "zoomorphic" allegory, the Animal Apocalypse, in which the participants in history from the first man to the new Jerusalem are symbolized by animals (chs. 85-90).[59] The first vision offers little additional information for the present inquiry. Collins notes that the vision of the coming flood is a vivid "paradigm of judgment, a reminder that the whole world could be destroyed" which certainly connotes the contingency of the world and its dependence upon the creator.[60] The first part of the second vision concerns a symbolic version of the Watcher legend (chs. 86-88). Particularly noteworthy are chapters 89-90 where the vision follows in chronological sequence the history of Israel from the flood and the deliverance of Noah to the last judgment. This sec-

---

[57] Collins thinks that this view demands too much of an "unduly rigid consistency." *Apocalyptic Imagination*, 225, n. 42. See his general discussion regarding apocalyptic language (11-13). Ch. 80 nevertheless has been adapted to the present context. Black, *1 Enoch*, 252.

[58] The reference to the transgression of the "chiefs of the stars" (v. 6) may indicate also a supernatural basis for the perversion of creation.

[59] This section is represented by Aramaic fragments of four manuscripts the oldest dating from 175 BC. Milik, *Books of Enoch*, 41.

[60] Collins, *Apocalyptic Imagination*, 54.

tion of the Animal Apocalypse presents the end times when the new Jerusalem and a new Eden will be established. Although the emphasis is more upon the transformation of God's people and a national restoration than on material renewal, one may argue that it is certainly implied in the reestablishment of God's reign in the land of Israel. A closer look at the judgment passage will determine the emphasis of this apocalypse.

Two judgments are described in 90.20-49. First, the fallen angels or "stars" and the seventy "angels" or shepherds in charge of Israel are judged followed by the "blinded sheep" or unfaithful Israelites. All are condemned to perish in the fiery abyss (90.21-27). Significantly, the place from which judgment is rendered is a throne "erected in the pleasant land, and the Lord of the sheep sat thereon" (v. 20).[61] Following the second judgment the writer describes the transformation of Jerusalem in Temple imagery and the renewal of the people of God.

> [28] Then I stood still, looking at that ancient house being transformed: All the pillars and all the columns were pulled out; and the ornaments of that house were packed and taken out together with them and abandoned in a certain place in the South of the land. [29] I went on seeing until the Lord of the sheep brought about a new house, greater and loftier than the first one, and set it up in the first location which had been greater and loftier than the first one, and . . . all its pillars were new. . . . All the sheep were within it (90.28-29).[62]

Does this refer to a heavenly Temple? The virtual identity of the Temple and Jerusalem makes this reading questionable. Further, the features of a new Eden--a new creation--reveal that earthly realities are intended. Even if a preexistent heavenly Temple is discerned in this passage, it is noteworthy that it must descend to

---

[61]Black's translation, *1 Enoch*, 81. "God's throne is set up in Jerusalem (vv. 28, 29)." Charles, *APOT*, 2:259.

[62]The figure of the Temple and city cannot be separated in this passage. The vision depicts the Temple expanding to include the whole City of Jerusalem to admit all dispersed persons returning to it. Shmuel Safrai, "The Heavenly Jerusalem," *Ariel* 23 (1969): 13.

the earth.[63] The characteristics of a new creation are especially evident in the portrayal of the birth of a snow-white cow with horns in verse 37.   Charles understood this to symbolize a messianic figure[64] but Milik and Black have argued effectively for interpreting the symbol as a new Adam (cf. 85.3).[65] Thus, the author's depiction of a new Jerusalem in a new Eden is completed with the arrival of the new or second Adam. The transformation of humanity ("all were transformed and became snow-white cows," v. 38), Jerusalem, and the world are clearly in mind. While there is no explicit mention of a new creation the features representing the concept are strongly suggested.

The Epistle of Enoch (chs. 91-108)

The final section of 1 Enoch is distinguished as an epistle written by Enoch "for all the offspring that dwell upon the earth, and for the latter generations which uphold uprightness and peace" (92.1; cf. 100.6). The primary emphasis of the Epistle, which is a complicated composition of literary sources, is clearly parenetic.[66] Exhortations to the righteous and woes for the wicked as in chapters 1-36 appropriately draw the theme of creation into consideration. In a section that Black labels a "nature poem" the author extolls the glory of God's creation (93.11-14).[67] As in the case of chapters 17-36 the motif of creation is given an eschatological focus. The wonders of creation serve to

---

[63]See further Davies, *Gospel and Land*, 143-44. R. G. Hamerton-Kelley argues that the source for the tradition of a heavenly Jerusalem which descends from heaven derives from Ezekiel's Temple vision (ch. 43). "The Temple and the Origins of Jewish Apocalyptic," *VT* 20 (January 1970): 4-6. The connection of the Animal Apocalypse with Ezekiel has been noted by Charles, *APOT*, 2:250.

[64]Charles, *Book of Enoch*, 215.

[65]Milik, *Books of Enoch*, 45; Black, *1 Enoch*, 20-21; idem "New Creation," 19-20.

[66]The Epistle proper includes chs. 91-105. Chs. 106-7 comprise fragments of Noah and an apocalyptic addition in ch. 108. See Black, *1 Enoch*, 21.

[67]Ibid., 216. The subject matter leads Milik to suggest that it is a eulogy of Enoch delivered following his journey reported in chs. 17-36. *Books of Enoch*, 270.

assure of God's just ways.

In 1 Enoch 101, a passage similar in language and purpose to chapters 2-5, the author enlists creation as a witness to God's authority. A series of questions attest that the power displayed by the natural elements point beyond to an even greater power who demands absolute obedience. Thus, the appeal to the natural order warns sinners who fear the mighty sea that they should rather fear its creator. "Did he not make the heavens and the earth and all that is in them? . . . Do not the sailors of the ships fear the sea? Yet the sinners do not fear the Most High." (101.8-9).

Embedded in the Epistle of Enoch is the significant book, the Apocalypse of Weeks (93.1-10; 91.11-17), so designated because it divides history into periods of ten "weeks" from creation to the *eschaton*.[68] It is generally agreed that the apocalypse is an earlier work rewritten, revised, and later incorporated into the larger epistle.[69] Milik, however, has assigned a date for both the epistle and the Apocalypse of Weeks toward the end of the second or beginning of the first century and further asserts that "no serious evidence exists to disprove that the author of this apocalypse of Weeks is the same author as composed the rest of the Epistle."[70] That the Apocalypse is a self-contained unit is evident but whether it circulated independently is uncertain. Like the Animal Apocalypse the impact of dividing history into progressive periods gives the impression of an ordered universe in which everything proceeds according to God's predetermined plan.[71] It also serves a literary function. The presentation of a linear succession of time helps direct attention toward the last judgment and the new creation.

---

[68]The Aramaic fragments confirmed what Charles earlier conjectured that the Ethiopic text had experienced extreme dislocation in the course of its transmission. In addition to several other dislocations Charles suggested that the apocalypse was comprised of 93.1-10 followed directly by 91.11-17. *Book of Enoch*, 218; Milik, *Books of Enoch*, 48, 247.

[69]Charles, Book of Enoch, 218, 221-27; Black, *1 Enoch*, 288-89; idem, "The Apocalypse of Weeks in Light of 4QEn^g," *VT* (October 1978): 464-69.

[70]Milik, *Books of Enoch*, 48, 255-56. VanderKam agrees but prefers the date between 175 and 167 BC. *Enoch*, 50.

[71]Collins, *Apocalyptic Imagination*, 50.

The rare phrase "new creation" was encountered in 1 Enoch 72.1, and it was also observed that the idea is implied in the Book of Dreams (90.20-49). However, among the early Enochic writings the Apocalypse of Weeks gives the clearest example of the concept in the judgment passage of chapter 91. The first seven weeks of this apocalypse surveys history until the election of the righteous in week seven. The last three weeks concern the final judgment and conclude with the vision of the new heaven. The eighth week witnesses the rise of a wicked generation at the end of which the righteous are given authority to exact punishment on the "oppressors and sinners" and an eschatological Temple is erected (vv. 11-13). In the ninth week the judgment widens to universal proportions. All works of iniquity "shall depart from upon the whole earth, and be written off for eternal destruction;[72] and all the people shall direct their sight to the path of uprightness" (v.14). Finally, in the tenth week the "watchers" or fallen angels are judged. The author then predicts the new creation.

> [16] And the first heaven will vanish and pass away, and a new heaven will appear, and all the powers of heaven will shine forever with seven-fold light. [17] And after this there will be many weeks without number forever in goodness and in righteousness, and from then on sin will never again be mentioned (vv. 16-17).[73]

The cosmic dimension of God's new creative act is demonstrated by the heavenly luminaries that will radiate light sevenfold.[74] The lack of any reference to a new earth leads Black to argue that this passage implies the doctrine of afterlife when

---

[72]Ethiopic mss B and C read: "and the world shall be written for destruction." Cf. Knibb, *Ethiopic Enoch*, 219-20. Note the Aramaic frg. 4QEn^g: "and all the workers [of impiety] shall entirely pass away from the whole earth, and they will be cast into the [eternal] Pit, . . ." Milik, *Books of Enoch*, 267. Black explains the variant as the Greek translator's misreading of ριφήσεται as γραφήσεται. *1 Enoch*, 294. Thus, this verse does not argue for world destruction.

[73]Knibb's translation, *Ethiopic Enoch*, 220-21.

[74]Cf. Isa. 30.26. Black explains that this is also a prophetic way of accentuating God's glory in salvation. "New Creation," 17.

the righteous will be received immediately into a transformed heaven where they will reside forever. As additional support Black adduces 1 Enoch 104.2 in which the righteous who have suffered affliction are promised that they "shall shine like the lights of heaven . . . and the windows of heaven shall be opened for you." Accordingly, the emphasis of this verse is not upon a transformed earth but the appearance of a new heaven as the eternal dwelling for the righteous.[75]

Although Black's observations may be correct, they are nevertheless open to criticism. Indeed, his appeal to a verse in the later (and as he has argued) independent work of the Epistle of Enoch greatly diminishes his argument. This may be the focus of 104.2 but it does not demand a similar interest in 91.16. Further, the *argumentum e silentio* is rather precarious since the assumption of a renewed creation including the new earth is actually strengthened by the context. In fact, the passage suggests a two stage purging process beginning with the reestablishment of universal order on the earth.[76] Judgment upon the earth and the establishment of an earthly order is depicted in verse 12. At the end of the eighth week it is stated that "the righteous will receive riches and a house shall be built," that is, a new Temple (v. 13).[77] There is every reason to believe that this Temple will reside upon the earth (cf. 90.27, 28). The reference is thus to a new Temple in the new Jerusalem.[78] In addition, it is

---

[75]Ibid., 17-18; Russell, *Jewish Apocalyptic*, 291-92.

[76]See the analysis of Ferdinand Dexinger. Part one: judgment on the earth (v. 12) consists of the new Temple (v. 13) and universal order (v. 14). Part two: judgment in the heavenly realm (v. 15) comprises the new heaven (v. 16) and the heavenly order (v. 17). Dexinger notes that the mention of the new earth in v. 16 would be an unnecessary duplication since it was dealt with previously in v. 14. Furthermore, the passage does not reflect a metaphysical dualism. It concerns not the abolition of an evil principle but the reversal of fortunes in a previously existing order. *Henochs Zehnwochenapokalypse und Offene Probleme der Apokalyptikforschung*, SPB (Leiden: Brill, 1977), 141-43, 185.

[77]Ethiopic mss B and C read: "and at its end they will acquire houses because of their righteousness." Cf. Knibb *Ethiopic Enoch*, 219. Charles sees this as the establishment of a temporary messianic kingdom and cites affinities of thought with Isa. 60.21-22 and Isa. 65.20-23. *APOT*, 2:264.

[78]But see the comments of Charles, *Book of Enoch*, 233 and Black, *1 Enoch*, 293.

stated that at the end of the ninth week "all the deeds of the sinners shall depart from upon the whole earth" (v. 14). Rowland
submits that in the apocalyptist's mind the eradication of evil
from the earth by the activities of the righteous is sufficient to
return the earth to God's original intentions.[79] Stage two centers
on the cleansing of the heavens. The primary concern of verse
15 is with the judgment of the fallen angels and the removal of
evil from the heavenly realm. The angel's domain has become
so infected that a total destruction of the old heaven and the creation of the new is demanded.[80] While a new earth is not explicitly mentioned in verse 16, the idea is nevertheless assumed. A
clear concern for the nation and the entire created order is therefore demonstrated in this passage.

The Similitudes (chs. 37-71)

The Similitudes, as noted in the introduction of this chapter, date to the mid first century AD. According to Black, these
parables, unlike the previous booklets, are "not a loose *mixtum
compositum* of disparate source traditions" but a generally unified piece of literary work based upon the previous visions of
Enoch in chapters 17-36.[81] This section consists of three parables each with a central focus. The first passage embraces the
appearance of the Righteous One and the judgment of the
wicked (chs. 38-44). The subject of the second parable is the
enthronement of the Elect One and the transformation of heaven
and earth (chs. 45-57). The third parable concerns the "glorious
lot of the righteous" (chs. 58-69).[82]

The influence of Enoch's heavenly tours in the Book of
the Watchers is readily evident in the references to the cosmic
wonders and secrets disclosed in this book (cf. chs. 40-41; 43-
44; 60-61). Particularly striking is an enigmatic text in which
heavenly bodies correspond in some way to the righteous on the

---

[79]Rowland, *Open Heaven*, 164-65.

[80]Ibid. Cf. Dexinger, *Zehnwochenapokalypse*, 142-43.

[81]Black, *1 Enoch*, 184-85.

[82]1 Enoch 70-71 are regarded as an epilogue. See the detailed analysis
of chs. 37-71 by Morna D. Hooker, *The Son of Man in Mark* (Montreal: McGill
University, 1967), 36-43.

earth and thus serve as prototypes.

> [1] And I saw other lightnings and the stars of heaven. And
> I saw how he called them each by their (respective) names,
> and they obeyed him. [2] And I saw the impartial scales for
> the purpose of balancing their lights at their widest areas. .
> . . Their revolutions produce lightning; and in number they
> are (as many as) the angels; they keep their faith each one
> according to their names. [3] And I asked the angel . . .
> "What are these things?" [4] And he said to me, "The Lord
> of the Spirits has shown you the prototype of each of them:
> These are the names of the holy ones who dwell upon the
> earth and believe in the name of the Lord of the Spirits for-
> ever and ever" (43. 1-4).

The exact nature of the correspondence is unclear. Equally vague is the purpose of the analogy.[83] The imagery suggests
that the heavenly bodies, hypostatised, have been "weighed in
the balance" and found righteous by virtue of their obedience to
God and correspondence to his design. Only in this manner can
they appropriately serve as prototypes of the holy ones on the
earth. That is to say, the thrust of the parallel is found in the
assertion that "he called them each by their (respective) names,
and they obeyed him" (v. 1). It is the obedience of the created
order which makes it possible for the natural elements to serve
as parables of holiness.

The wisdom poem of 1 Enoch 42 reveals the wicked state
of the world.[84] The poem portrays the descent of wisdom in
search of a resting place on the earth. The iniquity in the earthly realm prohibits a satisfactory dwelling and wisdom returns to
reside with the angels. This passage, according to Collins, aptly
illustrates the discontinuity between the earth and the heavens
and the present and new world. Wisdom is hidden to those on
the earth because iniquity dwells on the earth "like rain in a

---

[83]Note the comments of Black although he sheds little light on this passage. *1 Enoch*, 203-4. See also Stone, "Parabolic Use of Natural Order," 302-
3.

[84]The relation of the poem to the Similitudes is unclear. Black regards
it as an interpolation although its contents compliment the context concerning
cosmic secrets. *1 Enoch*, 203. Cf. Uhlig, *Henochbuch*, 584.

desert, like dew on a thirsty land" (42.3).[85] The passage, however, does not in anyway disparage the created order but force-
fully underscores the extent of evil which prevents humanity
from recognizing and receiving wisdom. Wickedness reigns in
the realm of human history.

The *locus classicus* for the concept of the new creation in
1 Enoch is found in chapter 45. The concern of this parable for
the destiny of the righteous and the judgment of the wicked naturally draws the subject of a new creation into the discussion.
The new heavens and a new earth are said to appear with the
enthronement of the Elect One.

> [4] On that day, I shall cause my Elect One to dwell among
> them, I shall transform heaven and make it a blessing of
> light forever. [5] I shall (also) transform the earth and make it
> a blessing, and cause my Elect One to dwell in her (45.4-5).

The passage offers little speculation regarding the exact character or description of this new creation. It is asserted that the new
transformed earth will become the residence for the "elect ones"
who will dwell in the presence of the Elect One but sinners will
be destroyed from the face of the earth (v. 6).[86] The nature of this

---

[85]Collins, "Cosmos and Salvation," 139-40.

[86]Black's comment that the concept of a transformed cosmos derives
from Isa. 65.17 and "ultimately no doubt, from Zoroastrian sources" is questionable. *1 Enoch*, 205. Cf. also Charles, *Book of Enoch*, 85. For Zoroastrian influence on Jewish apocalyptic see also, Geo Widengren, "Iran and Israel
in Parthian Times with Special Regard to the Ethiopic Book of Enoch," in *Religious Syncretism in Antiquity*, ed. Birger A. Pearson (Missoula, MT: Scholars,
1975), 85-129. Collins notes the difficulty in dating the Zoroastrian sources.
Apocalyptic Imagination, 22-28. S. Shaked observes that "the eschatological
conceptions of late Judaism and Christianity, . . . though they contain all the
essential themes which are present in Iran, do not possess a system of thought
which may link them together in a satisfactory manner." "Eschatology and the
Goal of the Religious Life in Sasanian Zoroastrianism," in *Types of Redemption*, ed. R. J. Zwi Werblowsky and C. Jouco. Bleeker (Leiden: Brill, 1970),
227. See further James Barr, "The Question of Religious Influence: The Case
of Zoroastrianism, Judaism, and Christianity," *JAAR* 53 (March 1985): 201-35
and W. S. McCullough, "Israel's Eschatology from Amos to Daniel," in *Studies on the Ancient Palestinian World*, ed. J. W. Wevers and D. B. Redford
(Toronto: University of Toronto, 1972), 86-101.

transformed world does receive treatment in chapter 51. While the expression "new creation" is absent, the scene once again centers upon the enigmatic Elect One and his enthronement in a renewed world. A picture of bliss and shalom is depicted as the mountains dance like rams and the angel's faces glow with joy. The statement that "the earth shall rejoice; and the righteous ones shall dwell on her" implies a transformation which assumes a new *earthly* existence (vv. 4-5).[87] The concept of deliverance is prominent in this description. The language is reminiscent of the Psalmist's praise of God's power in history and over creation in the Exodus (Ps. 114). This depiction goes beyond the language of God's epiphany by depicting the joy of the earth itself as a consequence of its redemption from the ravages of sin. The author hopes not in a spectral existence in a heavenly realm but a meaningful this-worldly experience in a creation free from iniquity.[88]

The Book of Jubilees

The second century BC writing of Jubilees is an expanded version of Genesis 1 through Exodus 12.[89] The title, "Jubilees," reflects the writer's division of the book into jubilee periods of forty nine years which in turn are divided into seven year-weeks from creation to the giving of the law at Mount Sinai.[90] An alternative designation attested in ancient writings, The Apocalypse of Moses, reveals its character as a direct revelation from God transmitted to Moses through an angel of presence (1.27). As such it is considered by some scholars as

---

[87]Note the comment of Black: "the prophecy about 'inheriting, possessing' the land is now to be fulfilled for the elect of the new Israel; cf. Ps.37.3, 9, 11, 29, 34, Mt. 5.5." *1 Enoch*, 214.

[88]Rowland, *Open Heaven*, 166.

[89]Paleographical analysis and historical allusions suggest the period between 161-152 or 170-150 BC. James C. VanderKam, *Textual and Historical Studies in the Book of Jubilees*, HSM, no. 14 (Missoula, MT: Scholars, 1977), 214-85; idem *The Book of Jubilees: A Critical Text and Translation*, CSCO, nos. 510-11 (Lovanii: Peeters, 1989), v-vi. Cf. Nickelsburg, *Jewish Literature*, 78-79.

[90]R. H. Charles, *The Book of Jubilees or the Little Genesis* (London: Black, 1902), xv.

an apocalypse.[91]   However, the work lacks several characteristics essential to apocalyptic. Wintermute lists the qualities it does not share with apocalyptic: bizarre imagery, limited esoterical appeal, and a prominence of apocalyptic eschatology.[92] In fact, Davenport's analysis reveals that only three passages have eschatological significance.[93] While the relationship of the entire work with apocalyptic is complicated, chapters 1-2 particularly reflect the revelatory character of apocalyptic even though there is little eschatological content. Moreover, the emphasis of chapter 23 upon *ex eventu* prophecy, cosmic transformation, and the afterlife of the righteous clearly marks it as an apocalyptic passage.[94]

As a rewriting of OT traditions Jubilees naturally demonstrates an interest in the created order. An expansion of the Genesis creation account occurs in chapter 2. One of the first acts of God, according to the author, was the creation of two classes of angels. The superior order, the angels of presence and angels of sanctification, share in the secrets and plans of God and even observe the sabbath. The concern for the entire creation is noted in the creation of an inferior class of angels to care for the natural elements of the world. They are described according to their various duties as "angels of the spirit of fire, and . . . of the clouds and darkness and snow and hail and . . . of his creatures which are in heaven and on earth" (v. 2). Each part of creation

---

[91]Rowland, *Open Heaven*, 51-52; Hartmut Stegemann, "Die Bedeutung der Qumranfunde für die Erforschung der Apokalyptik," in *Apocalypticism in the Mediterranean World and the Near East*, ed. David Hellholm (Tübingen: Mohr, 1983), 509. Collins observes that while Jubilees represents a borderline case its basic generic framework is an apocalypse. *Apocalyptic Imagination*, 66-67.

[92]O. S. Wintermute, "Jubilees," in *OTP* (New York: Doubleday, 1985), 2:37-38. Michael Testuz describes Jubilees as "un ouvrage de genre composite," combing historical, legal, chronological, apocalyptic, and the genre of the testaments. *Les Idées Religieuses du Livre des Jubiles* (Geneva: Droz, 1960), 11-12. Note that both Charles and Charlesworth omit Jubilees in their discussion of apocalypses.

[93]Jubilees 1.4b-26, 27-28; 23.14-31. Gene L. Davenport, *The Eschatology of the Book of Jubilees*, SPB (Leiden: Brill, 1971), 19-46.

[94]See Collins, "Jewish Apocalypses," 32-33.

is submissive to and dependent upon its supervising angel.[95] Jubilees also reveals a concern for the creation in other ways: the calendar,[96] geographical interests,[97] and its eschatology.

Two passages evince an eschatological intent. The primary purpose of Jub. 1.21-29 is to assure the readers that God's advent is near. The writer presents the history of Israel from creation to the new earth and new sanctuary.[98]

> And the angel of the presence, . . . took the tablets of the division of years . . . from [the day of creation until] the day of the new creation when the heaven and earth and all of their creatures shall be renewed . . . until the sanctuary of the Lord is created in Jerusalem upon Mount Zion. And all of the lights will be renewed for healing and peace and blessing for all of the elect of Israel and in order that it might be thus from that day unto all the days of the earth (1.29).

The passage does not disclose specifics regarding the transformation of the world. While it may suggest a sudden cataclysmic event, it is more likely a gradual transformation as in Jubilees 23. The reference to the establishment of the sanctuary and "all

---

[95]Testuz, *Idées*, 44-47, 75-77.

[96]In contrast to 1 Enoch 72-82, the author of Jubilees ferociously defends the observance of the 364-day solar calendar (6.32-38). The import of this solar, sabbatarian calendar appears to have been to keep the sabbath inviolate by not allowing any of the festivals or the beginning of the months to occur on the sabbath. See James C. VanderKam, "The Origin, Character, and Early History of the 364-Day Calendar: A Reassessment of Jaubert's Hypothesis," *CBQ* 41 (July 1979): 390-411; Joseph M. Baumgarten, "The Calendar of the Book of Jubilees and the Bible," in *Studies in Qumran Law*, SJLA, no. 24 (Leiden: Brill, 1977), 101-14. For an alternate view see Solomon Zeitlin, "The Judaean Calendar During the Second Commonwealth and the Scrolls," in *Studies in The Early History of Judaism* (New York: KTAV, 1973), 1:194-211.

[97]Testuz, *Idées*, 56-57; Philip S. Alexander, "Notes on the '*Imago Mundi*' of the Book of Jubilees," *JJS* 33 (Spring-Autumn 1982): 197-213.

[98]Davenport, *Eschatology*, 30. He notes three editions of Jubilees. The original angelic discourse of 2.1-50.4 dates prior to the Maccabean revolt and serves to affirm adherence to Torah. Jub. 1.4b-26, 29c and 23.14-31 dates to ca. 166-160 BC. Jub. 1.27-29 is the work of a "sanctuary-oriented redactor" in Qumran during the rule of Simon and John Hyrcanus. These verses were added to widen the scope of the eschatological teaching to include the establishment of the Temple (14-16).

the days of the earth" further implies that the author has in mind a temporal concept of the new creation. He anticipates not an end to history but its purification.[99]

Interestingly, in contrast to the depictions of the advent of the *eschaton* in previous writings, Jubilees 23 reveals a gradual transformation for the nation and creation.[100] Nickelsburg outlines four elements in the message of 23.16- 31: sin (vv. 16-21), punishment (vv. 22-25), the turning point (v. 26), and salvation (vv. 27-31).[101] The author views the present age as one of apostasy and wickedness. The people have abandoned Torah and the festivals and followed the way of the Gentiles (vv. 14-17). A great moral corruption therefore has overtaken the nation. God will punish Israel by sending them against the Gentiles.[102] The author depicts the plight of creation prior to renewal as one of futility because of the deeds of the faithless.

> Behold the land will be corrupted on account of their deeds, and there will be no seed of the vine, and there will be no oil. . . . And all of them will be destroyed together: beast, cattle, birds, and all of the fish of the sea on account of the sons of man (v. 18).

Therefore, according to the author of this apocalyptic section, the transgression of God's law leads not only to moral evil but also to creation's futility.

Jubilees 23 gives a detailed description of the messianic woes. The Israelites will experience great oppression symbolized by the deterioration of human life--gray hair, children appear as persons about one hundred years old, and of feeble stature (v. 25). Then Israel will return to God. A renewed devotion to Torah will usher in the day of salvation in a gradual manner rather than as a cataclysmic event. Longevity will increase to nearly one thousand years, youthful vigor will return, and

---

[99]Ibid., 31.

[100]1 Enoch 23 has been designated as an "historical apocalypse," Collins, "Jewish Apocalypses," 32-33.

[101]Nickelsburg, *Jewish Literature*, 77-78.

[102]The present crisis of vv. 16-25 describes the controversy over the hellenizing policies during the Seleucid period (175-165 BC). Ibid., 77.

Satan and his host will be destroyed. Israel then will rise up and drive out their enemies and peace will reign (vv. 28-30). The author also states that when death comes the bones of the faithful "will rest in the earth and their spirits will increase joy" (v. 31). The import of verse 31 is vague. Charles recognizes a reference to the immortality of the spirit.[103] It could also be a poetic statement suggesting that when death comes the pious can rest in peace knowing that God has vindicated Israel.[104] If this verse is understood in the latter sense, then the passage reflects a description of life on the renewed earth similar to that portrayed in Isa. 65.17-25 and thus its status as an apocalyptic text is questionable.

Charles further contends that this passage suggests the concept of a temporary messianic kingdom. The gradual transformation precludes the opportunity for judgment and thus a general assize at the end of the kingdom must be implied. He admits that this view contradicts the message of 1.17, 18, and 29 which asserts an eternal earthly kingdom.[105] This is an unnecessary attempt to systematize the eschatology of Jubilees. Logical consistency is not demanded.[106] It seems more cogent that the writer envisions in general terms the reestablishment of the new Jerusalem on the new earth. In either case a positive view of the creation's future is implied. Perhaps it is more reasonable that the author's primary concern is to provide hope by vividly depicting a new age in which Israel will live in complete obedience to God and Torah.[107]

The Qumran Literature

The role of the Qumran sectarians as *"the bearers, and in no small part the producers, of the apocalyptic tradition of Judaism"* makes the consideration of their works and thought

---

[103]Charles, *Jubilees*, 151. Cf. Nickelsburg, *Jewish Literature*, 78.

[104]Wintermute, "Jubilees," 102.

[105]Charles, *Jubilees*, 150.

[106]Davenport's attempt to resolve the issue by suggesting several levels of editorial activity has not been found entirely acceptable. See the comment of Collins, *Apocalyptic Imagination*, 228, n. 105.

[107]Rowland, *Open Heaven*, 167.

important for this study.[108] Some have argued that the appella-
tion "apocalyptic" does not adequately apply to the community
or the writings.[109] It is true that none of the writings produced by
the Qumran sectarians are in the literary form of an apocalypse.
Yet the QL shares many of the basic traits and concepts with the
larger apocalyptic corpus and thus offers an exceptional opportunity to evaluate the depth and scope of apocalyptic thought
especially with regards to the sect's eschatology.[110]

---

[108]Frank Moore Cross, *The Ancient Library of Qumran and Modern
Biblical Studies*, rev. ed. (New York: Doubleday, 1961; reprint, Grand Rapids:
Baker, 1980), 198 (italics original); Martin Hengel, *Judaism and Hellenism:
Studies in Their Encounter in Palestine During the Early Hellenistic Period*, 1
vol. ed., trans. John Bowden, (Philadelphia: Fortress, 1981), 218. Cross dates
the QL based on paleographical analysis from the third century BC to the third
quarter of the first century AD (118-21). A more precise dating is difficult
although Geza Vermes offers the following in his introductions to the major
manuscripts: 1QS, CD date ca. 100 BC, 1QH, 1QM date during the last century BC. *The Dead Sea Scrolls in English*, 3d ed. (London: Penguin, 1987). All
citations unless otherwise noted are from Vermes. Line and column references
follow A. Dupont-Sommer, *The Essene Writings from Qumran*, trans. Geza
Vermes (Oxford: Basil Blackwell, 1961).

[109]From a methodological perspective, Philip R. Davies challenges the
view that the community was an isolated, tightly knit group held together by
strong feelings of the imminence of the end since diverse eschatological beliefs
are manifested throughout the documents. "Eschatology at Qumran," *JBL* 104
(March 1985): 39-55. In response, one may note Collins' observation that the
writings of Qumran like apocalyptic in general "cannot be conceived as a consistent and univocal set of beliefs, even within a single community." John J.
Collins, "Patterns of Eschatology at Qumran," in *Traditions in Transformation*,
ed. Baruch Halpern and Jon D. Levenson (Winona Lake, IN: Eisenbrauns,
1981), 352. Rowland, e.g., questions whether the War Scroll can be accurately designated as apocalyptic. This, in part, is due to its lack of emphasis upon
"revelation," his major tenet of apocalyptic thought. *Open Heaven*, 38-42. See
Stegemann's reservation regarding this designation for the QL and his discussion of "possible" Qumran apocalyptic writings. "Bedeutung der Qumran-
finde," 498-501; 517-26. Cf. Jean Carmignac, "Qu'est-ce que l'Apocalyptique? Son emploi à Qumrân," *RevQ* 37 (September 1979): 22-33.

[110]Collins, "Patterns of Eschatology," 352. Collins lists several texts
that although they belong to a different literary genre nevertheless reflect an
apocalyptic worldview: the War Scroll, Rule of the Community, the *pesharim*
and related works such as the Melchizedek text. Only a few fragmentary texts
exist in the form of an apocalypse. Idem, "Jewish Apocalyptic," 48-49. The
Qumran community has been identified as providing important information

The QL is difficult to assess regarding a view of the created order and its future. Like the OT, the doctrine of creation is assumed rather than argued. As expected, a positive view similar to the biblical psalms is often found in the *Hodayot*.[111]

> [7] By Thy wisdom [all things exist from] eternity, and before creating them Thou knewest their works for ever and ever. [8] [Nothing] is done [without Thee] . . . Thou hast created [9] all the spirits . . . Thou hast spread the heavens [10] for Thy glory and hast [appointed] all [their hosts] according to Thy will; the mighty winds according to their laws . . . the heavenly lights to their mysteries, [12] the stars to their paths, [the clouds] to their tasks, the thunderbolts and lightnings to their duty and the perfect treasuries (of snow and hail) to their purposes, . . . [13] Thou has created the earth by Thy power and the seas and deeps [by Thy might] (1QH 1.7-13).

It is noteworthy that this hymn not only acknowledges that the creation exists for God's glory but the reality of an orderly and harmonious creation also provides the basis and framework for the apocalyptic doctrine of "determinism" or "predestination" (1QM 3.15-18).[112] The concept of determinism is a "leading characteristic of Jewish apocalyptic."[113] This psalm affirms

regarding the motivation and development of apocalypticism. Thus, Cross designates the sectarians as "an apocalyptic community, a *Heilsgemeinschaft*, imitating the ancient desert sojourn of Mosaic times in anticipation of the dawning Kingdom of God." *Library of Qumran*, 78-79. See also Hanson, "Apocalypticism," 31.

[111]Cf. 1QH 10.1-12; 13.1-10; 16.8; 11QPs[a] 26. The sectarians' interest in the world and the workings of the universe is also implied by their possession of the Enochic and Jubilee writings and the importance of the calendar.

[112]Eugene H. Merrill states that "predestination is one of the chief doctrines in 1QH, if not the most prominent." *Qumran and Predestination: A Theological Study of the Thanksgiving Hymns*, STDJ, no. 8 (Leiden: Brill, 1975), 12-13. Merrill prefers the term "predestination" to "determinism" as it avoids the concept of fatalism related to the "two spirits" of Zoroastrianism. The latter absolutely precludes human responsibility. The former connotes a providential arrangement of the universe which includes mankind and his destiny (14-15). Regarding the problem of determinism versus free will in apocalyptic see Russell, *Jewish Apocalyptic*, 230-34.

[113]Russell, *Jewish Apocalyptic*, 230. Cf. 1 Enoch 9.11; Jub. 1.27; 4.17, 19.

that the laws of the natural order were ordained or established (כון) at the beginning of creation.[114] The *Hodayot* thus takes the implications of the OT concept of God's sovereignty a step farther. Since the creation exists by God's absolute and immutable will, his decision at the beginning to create the world additionally determines every subsequent event. This absolute quality of God's rule is thus demonstrated by an orderly created order. As God has ordained the paths or laws for the natural elements so has he fixed the ways of humankind.[115]

Regarding the future of creation, a national, this-worldly eschatology by implication affirms the creation. The expectation of two messiahs who will occupy institutional roles in the new community underscores its historical and political character.[116] In addition, the depiction of restored *shalom* in Zion and the texts detailing the new Temple reveal that the sect fully expected a new Temple to be rebuilt in a new Jerusalem.[117] While not referred to in precise language, the QL describes the new age as "a time of salvation for the people of God" and the universal reign of the sons of light. This dominion will continue "eternally to the peace, blessing, glory, joy, and long life of all the sons of light" (1QM 1.5-9). 1QS 4.6b-8 depicts the life that awaits those who walk in the spirit of truth as consisting of "healing, great peace in a long life, and fruitfulness, together with every everlasting blessing and eternal joy in life without end, . . ." (cf. 1QM 19.1-8). While a new transformed age is

---

[114]The term כון occurs frequently in 1QH in contexts referring to the establishing of one's deeds and destiny. Cf. 1QH 1.14, 19, 2.17; 11.34; 15.14; 17.13; 19.22.

[115]J. Licht, "The Doctrine of the Dead Sea Scrolls," *IEJ* 6/1 (1956): 4-5; Helmer Ringgren, *The Faith of Qumran: Theology of the Dead Sea Scrolls*, trans. Emilie T. Sander (Philadelphia: Fortress, 1963), 52-56. Menahem Monsoor, *The Thanksgiving Hymns: Translation and Annotation with an Introduction*, STDJ, no. 3 (Grand Rapids: Eerdmans, 1961), 97-99.

[116]Cf. CD 12.23-13.1; 1QS 9.11. Qumran messianism is decisively this-worldly and reflects the political ideas of postexilic Israel. Shemaryahu Talmon, "Waiting for the Messiah--The Conceptual Universe of the Qumran Covenanters," in *The World of Qumran From Within* (Leiden: Brill, 1989), 294-300.

[117]5Q15; cf. 1QSb 4.24-28. See also Ringgren, *Faith of Qumran*, 165-66.

expected, the rewards are portrayed as this-worldly.[118]   The import of the land in the new age is evident in an eschatological midrash on Psalm 37 concerning the destiny of the wicked and the righteous.

> [9b] *But those who wait for the Lord shall possess the land.* Interpreted, this is the congregation of His elect who do His will. . . . [11] *But the humble shall possess the land and delight in abundant peace.* Interpreted, this concerns [the congregation of the] Poor who shall . . . be delivered from all the snares of Satan. Afterwards, all who possess the earth shall delight and prosper on exquisite food (4Q171 1.9b-11; cf. 3.21-22).

The Psalm also speaks of the renewed creation of the "penitents of the desert who, saved, shall live for a thousand generations and to whom all the glory of Adam shall belong, as also to their seed forever" (3.19b-20a).   One must note that although a change is expected, these passages even while using idealized terminology do not necessarily suggest an abrupt eruption or discontinuity in history.

The positive implications for the creation reflected by the this-worldly messianic conceptions appear compromised by apocalyptic motifs regarding the annihilation of creation.[119]   The

---

[118]See the comments of A. R. C. Leaney, *The Rule of Qumran and Its Meaning*, NTL (Philadelphia: Westminster, 1966), 152-53. Scholars are divided over whether the QL reveals a belief in resurrection and immortality. Matthew Black affirms a belief in a corporeal resurrection. *The Scrolls and Christian Origins: Studies in the Jewish Background of the New Testament*, BJS, no. 48 (New York: Scribner, 1961; reprint, Chico, CA: Scholars, 1983), 138-39. Dupont-Sommer contends for an immortality of the soul. *Essene Writings*, 81, n. 3. Ringgren resolves the problem by arguing that the sectarians felt that they already shared in eternal life and would continue to experience this in the new age. *Faith of Qumran*, 152-53.

[119]Mowinckel has noted that during the Second Temple period both a national, historical and an apocalyptic or transcendent type of eschatology often existed side by side. "They are always intermingled in a quite unsystematic combination, so that the main emphasis is put sometimes on the one aspect, sometimes on the other."   Sigmund Mowinckel, *He That Cometh*, trans. G. W. Anderson (New York: Abingdon, 1956), 267-71; Collins, "Patterns of Eschatology," 353-65. This is evident in the QL, but especially so in 4 Ezra. The QL, however, is less precise. The QL does not explicitly use

idea is found only in 1QH 3.19-36.[120]

> [29]The torrents of Satan shall reach to all sides of the world. In all their channels a consuming fire shall destroy every tree, green and barren, [30] on their banks; unto the end of their courses it shall scourge with flames of fire, and shall consume the foundations of the earth and the expanse of dry land. [31] The bases of the mountains shall blaze and the roots of the rocks shall turn to torrents of pitch; it shall devour as far as the great Abyss. [32] The torrents of Satan shall break into Abaddon, and the deeps of the Abyss shall groan amid the roar of heaving mud. [33] The land shall cry out because of the calamity fallen upon the world, and all its deeps shall howl. And all those upon it shall rave [34] and shall perish amid the great misfortune. For God shall sound His mighty voice, and His holy abode shall thunder . . . [35] and the world's foundations shall stagger and sway. [36] The war of the heavenly warriors shall scourge the earth; and it shall not end before the appointed destruction which shall be for ever and without compare (29-36).[121]

---

the terminology of "this age" and "the age to come." However, the present age is the "time of wickedness" (CD 6.10, 14; 12.23), and its limit is predetermined (1QS 3.19). While a transformation is implied in some passages, a radical disruption of history is not always clear. However, the following passages are suggestive.

[120]Hippolytus attributes the doctrine of conflagration to the sectarians: λέγουσι γὰρ καὶ κρίσιν ἔσεσθαι, καὶ τοῦ παντὸς ἐκπύρωσις, καί, τοῦ ἀδίκους κολασθήσεσθαι εἰς ἀεί (Hippol. *Haer.* 9.27). This testimony, however, does not suggest that Qumran adopted the Stoic tenet of ἐκπύρωσις. Hippolytus uses the same word to describe the eschatological beliefs of mainline Judaism (cf. Hippol. *Haer.* 9.30).

[121]Line 29 begins a new unit. A completely different vocabulary is introduced. However, in spite of this the section cannot stand alone. The third stanza of the hymn (26-28) demands a climax and this section lacks a satisfactory introduction which is provided by the preceding material. Thus, while it may have been originally an independent poem, as it now stands in the text it is part of a larger poem intended as a unified composition. For a structural analysis of the entire hymn see Bonnie Pedrotti Kittel, *The Hymns of Qumran: Translation and Commentary*, SBLDS, no. 50 (Chico, CA: Scholars, 1975), 57-76. Matthew Black contends that a division is demanded with line 31 since fire is merely a metaphor for the floods of Satan in lines 29-30 whereas in lines 31-36 "it is no metaphor, but a grim eschatological reality." *The Scrolls and Christian Origins*, 138, n. 1.

The thought of the entire hymn moves almost imperceptibly from the author's personal deliverance from distress (19-20), to the plight of mankind in a world dominated by Satan (24-33), and then fades into eschatological concerns, namely, the intervention of God who will defeat evil with his heavenly warriors, and bring destruction on the material universe (34-36). As the poem now stands it represents a mixture of both present and future reality.[122] The psalmist therefore can enjoy a present deliverance and fellowship within the community and also long for eternal fellowship with the "congregation of the Sons of heaven" in the new community established on earth.

The final section cited above is united by the central theme of the river of fire. Further, the incessant repetition of כל occurs six times and serves to stress the cosmic scope of the destruction: dry land and foundation of the mountains, the abyss, and the entire earth and inhabitants.[123] The language connoting a thoroughgoing conflagration has been linked to Iranian as well as Stoic conceptions. However, as Ringgren observes the idea of conflagration is Iranian but the passage "hardly presupposes more than the Old Testament prophecies concerning a punishment by fire."[124] In addition, the essential ideas related to the

---

[122]Helmer Ringgren notes the difficulty of determining where personal references stop and future concerns begin. "Der Weltbrand in dem Hodajot," in *Bibel und Qumran: Beiträge zur Erforschung der Beziehungen zwischen Bibel-und Qumranwissenschaft*, ed. S. Wagner (Berlin: Haupt-Bibelgesellenschaft, 1968), 177. As an eschatological community the *eschaton* had in some sense already begun and therefore the writer can speak of his deliverance as both a present and future reality (181-82). H. W. Kuhn, *Enderwartung und Gegenwärtiges Heil: Untersuchungen zu den Gemeindeliedern von Qumran mit einem Anhang über Eschatologie und Gegenwart in der Verkündigung Jesu.*, SUNT, no. 4 (Göttingen: Vandenhoeck & Ruprecht, 1966), 52-61; 181-85. Cf. Collins, "Patterns of Eschatology," 370-71 (cf. 1QH 16.8-9, 11.7-14). The reference to an eternal fellowship with the Sons of Heaven suggests a doctrine of resurrection.

[123]That the inhabitants are the last to be destroyed is not confusing since apocalyptic often utilizes the impact of imagery rather than the rules of logic or chronology. Kittel, *Hymns of Qumran*, 71-72.

[124]Ringgren, *Faith of Qumran*, 164; idem, "Weltbrand in den Hodajot," 177-80. Cf. Isa. 34.9; Amos. 1.3-4. See also observations on 1 Enoch 1.6-7 above. Regarding Iranian influence on Jewish eschatology see also comments above n. 86.

Stoic doctrine of ἐκπύρωσις are foreign to the biblical conceptions as well as the QL.[125] Yet the passage is not merely a weaving together of OT citations. It is the author's own vivid vignette. Kittel notes that the imagery "matches or surpasses in its conception of far-reaching destruction any eschatological description in either the Old or New Testaments."[126] It would be overstating the evidence to suggest that this one passage reflects a belief in a total annihilation of the world as in Stoic cosmology. Fire in the OT is closely associated with the concept of God's theophany and later as an element of his purifying judgment (Zech. 13.9; Mal. 3.2; 4.1).[127] This hymn no doubt stands in the same tradition. Cosmic language is utilized to stress the significance of historical occurrences. The hymn emphasizes the reality of a resolution to the problem of evil in the sect's experience and the world as a whole.

While it is all but impossible to systematize the teaching of the QL, it appears that the community expected some kind of universal renewal following God's visitation. In this regard,

---

[125]Although common Hellenistic features are attested in the QL, the essential conceptual matrix must be found in the OT. This is not to deny Hellenistic influence in Palestinian Judaism even among these more reclusive sectarians. See Hengel, *Judaism and Hellenism*, 228-47; idem, "Qumran und der Hellenismus," in *Qumrân: Sa piété, sa théologie et son milieu*, BETL, no. 46, ed. M. Delcor (Duculot: Louvain University, 1978), 333-72. The Stoic conception is based on an impersonal cyclical cosmology in which the universe dissolves periodically into fire, its basic constitutive element, from which the world is reborn. The cosmic process is thus an infinite series of finite periods of ἐκπύρωσις and διακόσμησις or παλιγγενεσία, that is, a destruction and reconstitution of the world (*SVF* 1:98, 107, 109). See the biological analogy of Chrysippus (*SVF* 1:604; cf. 2:412). For a general discussion see David E. Hahm, *The Origins of Stoic Cosmology* (Columbus: Ohio State University, 1977), 91-135, passim. On the logical difficulties of this system see Michael Lapidge, "Stoic Cosmology," in *The Stoics*, ed. John M. Rist (Berkeley: University of California, 1978), 161-85. An interesting rebuttal is also supplied by Philo (*De Aet. Mund.* 45-51). The Stoic teaching of a mechanical, infinitely repetitious occurrence stands in stark contrast to the Qumran conception of divine retribution. The earth experiences a final decisive judgment not as a natural development but as the consequence of the sin of humanity.

[126]Kittel, *Hymns of Qumran*, 72.

[127]*IDB*, s.v. "Fire," by M. E. Goodman, 2:269; *TDNT*, s.v. "Πῦρ" by F. Lang, 6:930; 935-36.

three passages are noteworthy. 1QH 11.3-14 extols the attributes of God and his graciousness bestowed upon humanity.

> [10] For the sake of Thy glory Thou hast purified man of sin that he may be made holy [11] for Thee, . . . that bodies gnawed by worms may be raised . . . [13] that he may stand before Thee with the everlasting host . . . to be renewed together with all the living and to rejoice together with them that know (10-14).

According to this passage the psalmist anticipates that humanity will be renewed with all that exists (להתחדש עם כל נהיה). It is unclear whether the writer has in mind a present mystical, personal renewal[128] or a reference to a future renewal of humanity and the creation as a whole.[129] Indeed, as an eschatological community one might expect an intimate association between personal and universal eschatology (cf. 1QH 3.20-22).

Toward the end of the *Hodayot* a hymn is presented praising God for the wonders of the creation and its renewal. This passage, fraught with lacunae, clearly echoes Isa. 43.18-19 and Isa. 65.17. God's works are said to

> [11] recount Thy victory throughout Thy dominion, for Thou didst show them that which no other fle[sh had seen]

---

[128]Theodor H. Gaster: "to be renewed with all things that are." *The Dead Sea Scriptures* (New York: Doubleday, 1956), 178, 221; Ringgren, *Faith of Qumran*, 164; Vermes, *Dead Sea Scrolls* (translation cited above). The concept of new creation in the QL like the NT has focused upon personal renewal to the exclusion of the creation. Most recently note John Duncan M. Derrett, "New Creation: Qumran, Paul, the Church, and Jesus," *RevQ* 13 (October 1988): 597-608.

[129]Monsoor translates the line: "to be renewed with all the Creatures." He notes that "creatures" or "beings" (הווה) reflects a common expression in the QL denoting the universe. *Thanksgiving Hymns*, 169. Unfortunately the end of line 14 in plate 45 is blurred. Svend Holm-Nielsen reads the last word in line 13 as נהיה rather than נהוה but does not attempt a translation: "to be renewed with all . . ." *Hodayot: Psalms from Qumran* (Aarhus: Universitetsforlaget, 1960), 185-88. In either case a universal renewal is implied. Dupont-Sommer translates simply: "to be renewed with all that is." *Writings from Qumran*, 237. Cf. Eduard Lohse: "zu erneuern mit allem, was ist." *Die Text aus Qumran*, 4th ed. (Munich: Kösel, 1986), 155.

before. [12] And to create new things, to destroy the established things of old and to [establish] the beings [הווה] forever for [Thou art a God everlasting] . . . and Thou wilt be.
. . . (1QH 13.11-12).[130]

The fragmented state of the text yields uncertain conclusions.
Gaster believes that the passage reflects the rabbinic doctrine of
creatio continua or periodic renewal.[131] The OT language suggests more likely that the writer like Isaiah believed that he was
standing on the threshold of a new redemptive event--a new creation.[132]

The clearest reference to a new creation is found within
the context of a discussion of the two spirits. 1QS 3.14-4.26
relates that two spirits created by God, the spirit of truth and evil,
are engaged in a constant struggle in the heart of every person.
An eschatological force is given to this section by the assertion
that "God has apportioned them in equal measure until the final
age [קץ נחרצה], until 'He makes all things new'" [ועשׂות חדשה]
(1QS 4.25).[133] Like 1QH 3.29-36 the concern of the passage is
the resolution of evil. God has predetermined a set period for
the activity of the spirit of evil at which time it will be destroyed
and all things, humanity and the universe, will be renewed.
Whether a national, historical or transcendent eschatology is
reflected in these passages, it is clear that the Qumran community fully expected a renewed existence on this earth. Further,
the focus of the passage regarding annihilation is clearly a
device to pledge the ultimate destruction of evil and hence not a
depreciating commentary upon the created order.

The Book of 4 Ezra

The depreciation of the creation is assumed particularly in

---

[130]Translation by Monsoor, *Thanksgiving Hymns*, 177-78.

[131]He cites the ancient prayer in the Jewish Daily Morning Service: "He
reneweth everyday continually the work of creation." *Dead Sea Scrolls*, 222.

[132]See Ringgren, *Faith of Qumran*, 165.

[133]Translation by Gaster, *Dead Sea Scriptures*, 46. Cf. Lohse: "und zur
neuen Schöpfung." *Text aus Qumran*, 17. The emphasis of the QL is not a
material-physical dualism but an ethical one.

those apocalypses that emphasize a distinction between the present and future age. The contrast between "this world" and the "world to come" is most striking in the late first century AD work of 4 Ezra.[134] The present world is often depicted as "corrupt" (4.11), "hastening swiftly to its end" (4.26), and "aging and passing the strength of youth" (5.55; 6.20). It is an age "full of sadness and infirmities" (4.27). The author also asserts that the full glory of God does not abide in the present world (7.112), and at the last days the earth which is corruptible will perish (7.31). In fact, it is said that God has "made not one world but two" (7.50). The writer therefore reflects a sense of gloom toward the present world. There is no hope for its improvement. Even God is said to despair over his world describing it as lost and in peril (9.20). Box concludes that the writer's pessimism leads him to believe that evil has so corrupted the earth that only its complete annihilation and the establishment of an entirely new order and a new creation is acceptable.[135] Yet the writer also affirms the importance of creation. Indeed, as the discussion will reveal the writer sometimes juxtaposes these contradictory viewpoints. The limitations of this investigation do not allow a thorough discussion of all pertinent passages. However, it will be demonstrated that 4 Ezra's doctrine of two ages does not disparage the creation.

The author certainly regards God as the only creator and displays an attitude of reverence and wonder in describing his acts of creation (cf. 6. 1-6, 38-54). Such an interest often appears in the dialogues between the angel and the seer.[136] In response to Ezra's query about the reason for Israel's suffering, the angel Uriel bids Ezra to "weigh for me the weight of fire, or

---

[134]Internal evidence dates 4 Ezra at the end of the first century AD. Michael E. Stone, *Fourth Ezra: A Commentary on the Book of Fourth Ezra* (Minneapolis: Fortress, 1990), 9-10.

[135]G. H. Box, *The Ezra-Apocalypse* (London: Pitman, 1912), xxiv, 30; idem, "IV Ezra," in *APOT*, ed. R. H. Charles (Oxford: Clarendon, 1913), 2:555.

[136]4 Ezra is composed of seven visions. Three are dialogues between the angel and Ezra concerning theodicy and three are symbolic visions. The final chapter consists of a narration regarding the commission of Ezra to preserve the ninety-four sacred books. An overview is provided by Nickelsburg, *Jewish Literature*, 287-94.

measure for me a measure of wind, . . ." (4.5). A listing of the marvelous elements of creation follows and serves to rebuke Ezra for presuming to understand the ways of God when he cannot comprehend the intricacies of nature (4.1-12). Attention is thus directed to God's wonderful creative works.

That the writer does not harbor a thoroughly pessimistic attitude toward the creation is evident especially in the parabolic use of the natural elements. This use was noted in the discussion of 1 Enoch 2-5.[137] Especially striking is that this work, which stresses the fragility of this world, utilizes the natural elements to underscore the regularity, stability, and faithfulness of God's creation. Following Uriel's rebuke of Ezra mentioned above, the angel further accentuates the inscrutable ways of God by recounting a parable about a conflict between the forest and the sea. The moral of the story is the folly of attempting to transgress one's natural abilities or boundaries. The parable therefore concludes: "For as the land is assigned to the forest and the sea to its waves, so also those who dwell upon earth can understand only what is on earth, . . ." (4.21). The lesson presents the creation as an exemplar of faithfulness to God's orderly design and thus affirms the goodness of creation.[138]

At the same time, however, the author reveals a realization that the world is unfit for the righteous and is even rapidly deteriorating. The most intriguing statements reflecting this view of God's creation are suggested in the idea of the two ages. Several questions may be posed to clarify the focus of this issue. What is the reason for the earth's corruption? Is the material or created order regarded as evil by the writer? Does the writing evince a material-spiritual opposition between this age and the age to come? That is, does 4 Ezra consider the physical world as corrupt and superfluous in light of the transcendental existence in the new age? Passages of note are those signifying "corruptibility" as a quality of the present world and those which speak of the passing of the present era and the advent and

---

[137]See above pp. 86-89.

[138]See Stone's discussion, "Parabolic Use of Natural Order," 304-7; idem, *Fourth Ezra*, 102.

description of the new age.[139]

The same passage cited above as an example of 4 Ezra's positive view of creation also suggests a negative perspective. The angel Uriel rebukes Ezra for presuming to understand the ways of God and concludes with the observation, "and how can one who is already worn out by the corrupt world understand incorruption?" (4.11).[140] Chapter 7 is especially fertile soil for this concept. Following a rehearsal of the great works of creation which God made for Israel Ezra inquires, "if the world has indeed been created for us, why do we not possess our world as an inheritance?" (6.59). The angel Uriel through several parabolic statements answers that the created world was indeed made for Israel. However, because of Adam "what had been made was judged. And so the entrances [paths] of this world were made narrow and sorrowful and toilsome, . . ." (7.12). Israel therefore must endure the difficulties of the present world in order to enjoy the blessings of the age or world to come. By contrast, the future world is characterized as an age "yielding the fruit of immortality" (7.13, cf. v. 96). There is a sharp distinction between the two ages. This one is treacherous and evil while the future age boasts of a life of ease and immortality. It is important to observe that Israel's suffering and the corrupt quality of the world is attributed to Adam and ultimately to humanity, not to a inherently fallen creation.

In another context God states that in the beginning before

---

[139]The ambiguity of the term "world" in 4 Ezra makes it difficult to determine whether the writer has in mind the "created world" or "world age." Stone's analysis of the extant versions of 4 Ezra in comparison with the LXX and the MT concludes that by the time of this writing the term "world" had experienced a shift in meaning toward the idea expressed by the Hebrew עולם ("age"). Where the meaning is not obvious, this study will attempt to alleviate the problem by using the terms noted above. However, sometimes a clear distinction is uncertain. The Latin *saecula*, the usual word for "world," often denotes both ideas and its meaning must be decided by context (cf. 6.59, 7.12, 13). This is perhaps due to the term itself which connotes a spatial as well as a temporal concept. See Michael E. Stone, *The Features of the Eschatology of IV Ezra*, HSS, no. 35 (Atlanta: Scholars, 1989), 147-80.

[140]Note Stone's emendation: "and how can one who is in a corrupt world . . ." (*et iam exeritus [extritus] corrupto saeculo*). *Fourth Ezra*, 78. Cf. the discussion of Box, *Ezra-Apocalypse*, 24.

humanity was created there was no opposition to his rule. The defiance of humankind brought corruption upon the world. The plight of the created world is characterized by God: "I considered my world [*saeculum*] and . . . it was lost, and my earth [*orbem*], and behold it was in peril because of the devices of those who had come into it" (9.20).[141] The writing does speak of the increased sinfulness of the world due to the rapid declining state of the material world (14.16-17; cf. 5.48-51); but as the discussion below reveals, this does not suggest that the creation itself is regarded as evil.

The author of 4 Ezra also recognizes that this present created world is passing away. In fact, the creation (*creaturae*) "already is aging and passing the strength of youth" (5.55). In chapter 6 the concept of the two ages is presented vividly in the context of Ezra's questions regarding the signs of the end of the present age. The notion of the end and a new creation is especially notable against the backdrop of the opening verses that depict the beginning of the world at which time God foreordained the events of the end. The very foundations of the earth are said to tremble in anticipation of the advent of God because the earth will understand that it will be changed at the end (vv. 15, 16).[142] The time preceding this advent is described as "when the humiliation of Zion is complete, and when the seal is placed upon the present age . . . " (6.20-21). The language of sealing aptly indicates the close or completion of the present age.[143] At the close of this era all will witness the salvation of God and "the end of my world" (v. 25). The imagery of the corruption of the world and the earth's deterioration must not be construed as a thoroughgoing disparagement of the creation. There is no suggestion that the suffering in the present age is related in any way to the material condition of the created order. The state of the present world--this age as well as the created order--is attributed to the activities of humans. The emphasis upon the approaching end and the senescence of the world likewise does

---

[141]See the comments of Jacob M. Myers, *I and II Esdras* (New York: Doubleday, 1974), 261.

[142] "*Et fundamenta terrrae intellegitur, . . .*"

[143]W. O. E. Oesterley, *II Esdras: The Ezra Apocalypse* (London: Methuen, 1933), 55.

not intimate the inherent sinfulness of the material world. It is dictated by the apocalyptic belief that the period of world history is fixed, predetermined, and rapidly moving toward the advent of the *eschaton*. Therefore, statements regarding the passing and aging of the earth serve primarily to remind of the hastening of the end.[144] Such are declarations of hope rather than negative assessments regarding the present creation.

How then is the new age depicted? Does the writer's view of the new age suggest a negative judgment upon the old especially with regard to the material order? The author of 4 Ezra maintains remarkable restraint regarding the details of the eschatological state.[145] Further, 4 Ezra does not present a logical, coherent eschatological perspective. Two types of eschatologies are displayed without any awareness of incompatibility: a universal, transcendental, other-worldly kind (cf. chs. 3-10) and a national, earthly eschatology such as found in the Eagle Vision (chs. 11-12).[146] The presence of this phenomena in one writing has led literary critics to distinguish several sources utilized by the final redactor.[147] Stone's analysis provides a more practical understanding of the eschatology of 4 Ezra much in keeping with the nature of apocalyptic language proposed in chapter one of this study. Stone argues effectively that logical or propositional consistency does not govern the eschatology of the writer. The different types reflect the use of traditional materials determined by the context, purpose, and related themes evoked by each passage. A consistent presentation is not always the primary intention of the writers.[148] The presence of a this-worldly, nationalistic perspective is particularly important to this study. This is espe-

---

[144]Cf. 4.36 and the comments on this verse by Box, *Ezra-Apocalypse*, 35. See Stone, *Eschatology*, 182-83; idem, *Fourth Ezra*, 420-21. Regarding the periodization of history in apocalyptic, see Michael A. Knibb, "The Exile in the Literature of the Intertestamental Period," *HeyJ* 17 (1976): 253-72.

[145]Rowland, *Open Heaven*, 172; Stone, *Fourth Ezra*, 206.

[146]See n. 119 above regarding this character of eschatology in the Second Temple Period. See Stone, *Eschatology*, 44-47; idem, *Fourth Ezra*, 206.

[147]Six sources are distinguished by Box: Salathiel-Apocalypse; Ezra-Apocalypse; Eagle-Vision; Son of Man Vision; Ezra-Piece; and the work of the final redactor. *Ezra-Apocalypse*, xxi-xxviii. See Stone's discussion, *Fourth Ezra*, 14-21.

[148]See Stone, *Eschatology*, 11-33.

cially evident in the Eagle Vision which depicts the defeat of the terrible eagle (Rome) and the reestablishment of the nation "so that the whole earth, freed from your violence, may be refreshed and relieved, and may hope for the judgment and mercy of him who made it." (11.46). Likewise, the vision of the Man from the Sea in chapter 13 offers a description of the Messiah who in the last days will "deliver his creation" (v. 26). Verse 29 makes it clear that this deliverance embraces humanity and the created order. While these passages clearly suggest a transformation, the seer envisions a renewal of Israel and the land rather than an entirely transcendent order. However, it will become clear that in 4 Ezra both types affirm the thesis of this study.

It has been observed that the writer often marvels at the wonders of creation. The descriptions of the end of the present world age and the dawning of the new also assert the importance of the created order.

[112] This present world is not the end; the full glory does not abide in it, . . . [113] But the day of judgment will be the end of this age and the beginning of the immortal age to come in which corruption has passed away, [114] sinful indulgence has come to an end, unbelief has been cut off, and righteousness has increased . . . (7.112-114).

The writer depicts the new age as entirely discontinuous with the present world order. Nevertheless, the characteristics of the new age in this passage clearly reflect a moral or spiritual distinction rather than a material contrast. The qualitative newness of the coming age is also expressed by the seer in the paradisal theme as he contemplates the blessed reward of the righteous--Paradise:

[52] Because it is for you that Paradise is opened, the tree of life is planted, the age to come is prepared, plenty is provided, a city is built, rest is appointed, goodness is established and wisdom perfected beforehand. [53] The root of evil is sealed up from you, illness is banished from you, and death is hidden; hell has fled and corruption has been forgotten, [54] sorrows have passed away, and in the end the treasure of immortality is made manifest (8.52-54).

Notably, while the contrast between the two ages or worlds is manifested, the focus is once again upon moral and spiritual aspects. The writer asserts not a spiritual-material dualism but a depiction of a future existence apart from corruption, death, and hardship.[149]   Indeed, these verses submit that the material realm is important in the world to come. An additional example may be seen in the notion of a temporary messianic kingdom. The messianic age is often seen as a compromise between the prophetical and apocalyptic eschatology.[150]

> [26] For behold, the time will come, when the signs which I have foretold to you will come to pass; the city which now is not seen shall appear, and the land which now is hidden shall be disclosed. [27] And everyone who has been delivered from the evils that I have foretold shall see my wonders. [28] For my son the Messiah shall be revealed with those who are with him, and those who remain shall rejoice four hundred years. [29] And after these years my son the Messiah shall die, and all who draw human breath. [30] And the world [*saeculum*] shall be turned back to primeval silence for seven days, as it was at the first beginnings; so that no one shall be left. [31] And after seven days the world [*saeculum*], which is not yet awake, shall be roused, and that which is corruptible shall perish. [32] And the earth [*terra*] shall give up those who are asleep . . . (7.26-32).

The concept of a temporary messianic kingdom not only provides hope for Israel but it also reflects God's concern for his creation. The land and the city previously hidden appear at the beginning of the kingdom and is a part of this world (v. 26). Box believes that this verse is an interpolation and in fact belongs to the depiction of the new age.[151] This view does not consider the

---

[149]This conclusion is vigorously argued by Stone. *Eschatology*, 76-83, 222-25. This writer is especially indebted to Stone's observations regarding the lack of a spiritual-material dualism in 4 Ezra as it pertains to the present study.

[150]Mowinckel, *He That Cometh*, 277-78; Box, *Ezra-Apocalypse*, 116; Stone, *Eschatology*, 57.

[151]Box, *Ezra-Apocalypse*, 108-9. He also identifies the land with Paradise although elsewhere it refers to Israel (cf. 5.25; 14.31). See Stone, *Fourth Ezra*, 214.

evocative power of the imagery intended to underscore the impact of the appearance of the Messiah upon the world. Evil cannot withstand the presence of God or his representative. Consequently, the messianic age is a time when the Messiah will stamp out all evil and restore felicity and fecundity to the land as well as among humankind. Both will enjoy a foretaste of the blessings of the new age free from evil's taint. The manifestation of the land and the return to primeval silence prior to the onslaught of humanity's voice of contention affirms God's concern for the present created order.

The radical difference of the new age is stressed by describing it as the age "not yet awake" (v. 31). Yet one may note a certain "material" continuity in the statement that in the new age "the earth shall give up those who are asleep in it; . . ." (v. 32). This suggests that the earth continues into the new age.[152] The concern for the material order does not stop with this age. Thus, while there is a distinction between the two ages, this passage as well as those previously studied focus upon the new "incorruptible" quality of the world to come. It is foremost a world devoid of evil, death, and suffering; but it is still a material one.[153] Furthermore, the material aspect of the new age and the process related in this passage strongly contend for the idea of the redemption or restoration of creation. The only explicit reference to the new creation in 4 Ezra occurs later in 4 Ezra 7. The seer requests additional information regarding the state of the dead "until those times come when you will renew the creation [*creaturam renovare*], . . ." (7.75). Stone opines that while these verses may well connote the idea of renovation, this

---

[152]Note that Box's translation adds: "and the dust those that are at rest therein" (v. 32). *Ezra-Apocalypse*, 119. This passage appears to indicate that the old age passed away in v. 29 with the death of the Messiah and all the living. See Stone, *Eschatology*, 56-57. It is often difficult to locate the exact time of "the end" in the eschatological sequence of events in 4 Ezra. Its precise location is determined primarily by the context and purpose of the passage. It therefore serves as a technical term for the "decisive point in the eschatological sequence" (83-87). Idem, "Coherence and Inconsistency in the Apocalypses: The Case of 'The End' in 4 Ezra," *JBL* 102 (June 1983): 229-43.

[153]Stone, *Eschatology*, 56-58, 182. Contrary to Stone, the term *saeculum* is used to denote the "created world" (v. 30) and "age" (v. 31).

expression may only mean "a setting in order, and establishment of the full divine constitution of the world."[154]

To summarize: while some have thought that the concept of two ages devalues the created order, a closer investigation reveals the opposite conclusion. Whereas a radical discontinuity is maintained between the two ages, there is no hint of a material-spiritual dualism. The new age is characterized by the absence of iniquity, hardship, and death. Furthermore, the writer does not argue that the material order is unimportant in the future age. Indeed, the opposite view often is indicated. Even the earth is said to continue into the new age. The use of the term "world" to denote both spatial and temporal qualities underscores the importance of the material world. The idea of two ages, then, actually affirms rather than depreciates the creation. While the author realizes that this age brings suffering and thus longs for the advent of the new, he does not intend to nullify the creative intentions of God.

Apocalyptic Literature of Diaspora Judaism

The Sibylline Oracles

The Jewish Sibylline Oracles are representative of apocalyptic tradition in the diaspora, and while they cannot be described as true apocalypses, the sibyllines reflect principally in their eschatology affinities with apocalyptic works previously encountered.[155] The entire corpus of the sibyllina cannot be considered since the individual books reveal divergent traditions,

---

[154]Ibid., 78-79. Cf. 2 Baruch 32.6; 44.12; 57.2.

[155]The Sibylline Oracles are listed as apocalyptic works in the major reference works (*OTP, APOT,*). John J. Collins, however, argues that they cannot be accepted fully as apocalyptic. One chief characteristic is noteworthy, i.e., cosmic destruction. However, with only a few exceptions there is little emphasis upon the world beyond or immortality or resurrection. The sibyllina lie closer to the OT proto-apocalyptic traditions (Isaiah 34-35) and moreover this suggests that their eschatology was derived not from Judaism in the Hellenistic period but was an independent development. Collins thus designates only Sib. Or. 3 and Sib. Or. 5 as "incipient apocalyptic." *The Sibylline Oracles of Egyptian Judaism*, SBLDS, no. 13 (Missoula, MT: Scholars, 1974), 110-11; idem, "Jewish Apocalypses," 46-47.

dating, provenance, and some with extensive Christian redac-
tions.[156] However, the Sibylline Oracles books 3 and 5 represent
respectively the earliest and latest traditions from Egyptian Judaism.[157] Book 4 corresponds more closely with the eschatology of
Jewish apocalyptic but appears to be a late first century AD Jewish revision of an original anti-Macedonian oracle.[158]

The Sibylline Oracles books 3 and 5 contribute little if any
additional information for this study. The composite nature of
the individual oracles make it impossible to systematically
arrange the views regarding creation and its future. However,
with this caveat in mind, general observations may be made.
There is no interest in the importance of the natural order in
itself. The prominent motif of these sibyllina is the fiery
destruction of the world like that encountered in 1QH 3.29-36.
Book 3 is more restrained in its expression of the motif of conflagration.[159] The primary stress is upon the establishment of an
ideal king or kingdom preceded by cosmic upheavals. World
transformation at the advent of this king and the restoration of
the Temple is clearly drawn from OT traditions. A time of
restored fruitfulness to the earth follows the exaltation of the
king (vv. 619-623) and universal peace that embraces even the
animal kingdom (vv. 767-95; cf. Isa. 11.6-8). This imagery,
however, does not extend beyond the bounds of history and thus
does not denote an entirely new creation.[160] The use of OT
motifs asserts not a particular view of the sibyl but serves to fill
out the picture.

Book 5, however, evinces a more intense speculation
regarding eschatological disturbances in nature (vv. 477-80) and

---

[156]See the general introduction by John J. Collins, "Sibylline Oracles,"
in *OTP*, ed. James H. Charlesworth (New York: Doubleday, 1983), 1:318-34.

[157]Book 3 dates from ca. 160-50 BC while Book 5 derives from the end
of the first century AD and collected under Hadrian. Collins, *Sibylline Oracles*, 21, 73-75.

[158]Collins, "Jewish Apocalypses," 47.

[159]The motif occurs in vv. 75-92, but this section belongs to book 2.
Collins, "Sibylline Oracles," 360. Regarding the development of conflagration
from OT ideas in relation to the Sibylline Oracles see Rudolf Mayer, *Die biblische Vorstellung vom Weltbrand: Eine Untersuchung über die Beziehungen
zwischen Parismus und Judentum* (Bonn: Bonn University, 1956), 134-35. Cf.
Collins, *Sibylline Oracles*, 109-10.

the universal fiery destruction of the world (vv. 155-161). This book concludes with an oracle of the total collapse of the world and thus appears to reflect a thoroughly pessimistic perspective with no hope for the future (vv. 511-31). As noted, the eschatological ideas of the sibyllina are complex. Total conflagration is only one conception. Often it is only the wicked who are destroyed (vv. 375-85; cf. 3.505-10, 540-44, 761). Further, two passages present a picture of a restored Jerusalem on the earth (vv. 249-55; 420-27).[161] It is difficult to argue that the sibyllina held to a firm belief in the entire destruction of the universe. The sibyllists' eschatology reflects neither a regard for nor a negative assessment of the future of this world. Instead, the writers borrowed freely both Jewish and Hellenistic ideas in order to express their beliefs regarding judgment in their respective religio-political environments.[162]

The Book of 2 Enoch

2 Enoch like 1 Enoch reveals a positive interest in the creation, but more so.[163] 2 Enoch affirms a belief in God as sole creator "who laid the foundation of the unknown things and who spread out the heavens above the invisible things" (47.4). An intense interest in the elements of creation is reflected in the account of the angel Vreveil who is said to have instructed Enoch for thirty days concerning all the "deeds of the Lord, the earth and the sea, and all the elements and the courses and the life, and the changes of the years . . . and everything that is

---

[160]Collins, *Sibylline Oracles*, 45.

[161]See the comments of H. C. O. Lanchester, "The Sibylline Oracles," in *APOT*, ed. R. H. Charles (Oxford: Clarendon, 1913), 2:375.

[162]See Collins, *Sibylline Oracles*, 111.

[163]The provenance of 2 Enoch is unclear. F. I. Andersen contends that it hardly stands in the mainstream of either Christian or Jewish religions. He notes that "if the work is Jewish, it must have belonged to a fringe sect." "2 Enoch," in *OTP*, ed. James H. Charlesworth (New York: Doubleday, 1983) 1:95-96. Collins accepts the general view that it is Jewish dating from no later than the first century AD and derives from Egypt. *Apocalyptic Imagination*, 195. 2 Enoch has survived in two Slavonic recensions. The shorter one (A) is considered as the more original and devoid of Christian elements that are evident in the longer recension (J). The references in this study unless otherwise noted are to A.

appropriate to learn." These Enoch recorded in 360 books (23.1-6; 40.1-12). Further, the 364-day calendar surfaces again in 2 Enoch and draws attention to the wonders of the created order (13.1-5; 16.1-8; 48.1-5 J). Also like the cosmic journeys of 1 Enoch cosmology and eschatology are intimately related as human destiny is seen as inherent in the creation (49.2).[164]

An account of creation is given by God himself although much different from the Genesis account. The world is brought into existence through two mythical beings, Adail and Arukhas, who bear in their bellies the entire creation (25.1-26.3).[165] A recounting of the elements created during the first week follows (chs. 27-33). The longer recension account of the Fall explicitly denies that Adam's act of rebellion affected the earth: "Neither mankind I curse, nor the earth, nor any other creatures, but only mankind's evil fruit-bearing" (31.7, J). Thus, humanity is not cursed but only ignorance and sin. A unique and intriguing passage reflects the author's interest in the animals and even their afterlife. Chapter 58 recounts that humanity will be held responsible in the "great age" for the treatment of animals.[166]

> [3b] The Lord created mankind to be lord of all his possessions. [4] And the Lord will not judge a single animal soul for the sake of man; but human souls he will judge for the sake of the souls of their animals. [5] In the great age there is a special place for human beings. [6] And just as every human soul is according to number, so also it is with animal souls. . . . And every kind of animal soul will accuse the human beings who have fed them badly (vv. 3b-6 J).

The souls of animals are preserved in order to render testimony against humanity for any harsh treatment. Furthermore, that the afterlife of animals are placed on par with humankind reflects a concern for all of God's creation. It is therefore clear that 2

---

[164]Despite the occasional similarities 2 Enoch is independent of 1 Enoch. Collins, *Apocalyptic Imagination*, 195.

[165]See the comments of Arie Rubinstein, "Observations on the Slavonic Book of Enoch," *JJS* 13/1 (1962): 16-17.

[166]Gowan also cites and comments on this text. "Fall and Redemption of the Material Order," 101.

Enoch reveals a positive concern for the created order.

Summary and Conclusions

Two issues are of special importance for understanding the apocalyptic view of creation and cosmic hope: the apocalyptists' attitude toward the created order and the related question of whether the anticipation of the new creation depreciates the present world. With the exception of the Sibylline Oracles, the writings investigated reveal an intense interest in the natural order. The apocalyptists' view of the heavens as the dwelling of God and hence the source of divine secrets is no doubt the basis for much of their cosmological speculations. However, one also must understand that the interest in the movements of heavenly bodies as well as geography betrays the importance of God's good creation--the only stable, obedient, and trustworthy aspect of a world otherwise in a state of disrepair and rebellion. While one may detect additional reasons for the references to the created order, the following primary functions may be noted. The apocalyptists noted the created order (1) to draw attention to the wonders of God's creation, (2) to serve as exemplars of obedience for humanity, (3) to underscore God's absolute will in human history, (4) to relate cosmology and individual eschatology, (5) to accentuate the pervasiveness of sin and its effects, and (6) to provide hope for a new world free from the ravages of sin.

The longing for a new creation even in the later first century writing of the Similitudes does not demonstrate a hopelessness for the present creation. It attests the intense desire to see all creation relieved from the suffering caused by human sin. The writers, especially in their references to the examples of the obedient creation, are primarily concerned about righteous living in the present world. In this regard, Coughenour contends that 1 Enoch's eschatology is less dualistic than usually assumed. While the first reference to "the world to come" in Jewish literature occurs in 1 Enoch 71.15, little emphasis is placed on "this age" in contrast to "the age to come." The primary concern is for righteous living in the present world rather

than an escape beyond history.[167] Even those texts with a transcendent eschatology have not abandoned the material order. 4
Ezra even reveals a material continuity with the present creation.
The distinction is upon a world devoid of evil and suffering
rather than an immaterial existence. Therefore, with the possible exception of those passages which can be construed as suggesting the immortality of the soul, the expectations of the
apocalyptists are for a future existence in *this* renewed world.

　　Apocalyptic writings therefore maintain an interest in
creation. Further, there is no hint of disparagement concerning
the natural order. The terminology of a fallen creation does not
appear. Indeed, one writing explicitly states that God has not
cursed the earth. However, the frequent statements regarding
the earth's restored fecundity in the messianic or the new age
reveals that the apocalyptists like the OT authors realized that
the creation had been impaired in some way by an act of human
or supernatural rebellion. The primary emphasis is upon corruption within human history. Nevertheless, while we recognize
the general accuracy of this statement, one should be careful not
to distinguish too sharply between God's acts in human history
and the creation. The solidarity of humanity and creation is
affirmed not only by the effects of sin upon the creation but also
by the apocalyptists' portrayal of judgment upon humanity
which takes the form of a cosmic catastrophe.

　　The apocalyptists thus stand firmly within the OT dialectic of a good yet perverted creation and long for its ultimate
release from the bondage imposed by human sin. Although
there is only one mention of the "deliverance" or redemption of
creation, this may be implied in the concept of renewal. It seems
reasonable, then, that the motif of renewal or the "new heavens
and new earth" evoked in the minds of the apocalyptists the
anticipation of God's holistic salvation embracing humankind
and the universe rather than a negative view of the creation. The
restoration of the community within history or in an entirely
transformed new age is still presented in this-worldly language
and thus serves to affirm God's original creative intentions. The

---

[167]Coughenour, "Enoch and Wisdom," 164. Cf. Charles, *Book of Enoch,* 145.

apocalyptic writers did not renounce the created order. It therefore can be stated with confidence that the apocalyptists clearly were not disposed toward a spiritual-material dualism. In fact, as demonstrated in this chapter, they viewed God's creation as above all "perfectly good."

CHAPTER IV
CREATION AND REDEMPTION IN
THE NEW TESTAMENT

Introduction

The theme of creation in the field of NT has been over-shadowed historically by an individualistic, anthropocentric emphasis. Particularly, the focus in Pauline studies on justification by faith has encouraged the general neglect of a balanced treatment of creation and redemption. The tendency therefore has been to stress personal salvation without adequately addressing the redemption of the material creation in a meaningful way. The current environmental crisis no doubt has contributed to a revival of interest in this subject in biblical studies.[1] Moreover, as noted in chapter one the renewed appreciation for apocalyptic with its universal stress also has provided a new avenue for pursuing the cosmic aspects of God's redemptive work.[2]

The relationship of apocalyptic and Christianity has been tentative at best. NT scholars have been hesitant to relate Jesus

---

[1]In the midst of the environmental revolution of the 1960s James Perry Martin observed that the individualistic narrowing of salvation to sin and guilt stands in stark contrast to Paul's cosmic perspective. He goes so far as to say that "individualistic Christology is an evangelical relic of Greek dualism. It can say nothing about nature, creation, and the cosmic eschatology." "Cosmic Christ and Cosmic Redemption," *Affirmation* 1 (July 1967): 28.

[2]See discussion above pp. 18-23.

and the early church too closely with apocalyptic.[3] Goppelt acknowledges that while Jesus freely made use of apocalyptic motifs and categories, he certainly was not an apocalyptist since "he did not think with the framework of typically apocalyptic categories."[4] However, since the declaration by Käsemann that "apocalyptic was the mother of all Christian theology," students of the NT nevertheless have become increasingly convinced that Jewish apocalyptic played a decisive role in the message of Jesus and the early church.[5] Rowland, whose essential element of apocalyptic is divine disclosure, comments that it would be a mistake to believe that Jesus was unaffected by apocalyptic. "Indeed, there is evidence to suggest that on certain occasions Jesus did receive visions which resemble the visions of apocalyptic."[6] Dunn likewise contends that apocalyptic language and imagery is so pervasive in the Gospel tradition that to remove it would alter the very character of Jesus' message.[7] Recently, in Pauline studies, Beker has argued that apocalyptic is clearly a constituent part of Paul's thought rather than a peripheral curiosity which underscores the cosmic emphasis. Paul's focus is found in the resurrection of Christ "an event that not only negated the old order but also initiated the hope for the transformation of the creation that has gone astray. . . . "[8]

---

[3]See Koch's discussion regarding the attempt to save Jesus from apocalyptic. *Rediscovery of Apocalyptic*, 57-97.

[4]Leonhard Goppelt, *Theology of the New Testament*, ed. John Alsup, trans. Jürgen Roloff (Grand Rapids: Eerdmans, 1981-82), 1:28.

[5]Käsemann, "Beginning of Christian Theology," 102. Käsemann's thesis, however, requires modification. I. H. Marshall notes that while the theme of an imminent parousia formed "an important part of the horizon of early Christianity" it did not *eclipse* the centrality of the resurrection in the message of the early church. "Is Apocalyptic the Mother of Christian Theology?" in *Tradition and Interpretation in the New Testament*, ed. Gerald F. Hawthorne and Otto Betz (Grand Rapids: Eerdmans, 1987), 33-41. See other early responses to Käsemann especially those of G. Ebeling and E. Fuchs in *Apocalypticism*, JTC, no 5, ed. Robert W. Funk (New York: Herder & Herder, 1969).

[6]Rowland, *Open Heaven*, 358.

[7]James D. G. Dunn, *Unity and Diversity in the New Testament*, 2d ed. (London: SCM, 1990), 322. What distinguishes Jesus from the Jewish apocalyptists is his refusal to calculate a timetable for the end and the element of realized eschatology (321).

[8]Beker, *Paul the Apostle*, 149.

It is therefore acknowledged that while Revelation is the only true apocalypse in the NT, the NT as a whole reflects a general apocalyptic orientation in its revelatory character as well as in its anticipation of a radical transformation of the present world order accomplished through the supernatural agent of God. That apocalyptic provides much of the language and structure of the message of the NT affirms further that the cosmic perspective, so much a part of apocalyptic, inheres to the very substance of the message of the NT and therefore provides a much needed corrective for the imbalance of the themes of creation and redemption in biblical studies.[9] The apocalyptic motif of the new heavens and new earth underscores the unity of humanity and creation in God's redemptive plan. In the words of Paul (but with a more *cosmic* focus), as long as creation groans awaiting liberation from bondage, the children of God will likewise "wait eagerly for our adoption as sons, the redemption of our bodies" (Rom. 8.20-23). Humanity is truly a microcosm of the greater macrocosm or universe, and thus a balanced understanding of creation is indispensable for a true wedding of the soteriological and cosmic dimensions of redemption in biblical theology.

The purpose of this chapter therefore is to demonstrate that the apocalyptic perspective of cosmic redemption played an important and positive role in the NT writers' view of creation. The authors did not renounce the creation in their stress on personal salvation. Indeed, it is clear that even the soteriological concerns of the NT take on a cosmic, universal significance like that reflected in apocalyptic writings. The apocalyptic concept of the coming kingdom of God and the new creation received further emphasis, albeit modified by the stress upon the person of Jesus as the inaugurator of the kingdom, which served to underscore the importance of the created order in God's redemptive plan. Salvation is therefore not depicted as an escape beyond a this-worldly existence; it is rather holistic and rooted in the foundational teaching of God as creator.

---

[9]See Dunn's discussion of the features of apocalyptic in early Christianity. *Unity and Diversity*, 322-25. Chief among these was the conviction that the events of the *eschaton* had already begun in the ministry of Jesus.

Limitations imposed on this study permit only a survey of motifs and passages from the Gospels while more attention will be given to other NT "creation" texts. Yet these provide sufficient information in support of our thesis. Examples of the NT understanding are derived from a study of creation themes in the Gospels, two important passages in the Pauline (and deutero-Pauline) tradition, the 2 Peter message of the "new heavens and new earth," and a presentation of the role of the creation motif in the book of Revelation.

Jesus, the Kingdom, and Creation

Jesus and the Kingdom

That the kingdom of God forms the center of Jesus' teaching is evident from the Gospel accounts. As Goppelt notes, "everything else is related to it and radiates from it."[10] It may be noted that while the term "kingdom of God" is not common in apocalyptic writings, the idea is implicit in the various motifs and language depicting the rule of God that would be manifested in the eschatological kingdom.[11] The ideas regarding the concept of the kingdom in apocalyptic writings are complex. The future kingdom is often associated with the idea of the new age while in other texts the messianic kingdom receives prominent treatment sometimes as an eternal kingdom while at other times it is regarded as a transitory stage (cf. 1 Enoch 45.4-5; 4 Ezra 7.26-32). Nevertheless, while a variety of speculations surround the concept in apocalyptic literature of the Second Temple period, Perrin has noted the scholarly consensus that Jewish apocalyptic forms the interpretive background for Jesus' teaching. Chief among these concepts is that the imminent advent of God

---

[10]Goppelt, *Theology of the New Testament*, 1:43.
[11]Cf. 1 Enoch 25.3; 84.2; Sib. Or. 3.47-48; 1QM 12.7; 1QSb 4.25-26. See John J. Collins, "The Kingdom of God in the Apocrypha and Pseudepigrapha," in *The Kingdom of God in 20th Century Interpretation*, ed. Wendell Willis (Peabody, MA: Hendrickson, 1987), 81-96; Michael Lattke, "On the Jewish Background of the Synoptic Concept 'the Kingdom of God,'" in *The Kingdom of God in the Teaching of Jesus*, ed. Bruce Chilton, IRT, no. 5 (Philadelphia: Fortress, 1984), 92-106.

to establish his reign results not from any human endeavor but from God's mighty intervention.[12] This is certainly one emphasis of the parables of growth (Mark 4.26-34).[13]

It is unnecessary and impractical at this juncture to raise in detail the issues surrounding the debate regarding the kingdom of God in NT studies. The history of interpretation has witnessed at various periods a radical swing of the pendulum from one extreme of the kingdom as entirely future to the opposite view of the kingdom as a present reality. Mediating approaches affirming both aspects likewise have been expressed.[14] Further, in an attempt to integrate and interpret these two emphases some scholars have turned to linguistics.[15] The Synoptic Gospels clearly present a "future in the present" perspective. Jesus' understanding undoubtedly corresponded to the apocalyptic notion of the future erection of a kingdom in the new age in a renewed cosmos. Only in this way would his message communicate to the audience. The temporal dualism of two ages, however, experienced radical modification by affirming that the eschatological kingdom was in some way operative in Jesus' words and works.[16] Jesus' preaching affirmed that

> The reign of God is not an awareness of God's sovereign
> power over the universe or of God's kingship over Israel,
> long established and still enduring, though both these con-
> cepts are presupposed. It is the announcement of God's
> kingship in its full realization, fully active, eschatologically

---

[12]Norman Perrin, *The Kingdom of God in the Teaching of Jesus* (Philadelphia: Westminster, 1963), 56-57.

[13]See W. G. Kümmel, *The Theology of the New Testament*, trans. John E. Steely (Nashville: Abingdon, 1973), 36-39.

[14]See Goppelt's discussion, *Theology of the New Testament*, 1:51-55; Eldon Jay Epp, "Mediating Approaches to the Kingdom: Werner Georg Kümmel and George Eldon Ladd," in *The Kingdom of God in 20th Century Interpretation*, ed. Wendell Willis (Peabody, MA: Hendrickson, 1987), 35-52.

[15]Norman R. Perrin, *Jesus and the Language of the Kingdom: Symbol and Metaphor in New Testament Interpretation* (Philadelphia: Fortress, 1976).

[16]One only need to recall the perspective of the Qumran community to understand that this was not entirely unprecedented. See above nn. 118, 122, and pp. 114-115. However, the unique distinction is grounded in Jesus' claim that the presence of God's kingdom is established only in his person and work. Kuhn, *Enderwartung und Gegenwärtiges Heil*, 204.

irrevocable.[17]

While perceptible only to those with eyes of faith, Jesus proclaimed that the kingdom of God had broken into the present age (Matt. 12.28). Moreover, the kingdom of God inaugurated by the ministry of Jesus and made effective "in power" (Mark 9.1; cf. Rom. 1.4) in the resurrection also awaits full realization of God's rule over his creation.[18] Thus, the future kingdom was in the process of being actualized in Jesus.

Jesus, the Inaugurator of the New Creation

The apocalyptic expectation of the universal and cosmic reign of God with the new heavens and new earth as an acceptable setting has far-reaching implications for the NT understanding of creation and cosmic hope. As argued in the previous chapter, the apocalyptists did not abandon the created order for a realm beyond the material world. Further, whether a new creation was depicted in this age or in the age to come is of little import. In either case it affirms that the material creation remains a significant object of God's redemptive activity and moreover receives greater value in light of the goal of cosmic renewal. The creation had not become superfluous in view of national or individual salvation. The NT writers likewise affirm the creation. The natural order even in its impaired condition is viewed as God's creation.[19] The decisive and revolutionary new

---

[17]Rudolf Schnackenburg, *God's Rule and Kingdom* (New York: Herder & Herder, 1963), 82. See also the important works of W. G. Kümmel, *Promise and Fulfillment: The Eschatological Message of Jesus*, rev. ed., trans. Dorothea M. Barton (London: SCM, 1957); George E. Ladd, *The Presence of the Future: The Eschatology of Biblical Realism*, rev. ed. (Grand Rapids: Eerdmans, 1974); G. R. Beasley-Murray, *Jesus and the Kingdom of God* (Grand Rapids: Eerdmans, 1986).

[18]See the discussion of I. H. Marshall, "The Hope of the Age: The Kingdom of God in the New Testament," in *Jesus the Saviour: Studies in New Testament Theology* (Downers Grove, IL: InterVarsity, 1990), 213-38.

[19]Note Hans Bald's unfortunate statement that in the NT the world even in its spoiled condition remains God's creation and "can neither be devalued in the apocalyptic manner, nor made absolute." "Eschatological or Theocentric Ethics? Notes on the Relationship between Eschatology and Ethics in Jesus'

emphasis of the NT writings is the assertion that the reign of God for which the apocalyptists longed at the end of the age has become a present reality in the person of Jesus. Significantly, the Gospel writers declare in various ways that in Jesus God already had begun his work of renewal--a new creation. Indeed, the cosmic relevance of Jesus is revealed by the writers' depiction of his incarnation, life, and ministry as a new creation. Thus it is clear that the reality of the kingdom and the renewal of creation are intimately related. In Jesus the kingdom of God is already present and hence the beginning of a new creation.

Language reminiscent of the original creation account surfaces often in the Gospels linking Jesus and the creation in a remarkable way.[20] Such is not accidental but appropriate in light of apocalyptic anticipation of an eschatological redeemer and the return of creation to God's original intention (cf. 4 Ezra 7.30). Thus, as noted early on by Burney, this association especially with regard to the incarnation can be traced to the belief of Jesus' appearance on earth as a new creation that would rectify the travail suffered by the old.[21] For example, that the early church saw the birth of Jesus as a new creation is reflected in Matthew's opening genealogy. Davies and Allison argue that γένεσις, usually understood as introducing the ancestry of Jesus (Matt. 1.2-17), functions rather as a title to the entire Gospel account. Γένεσις in this context carries the meaning "history" or "genesis," that is, "new creation" and therefore should be read as a general title: "Book of the New Genesis by Jesus Christ, son of

---

Preaching," in *The Kingdom of God in the Teaching of Jesus*, ed. Bruce Chilton, IRT, no. 5 (Philadelphia: Fortress, 1984), 146.

[20]Eric C. Rust presents a more thorough discussion of creation motifs in the Gospels. *Nature and Man in Biblical Thought* (Philadelphia: Fortress, 1953). Due to the limitations of this study, we only mention those which have not been greatly emphasized in literature.

[21]C. F. Burney, *The Aramaic Origin of the Fourth Gospel* (Oxford: Clarenden, 1922), 43. The eschatological significance of John's prologue is seen in the linking of the concepts of creation and redemption. For the cosmic significance of Jesus in the prologue see Loren Wilkenson, "Cosmic Christology and the Christian's Role in Creation," *CSR* 11 (Spring 1981): 18-40. The eschatological import of Jesus in relation to creation is more evident in Heb. 1.1-3 and Col. 1.15-20. See Dahl, "Christ, Creation and the Church," 432-33.

David, son of Abraham."[22] The cogency of this view is strengthened since Matthew's use of Βίβλος γενέσεως would have reminded Jewish Christian readers of the first book of the Torah (cf. Gen. 2.4; 5.1) and the beginning of creation. Matthew thus offered his story as a counterpart to the story of Genesis (cf. Luke 3.38).[23] The eschatological significance of Jesus in relation to the creation is more pointed in Luke's birth narrative. It has been suggested that the angel's statement to Mary that the "Holy Spirit will come upon you" (Luke 1.35) reflects a new creation motif. As such Luke alludes to the Spirit of God depicted in Gen. 1.2 hovering over the surface of the celestial waters and hence the Spirit active in the original creation is the same agent through whom the new creation is effected.[24] The role of the Holy Spirit in the birth narrative is therefore seen as the fulfillment of God's promised redemption of creation analogous to that of the Genesis account.[25]

The NT conception of Jesus as inaugurating the kingdom and a new creation is reflected also in the baptismal event (Mark 1.9-11 pars.). Eschatological features abound in the account: the open heaven, a common feature of apocalyptic (cf. 2 Bar. 22.1; Rev. 19.1), the heavenly voice, and the descent of the Spirit--the promised gift of the last days (Joel 2.28-29). The synoptic writers are in agreement in marking this event as the initiation of the new age and Jesus' initiation into his new role within the new era. Dunn comments, "in short, a decisive 'shift in the aeons' has taken place. And if we inquire, At what point? the answer is clearly, At Jordan, when Jesus was anointed with the Spirit. It is after that event that the note of fulfillment enters: . . . "[26] That this marked a new epoch makes even more appropriate the presence of creation motifs in this event.

---

[22]W. D. Davies, and Dale C. Allison, *The Gospel According to Saint Matthew*, ICC (Edinburgh: T. & T. Clark, 1988), 1:149-55.

[23]Ibid., 151.

[24]Burney, *Aramaic Origin of the Fourth Gospel*, 44; E. Earle Ellis, *The Gospel of Luke*, 2d. ed. (Greenwood, SC: Attic, 1974), 74.

[25]C. K. Barrett, *The Holy Spirit in the Gospel Tradition*, 2d ed. (London: SPCK, 1966), 17-24.

[26]James D. G. Dunn, *Baptism in the Holy Spirit*, SBT, no. 15 (Naperville, IL: Allenson, 1970), 26.

The imagery of the dove, for example, is given eschatological significance as representing hope for the new creation. The precise intention of the dove imagery has been the subject of vigorous debate. Problematic is that Mark and Matthew's ambiguous ὡς περιστεράν is objectified by Luke who attests that the Spirit descended σωματικῷ εἴδει (Luke 3.22; cf. John 1.32). Marshall, however, notes that Mark 1.10 is naturally interpreted as depicting the visible descent of the Spirit in the appearance of a dove.[27] The background for the association of the dove and the Spirit nevertheless remains uncertain.[28] The attempt to draw Hellenistic parallels has proven interesting but unconvincing.[29] In addition, the suggestion that the dove is Israel in Jewish symbolism and thus presents Jesus as the true Israel is questionable in this text since the comparison is made between the dove and the Spirit rather than with Jesus.[30] Also of little aid is that the dove symbolizes purity, innocence, and loveliness and represents "the nature of that holy and lovely Spirit" upon Jesus.[31] It is noteworthy that the rabbis explained the movement of the Spirit over the waters in Gen. 1.2 as like the brooding of a dove (b. Hag. 15a). Nevertheless, the evidence for a widespread concept in early Judaism is weak.[32] However, Rowland contends that if the dove and the Spirit were associated in the eschatological preach-

---

[27]I. H. Marshall, *The Gospel of Luke*, NIGTC (Grand Rapids: Eerdmans, 1978), 153.

[28]Leander E. Keck provides a thorough discussion of the various alternatives and concludes that Luke's reading originated in the process of transmission from an originally adverbial phrase specifying the action of the Spirit descending with dove-like descent. "The Spirit and the Dove," *NTS* 17 (October 1970): 41-67.

[29]Rudolf Bultmann, *The History of the Synoptic Tradition*, rev. ed., trans. John Marsh (New York: Harper & Row, 1963), 249-50.

[30]See Morna D. Hooker, *Jesus and the Servant: The Influence of the Servant Concept of Deutero-Isaiah in the New Testament* (London: SPCK, 1959), 72-73. The argument is strengthened if one recognizes a new Exodus motif in the waters of baptism. But see W. D. Davies, *The Setting of the Sermon on the Mount*, BJS, no. 186 (Atlanta: Scholars, 1989; reprint, Cambridge: Cambridge University, 1966), 36-45.

[31]Norval Geldenhuys, *Commentary on the Gospel of Luke*, NICNT (Grand Rapids: Eerdmans, 1952), 146.

[32]Marshall, *Luke*, 153.

ing of John, then this might have led Jesus to link the Spirit mentioned by John with Gen. 1.2. Such beliefs most certainly
included the presence of the Spirit and apocalyptic notions of the
return of creation to its original state in the last days. This Spirit of the eschaton was then no other than the Spirit of God active
in the original creative event.[33] Dunn suggests that the dove was
an allusion to Noah's dove especially if John's baptism was
understood to symbolize the coming flood of judgment and the
dove, the beginning of the new era of grace.[34] A new creation
motif also may be implicit in the words of the heavenly voice
reminiscent of Ps. 2.7,[35] a royal psalm celebrating the victory of the
Davidic king over the nations understood as a repetition of God's
victory in the beginning.[36] Whatever the exact nature of the

---

[33]Rowland, *Open Heaven*, 361-63; Dunn, *Baptism in the Holy Spirit*,
27.

[34]Dunn, *Baptism in the Holy Spirit*, 27.

[35]The closest parallel to Mark 1.11 (σύ εἶ ὁ υἱός) is Ps. 2.7 (υἱός
μου εἶ σύ LXX). The change in word order directly designates Jesus as
God's son. Marshall, *Luke*, 155-57; idem. "Son of God or Servant of Yahweh?:
A Reconsideration of Mark 1.11," *NTS* 15 (April 1969): 326-36. Luke 3.22 is
a direct citation of Ps. 2.7. D and a few OL manuscripts and a number of
Church Fathers add the remainder of Ps. 2.7 but the major weight of the manuscript evidence precludes its inclusion. See Metzger, *TCGNT*, 120. The
heavenly voice is actually a conflation of Ps. 2.7 and Isa. 42.1 (ἐν σοὶ
εὐδόκησα) and stresses Jesus' role as the eschatological king over his creation and the Spirit endowed servant of Yahweh.

[36]Anderson, *Creation Versus Chaos*, 102-3. Walter Harrelson observes
that behind the portrayal of the raging nations in Psalm 2 lies the mythological
imagery of the gods' raging against the chief god who is proclaimed lord over
the universe. *From Fertility Cult to Worship* (Garden City, NY: Doubleday,
1969), 86-87. Many scholars following Sigmund Mowinckel have identified a
group of Royal psalms composed for use in the autumn festival of the Feast of
Tabernacles--a New Year's feast. (Pss. 2; 18; 20; 28; 45; 65; 110; etc.). According to Mowinckel, this festival reflected the character of an annual Egyptian or
Babylonian New Year celebration the central theme of which was the enthronement of the chief god above all others and the triumph over evil and chaos.
Similarly, Israel marked the enthronement of Yahweh. It was a cultic drama in
which God made all things new by repeating his triumph over the primeval
chaos and his work in creation and hence it was a new beginning. Accordingly,
God renewed his covenant with the Davidic king who as God's "son" or representative mediated world order in the political, social, and cosmic realms. The
idyllic hopes for the king, however, were never realized and were transferred

individual features surrounding the baptismal experience, it meant a new beginning. Barrett opines that this event, like the birth narratives, focuses upon the creative activity of the Spirit: "a new thing was being wrought in the waters of baptism comparable with the creation of heaven and earth out of primeval chaos."[37]

The New Creation in the Words and Works of Jesus

Such passages reflecting an association of the Spirit, Jesus, and creation motifs especially as noted by Luke are not accidental but rooted in the conviction that the new creation, like the old, would be effected by the powerful operation of God's Spirit. The anointing of Jesus as God's agent in bringing about God's kingdom and new creation also is set forth powerfully in Jesus' preaching. Noteworthy is the inaugural sermon at Nazareth (Luke 4.16-30).[38] It could well be that the announcement of the "favorable year of the Lord" has far more implica-

---

into the future to be fulfilled by a descendent of David. *The Psalms in Israel's Worship*, trans. D. R. Ap-Thomas, (New York: Abingdon, 1962), 1:47, 62-64, 106-92; idem. *He That Cometh*, 64-81. The lack of evidence for an enthronement festival in Israel and the excesses of the so-called "Myth and Ritual School" while diminishing this argument does not preclude the influence of the language and imagery of the motif in Israel's concept of kingship. Furthermore, the enthronement was only one aspect of the Feast of Tabernacles, which as A. R. Johnson observes, was itself a celebration that affirmed God as creator and "found its focus in the worship of Yahweh as king and even perhaps the universal king" (Zech. 14.16-17). *Sacral Kingship in Ancient Israel* (Cardiff: University of Wales, 1955), 49-52. See the balanced discussion of H. H. Rowley, *Worship in Ancient Israel: Its Forms and Meaning* (Philadelphia: Fortress, 1967), 184-202. Whether or not Psalm 2 is to be understood against this background, the gospel writers certainly recognized that this was Jesus' anointing as the *universal* Davidic king.

[37]Barrett, *Holy Spirit in the Gospel Tradition*, 39.

[38]The narrative is unique to Luke in terms of content and its placement at the beginning of Jesus' ministry (cf. Mark 6.1-6; Matt. 13.53-58). This has raised the question of its historicity. In an attempt to harmonize the accounts W. L. Lane has posited two distinct visits to Nazareth. *Commentary on the Gospel of Mark*, NICNT (Grand Rapids: Eerdmans, 1974), 201 n. 2. Bultmann regards it as a Lucan composition based upon Mark. *Synoptic Tradition*, 31-32. It seems best to credit it to Luke's special source with Marshall, *Luke*, 178-80 and John Nolland, *Luke 1-9.20*, WBC (Dallas: Word, 1989), 189-93.

tions for the redemption of creation than generally has been recognized. Moltmann has noted that the sabbath as the completion and crown of creation points beyond itself to the sabbatical year which in turn points to the messianic era--the announcement of the Jubilee year. As such "every sabbath is a sacred anticipation of the world's redemption," and according to Luke, it was with this proclamation that Jesus' ministry began. Through his life and ministry the kingdom of God was initiated, and what is more, his resurrection "shines as a messianic light on the whole sighing creation, giving it, in its transience, an eternal hope that it will be created anew as the 'world without end.'"[39] In fact, this emphasis is more evident since Luke's placement of the narrative at the beginning of Jesus' ministry serves a programmatic purpose summing up the significance of his ministry: the presence of the new era of salvation.[40] The proclamation of the "release" declared that all the hopes and dreams expressed by the jubilee imagery were fulfilled in the person and preaching of Jesus.

It is true that Jesus does not explicitly proclaim a reconstitution of the land any more than he intended his message as a social manifesto.[41] The use of the jubilary motif as seen at Qumran (11Q Melch.) above all proclaims the arrival of the era of salvation which the NT writers interpreted as fulfilled *today* in the person of Jesus. However, both the original Mosaic and Isaianic eschatological backgrounds for the jubilee imagery affirm the importance of the land and all creation. The imagery, regard-

---

[39]Jürgen Moltmann, *God in Creation: A New Theology of Creation and the Spirit of God*, trans. Margaret Kohl (San Francisco: Harper & Row, 1985), 6-7, 291.

[40]See Robert B. Sloan, *The Favorable Year of the Lord: A Study of Jubilary Theology in the Gospel of Luke* (Austin: Schola, 1977), 159-65 passim.

[41]The theme of the jubilee year in Luke 4.16-30 has been pressed into service by those with political, social, and economic interests. See John H. Yoder, *The Politics of Jesus* (Grand Rapids: Eerdmans, 1972); Pace Andre Trocme, *Jesus and the Nonviolent Revolution*, trans. Michael H. Shark and Marlin E. Miller (Scotsdale: Herald, 1973). However, its implications for the creation has been all but overlooked. The passage is cited without further discussion by both Brueggeman, *The Land*, 172 and Austin, *Hope for the Land*, 115.

ed by most as primarily that of humanitarian concern, cannot be understood apart from its historical referent to the land. Indeed, as noted in chapter two, the jubilary slave release law is better understood as predicated upon the agrarian principle of the sabbath rest for the land--a constituent part of the jubilee legislation.[42] Certainly the theme as filtered through Isaiah 61, which Jesus cites in part,[43] would have evoked thoughts not only of the prospect of personal release and prosperity but also the eschatological hope for the restoration of Zion in a renewed land. It is significant that Isaiah 61 is couched within the context of the promised restoration of Jerusalem and the land (chs. 60-62) which is given a universal emphasis in Isa. 65.17-25.[44] Especially noteworthy is Isa. 60.19-22 in which the prophet pictures future salvation in personal, economic, and material aspects (cf. Isa. 61.7). It is thus pivotal that the prophet's announcement of the good news of release comes on the heels of such a statement and affirms what has been argued throughout this study that for Israel salvation is not genuine apart from the material aspects.[45] That this is not an overly optimistic estimation of the evidence is revealed in the beatitudes of Matthew, a jubilary text which explicitly proclaims the earth as an eschatological gift for God's

---

[42]The jubilee legislation forms part of the Holiness Code (Leviticus 17-26). Lev. 25.1-7 is devoted to the sabbath year provisions while vv. 8-55 concerns the jubilee year which every fiftieth year coincided with the ordinary sabbatical year. Four provisions are set forth: the restoration of all land according to original Mosaic distribution, the release of all Israelite slaves, the cancellation of all debts, and in keeping with the sabbath year, a fallow for the land. Sloan, *Favorable Year*, 4-9; Margaret Rodgers, "Luke 4.16-30; A Call for a Jubilee Year?" *RTR* 40 (September-December 1981), 72-82. Regarding the sabbath rest for the land see the discussion above ch. 2, pp. 51-55 and n. 44.

[43]The text cited by Jesus in Luke 4.18 is in fact a combination of Isa. 61.1 and Isa. 58.6 joined midrashically on the basis of the common word ἄφεσις. James A. Sanders, "From Isaiah 61 to Luke 4," in *Christianity, Judaism, and Other Greco-Roman Cults*, ed. Jacob Neusner (Leiden: Brill, 1975), 1:97.

[44]Westermann's contention that originally Isa. 65.16b-25 followed directly upon Isaiah 62 is suggestive but hardly applicable to Jesus' audience. *Isaiah*, 411.

[45]See the comments of George A. F. Knight, *The New Israel: A Commentary on the Book of Isaiah 56-66*, ITC (Grand Rapids: Eerdmans, 1985), 48-50.

people: the meek "shall inherit the earth" (Matt. 5.5).[46]

The authenticity of this verse and hence its promise is immediately compromised due to the problems of source, language, and text-critical matters. This third beatitude is peculiar to Matthew (cf. Luke 6.20-23). The place of verse 5 is also unclear in the series of beatitudes. Moreover, since the terms for "poor" (v. 3) and "meek" (v. 5) translate the same Hebrew term, עֲנָו, in Isa. 61.1 and Ps. 37.11 (on which verse 5 is based) it is considered unlikely that two virtually identical beatitudes existed in a Hebrew or Aramaic original.[47] Accordingly, these considerations provide weighty evidence for some that verse 5 is a later interpolation and does not belong to the earliest tradition. Gundry, for example, attributes its inclusion to Matthew's own hand as redactor in order to preserve Luke's eightfold design of beatitudes and woes. It is thus highly questionable that the beatitude of Matt. 5.5 can be traced to Jesus himself.[48]

Such arguments are predicated upon the confident ability to locate the core of the beatitudes by comparing the Gospel parallels.[49] The original beatitudes of Matthew, in comparison to Luke, then, comprise verses 3, 4, and 6. The others must be

---

[46]Scholars are in general agreement that Isaiah 61 serves as the inspiration for the beatitudes of Luke and Matthew. See Matthew Black, *An Aramaic Approach to the Gospels and Acts*, 3d ed. (Oxford: Clarendon, 1967), 156-58. Robert A. Guelich has argued that Matthew has deliberately modified his beatitudes to more directly parallel Isa. 61.1-3. "The Matthean Beatitudes: 'Entrance Requirements' or Eschatological Blessings?" *JBL* 95 (September 1976): 431-33.

[47]See Guelich, "Matthean Beatitudes," 423.

[48]Robert H. Gundry, *Matthew: A Commentary on His Literary and Theological Art* (Grand Rapids: Eerdmans, 1982), 69; Bultmann, *Synoptic Tradition*, 123; Davies, *Gospel and Land*, 361. Georg Strecker notes that since πραΰς is characteristically Matthean v. 5 must belong to the hand of the evangelist. Likewise v. 5 is set apart from the rest of the beatitudes by its verbatim citation of Ps. 37.11. *The Sermon on the Mount: An Exegetical Commentary*, trans. O. C. Dean Jr. (Nashville: Abingdon, 1988), 35. Note, however, that v. 5 agrees with Isa. 61.7 (κληρονομήσουσι τὴν γῆν) against Ps. 37.11 (κληρονομήσουσι γῆν) in its inclusion of the article.

[49]See Davies and Allison with regard to the stages of the traditioning process in the beatitudes. *Matthew*, 1:434-36.

attributed to Matthew's own special source or to his creative genius as redactor. In response, while the textual evidence reveals two different places for the third beatitude, there is no evidence for its omission. In addition, the textual attestation for the usual order followed by most every translation of verses 4-5 is notably superior to that of verses 5-4 supported by the Western reading (cf. NJB). The latter provides a striking antithesis of heaven and earth (vv. 3, 5) which, however, appears to preclude the likelihood of scribal tampering by the insertion of verse 4 if that were the original order. The order of verses 4-5 therefore appear to be the more original which Second Century copyists reversed to produce the antithesis.[50] The attempt to determine the extent of the tradition and the editorial activity of the evangelist, at least in this instance, may create more problems than it resolves.[51] It is entirely conceivable that two different versions of the beatitudes existed and in the course of transmission were elaborated to communicate more effectively to the audience of each evangelist. This possibility notwithstanding, such arguments appear to dismiss too readily the equally reasonable assumption that the two various formulations of the first and

---

[50]Metzger, *TCGNT*, 12. The order vv. 4-5 is supported by ℵ B C and most uncials and minuscules in *f*¹ *f*³ 28 Tertullian *al*. Vv. 5-4 is read by D 33 OL Clement Origen *al*.

[51]Guelich, favors attributing v. 5 to Matthew's source rather than to his own creation. In doing so he attempts to resolve the problems of source and location. The introduction of the πραεῖς beatitude parallel to v. 3 in the secondary stage of the pre-Matthean tradition served to interpret and preserve the religious meaning of πτωχοί which usually carried socio-economic connotations. The later inversion was due to "the loss of the epexegetic character of the parallelism to a Greek-speaking audience" and thus required the addition of "in the spirit" as a qualifier. This view is more acceptable, according to Guelich, since it is inconceivable that the evangelist would have created both the interpretive comment of v. 3 and the third beatitude. This would have resulted unnecessarily in a redactional redundancy between "in the spirit" and "meek" making the two virtually identical. "Matthean Beatitudes," 424-26. However, Matthew's use of this beatitude already embedded in the earlier tradition yields the same result. Guelich's argument itself appears redundant. Furthermore, while Matthew's proclivity for interpretive additions is acknowledged, the phrase "poor in spirit" is witnessed in 1QM 14.7 and is not necessarily a Matthean expansion. Regarding Matthew's interpretive penchant see Robert H. Mounce, "Synoptic Self Portraits," *EvQ* 37 (October-December 1965): 212-17.

third beatitudes could have originated with Jesus himself. As Beasley-Murray explains, this is a simpler possibility.

> If the beatitudes were spoken by Jesus on various occasions, there is no reason why he should not have uttered *both* beatitudes. While the first accords with his frequent citation of Isaiah 61.1, the formulation of inheritance in the kingdom in terms of Psalm 37.11 more clearly conveys the thought of Isaiah 58, and constitutes a vivid alternative expression of the promise of the first beatitude (and of the rest!).[52]

The problem of arrangement nevertheless remains unresolved. If, as Black has theorized, verses 3 and 5 originally formed a four line stanza of two lines each in synthetic parallelism, it is clear that the second couplet, verse 5, seems to further interpret and explain the meaning of the first. The poetic quality of this order is remarkable.

[τῶν οὐρανῶν.
μακάριοι οἱ πτωχοὶ τῷ πνεύματι, ὅτι αὐτῶν ἐστιν ἡ βασιλεία
μακάριοι οἱ πραεῖς, ὅτι αὐτοὶ κληρονομήσουσιν τὴν γῆν.
μακάριοι οἱ πενθοῦντες, ὅτι αὐτοὶ παρακληθήσονται.[53]

If this view is preferable, it certainly accents the relationship of the kingdom of God (or heaven) to the promise of inheriting the earth. However, as mentioned the virtual synonymy of πτωχ-οί and πραεῖς makes it likely that they were originally separated by verse 4. In any case, as noted in the quotation above the third beatitude nevertheless provides a "vivid alternative expression" to the promise of the first. How then does one interpret verse 5? Davies argues vigorously that the promise of the land to Israel was later spiritualized and divorced from all geographical connotations with reference to Palestine. The key for Davies is not only the diminished significance of the "Holy Land" for early Christianity but also the implications of the synonymous parallelism (he accepts the Western text) that links verse 5 with the promise of the kingdom of God which most certainly transcends all local dimensions. To inherit the earth is merely anoth-

---

[52]Beasley-Murray, *Jesus and the Kingdom*, 158.
[53]Black, *Aramaic Approach*, 156-57.

er way of saying, "the one who humbles himself will be exalted (in the kingdom of God)."[54] Strecker agrees and observes that the land of Palestine would have little significance for the Matthean community.[55]

Assuming for the moment the validity of this view, is it not more reasonable to expect that the evangelist would have chosen a more neutral image than the theologically value laden concept of the land or earth? Indeed, his words were more incisive precisely because the land had become a powerful eschatological image expressing in part the universal reality of the kingdom of God. This was the case with the apocalyptists (1 Enoch 5.6, 7, 8; 4Q**171** 1.9b-11). Otherwise one would think that a more suitable passage could have been found rather than Psalm 37 with its incessant echo of "they shall inherit the earth" (vv. 11, 22, 29, 34). However, if with Aalen one recognizes that the concept of the kingdom of God in the NT has not only the abstract meaning of "reign" but in certain contexts connotes "realm," the spatial and physical aspects of the kingdom cannot be overlooked or spiritualized.[56]

Moreover, while Matthew's beatitudes may be more religiously oriented than Luke's, they do not transcend the material aspects but are couched in concrete eschatological language. The πτωχοί beatitude like its Lucan parallel never completely rejects its socio-economic aspect even with the qualification. Indeed, it is the meaning of the term itself which gives significance to its interpretive "in the spirit." Those who are poor are not only destitute but are oppressed, miserable, and humiliated. Only the hope for the ultimate reversal of this plight can provide

---

[54]Davies, *Gospel and Land*, 361-62; Davies and Allison, *Matthew*, 1:450-51.

[55]Strecker, *Sermon on the Mount*, 36. However, note T. W. Manson's view that v. 5 is a late Jewish Christian interpolation since Jesus did not envision a messianic kingdom on earth. *The Sayings of Jesus* (London: SCM, 1949), 152.

[56]Sverre Aalen, "'Reign' and 'House' in the Kingdom of God in the Gospels," *NTS* 8 (April 1962): 215-40. Aalen contends that Jesus' language of the kingdom always refers to a local sphere. Joachim Jeremias appropriately recognizes that the biblical idea of the kingdom is neither primarily spatial nor abstract but a dynamic concept. *New Testament Theology*, trans. John Bowden (New York: Scribner, 1971), 1:98.

blessing.   Similarly, while Matthew uses the more general expression "mourning" to Luke's "weeping" the basic meaning remains the same. The assurance for the readers of Matthew and Luke rests on the anticipation of the eschatological reversal of fortune. This is even more pointed in Matthew's use of πενθέω derived from Isa. 61.2 where the "mourning" is not over personal sins but the plight of Israel. The mourners shall be comforted only by the advent of the new era of salvation and the restoration of the former glory of Jerusalem.[57] Sloan likewise has noted this material aspect. He opines that given the Isaianic background and the social and material perspective of the Lucan beatitudes it was most appropriate for Jesus' audience "to understand the ὅτι promise of 'the kingdom of God' as analogous to, i.e., drawing its metaphorical content from, the restoration of lands that was to occur in the jubilee."[58]

The concept of the kingdom, then, can in various contexts include spiritual, historical, and physical or local connotations. The language of Matthew's third beatitude therefore cannot be accepted as merely a figurative expression for blessing in the kingdom. The promise, although universalized as the "earth," presents an important eschatological image regarding the importance of creation.[59] The promise expressed here has clearly transcended all national and political aspirations. Yet the hope of a transformed world for Judaism cannot be attributed merely to nationalism; it is rooted in the understanding of God as creator. God will not negate his creation. Such would pronounce a "not good" over his creative work. As argued in chapter three,

---

[57]See the comments of Ulrich Luz on these verses, *Matthew 1-7: A Commentary* (Minneapolis, MN: Augsburg, 1985), 231-35; Brueggemann, *The Land*, 176.

[58]Sloan, *Favorable Year*, 126.

[59]To translate γῆ as "land" or "earth" must be determined by context. With this in mind, it may be noted that Matthew usually utilizes the anarthrous construct for "land" or "soil" and the articular construct to designate "the earth." The LXX commonly uses the articular but the context decides the meaning. H. Sasse comments that the reader of Matthew 5.5 only could have understood γῆ as "the earth." *TDNT*, s.v. "γῆ," 1:678. That the concept of inhertance was sometimes spiritualized in the OT (cf. Ps. 15.5) and the QL (1QS 11.7-8) does not detract from the importance of the land motif.

the salvation of God does not reject a this-worldly outlook. The
hope of a new world is often expressed in materialistic or "land"
categories. Therefore, whether expressed in nationalistic or
transcendental "new world" patterns, the apocalyptists and biblical writers fully expected a new earth co-extensive with the
kingdom as vividly revealed in Matt. 5.5.[60]

> The earth, not only the land Israel, will belong to those
> who are kind, for the traditional promise of the land had
> long been transposed into the cosmic realm, but not also to
> the beyond, for the promise of the earth makes clear that
> the kingdom of heaven also comprises a new "this
> world."[61]

To be sure, the fullness of the promise is future. But what
of the present? The beatitudes of Matthew and Luke reflect both
a present and future orientation. Although Matthew's first beatitude promises that αὐτῶν [ὑμερτέρα] ἐστὶν ἡ βασιλεία
τῶν οὐρανῶν [θεοῦ] (cf. Luke 6.20), the statement is best
taken in relation to the ensuing future tenses as a proleptic present "expressing vividness and confidence" and reflecting that
the kingdom is in some sense present but awaiting fulfillment.[62]
Thus, Jesus' announcement of the favorable year of the Lord, the
kingdom of God--the new creation, which will remedy the plight
of God's people and creation, is presented as an eschatological
reality in the process of realization.

If the announcement of the kingdom in Jesus' preaching
has implications for creation then it is equally apparent in his
works. The miracles offer merely another perspective of the
same message of Jesus. As Kallas observes, the proclamation of
Jesus concentrated on the announcement of the kingdom while
the miracles demonstrated what it would be like. "The parables

---

[60]W. L. Lane interprets v. 5 as "the earth purified from sin and purged
of the ungodly, who now oppress the 'poor' will then be *co-extensive* with the
kingdom" (emphasis mine). *The Gospel According to St. Matthew*, 3d ed., ICC
(Edinburgh: T. & T. Clark, 1912), 42. See also the comments of Adolf Schlatter, *Der Evangelist Matthäus* (Stuttgart: Calwer, 1959), 136

[61]Luz, *Matthew*, 236.

[62]Davies and Allison, *Matthew*, 1:446.

and preaching were verbal announcements: the miracles were physical anticipation."[63] This is evident in Mark's placement of the parable collection (4.1-34) in connection with the miracle section (4.35-5.43) and thus portrayed the person of Jesus through word and deed. In regard to the creation, it is notable that Jesus' reply to the query of John the Baptist (Matt. 11.5 par.) is expressed as a list of miracles reminiscent of Isaiah's portrayal of the new age (Isa. 61.1-2; 35.5-9).[64] The use especially of Isaiah 35 recalls the salvific work of God in which the natural world is transformed concomitantly with the deliverance of Israel. At the appearance of the Lord not only will the lame leap like the deer and the dumb shout for joy but the wilderness will blossom and water will spring forth in the wilderness and the desert (Isa. 35.1-10). Are these merely metaphorical statements? As argued previously, the reality to which such language refers is a salvation that brings not only spiritual, personal blessing but the redemption of creation. God's salvific work is holistic.

The impact of the kingdom in Jesus' ministry upon the created order is most prominent in the so-called "nature miracles" which assert unequivocally Jesus' authority over creation contrary to ordinary appearances. The most instructive of these is the account of the stilling of the storm (Mark 4.35-41). The vividness of Mark's details in the story is reflective of personal reminiscence and is probably to be attributed to an eyewitness, perhaps Peter.[65]

---

[63]James Kallas, *The Significance of the Synoptic Miracles*, (Greenwich, CT: Seabury, 1961), 77.

[64]Jeremias, *New Testament Theology*, 1:104. That Jesus adds to the list the lepers and the dead indicates that the present era of salvation far exceeds that of Isaiah's promise (105).

[65]Vincent Taylor, *The Gospel According to St. Mark* (London: Macmillan, 1957), 272. While most agree that Mark's account is derived from the best traditions, it hardly represents an historical account. Bultmann, noting the non-Christian parallels, regards it as an alien miracle story transferred to Jesus. *Synoptic Tradition*, 235. Such a view is hardly related only to this account but is indebted to a general skepticism toward miracles. The prevailing view is summarized by Reginald H. Fuller who admits that while the tradition that Jesus performed miracles "is very strong . . . we can never be certain of the authority of any actual miracle story in the gospels." *Interpreting the Miracles* (Philadelphia: Fortress, 1963), 38-39. Briefly, with respect to this account, the non-Christian parallels adduced as influential reveal common themes but do

The import of this miracle is best understood against the OT background of the *chaoskampf* imagery. The motif of God's victory over the demonic dragon and the sea is often associated with creation in the OT. Order usurped is divinely restored out of chaos. The sea thus became in Israel's faith representative of all evil forces in opposition to God's reign. Significantly, in the stilling of the storm Jesus is portrayed as accomplishing only what the God of the OT could do. As order was brought out of chaos at the beginning of creation by the command of God, so the wind and the chaotic sea were once again overcome by the authoritative word of Jesus (cf. Ps. 74.12-17; 84.9-10).[66]

Furthermore, the use of ἐπιτιμάω indicates that the story is also a type of exorcism account. Kee's examination of Semitic texts reveals that גער, translated by ἐπιτιμάω ("rebuke"), occurs as a technical term for the authoritative word spoken by God or his representative by which evil powers are subdued in order to prepare for the establishment of God's reign. The term גער occurs often in the OT referring to God's "rebuke" of the waters of chaos (cf. Isa. 51.20). In the QL, moreover, גער is used of overcoming evil spirits that God's rule might be effected. A striking association is revealed between the exorcism account of Mark 1.25 and the stilling of the storm by using ἐπιτιμάω to relate Jesus' authoritative word of rebuke to the demon and the wind (Mark 4.39) and the rebellious sea (Matt. 8.26; Luke 8.24). As Kee observes, in the stilling of the storm Jesus speaks a word by which

---

not reflect any significant correlation to the main point of the story. The focus of the story is upon the person of Jesus as revealed by what he does rather than merely his actions as a miracle worker. Goppelt, while noting the verbal connection with the Jonah story, nevertheless observes that the focal point of the account has no counterpoint in the OT story. Furthermore, the impossibility of detecting any great influence of the OT miracles upon the stories of Jesus' miracles affirm the "historical veracity of the tradition." *Typos*, 72-73; Nolland, *Luke*, 398-99. One's view of miracles and of the entire biblical record derives ultimately from one's view of the person of Jesus. This, in fact, is the thrust of this very account! "Who then is this, that even the wind and the sea obey Him?" See also the important discussion of Craig L. Blomberg, "The Miracles as Parables," in *The Miracles of Jesus*, Gospel Perspectives, vol. 6, ed. David Wenham and Craig L. Blomberg (Sheffield: JSOT, 1986), 327-60.

[66]Paul J. Achtemeier, "Person and Deed: Jesus and the Storm-Tossed Sea," *Interp* 16 (April 1962): 174-75.

the demon representing all forces opposed to God are subdued in order that his rule might be established.[67] That Jesus addresses the elements as if they were a demonic force is not foreign to apocalyptic in which angelic beings are pictured as controlling the natural world and even disrupting the creation in the end times (1 Enoch 80.6-8).   In addition, the triumph of Jesus conveyed through the chaos imagery reflects the eschatological promise that at the *eschaton* God would judge the Leviathan (Isa. 27.1).   Therefore, the background of this event was "nothing less than the cosmic plan of God by which he was regaining control over an estranged and hostile creation which was under subjection to the powers of Satan."[68]

The story, then, performs a Christological function revealing Jesus as Lord over all nature. Certainly, the NT writers were not oblivious to the continual effects of sin upon the world even if Jesus had begun to reclaim his creation. Storms continue to rage, birds "fall," flowers fade, and people suffer from malnutrition and other diseases.[69] However, as Goppelt observes, a positive perspective reigns since in the coming of the kingdom "the real nature of God's creation finds its illumination." Goppelt notes further that Jesus' sayings regarding the lilies of the field and the birds of the air as examples of God's goodness are meaningful only because they are placed within the context of Jesus' kingdom preaching.[70] Thus, Jesus' message of the present and future coming of the kingdom not only speaks to the lost condition of humanity but illuminates the ultimate aim to bring

---

[67]Howard Clark Kee, "The Terminology of Mark's Exorcism Stories," *NTS* 14 (January 1968): 232-42.

[68]Ibid., 244-46.

[69]See Bo Reicke, "Positive and Negative Aspects of the World in the NT," *WTJ* 49 (Fall 1987): 351-69.

[70]Goppelt, *Theology of the New Testament*, 1:73-75. It is noteworthy that Jesus' comments regarding the new age are void of the vivid depictions characteristic of apocalyptic. There is no elaboration of a return of fertility, the rejoicing of creation and the like. However, the nature miracles serve a "proleptic" purpose depicting the beginning of the return to wholeness for the creation in the new age. Especially evocative are the miracles of the new wine (John 2.1-12), the feeding of the four and five thousand (Mark 6.33-44; 8.1-9 par.), and the great catch of fish (Luke 5.4-7; John 21.6; cf. 1 Enoch 10.18-20; 2 Baruch 29.5-8; Rev. 22.2).

all of creation under the reign of God.

The Παλιγγενεσία

The radical reversal of the present situation for both humankind and creation at the consummation of the kingdom is proclaimed in Jesus' message of the παλιγγενεσία (Matt. 19.28, "regeneration" NASB; "renewal of all things" NIV; "in the new world" NRSV).[71] In Matthew's account Jesus announces in concrete terms a reversal of both the plight and position of the faithful. The twelve are promised a functional role in the kingdom as well as eternal life (v. 29). Jesus states that in the new world or age when the Son of Man will sit on his throne the twelve also will sit on thrones and participate in judging Israel. Two considerations are of concern in this passage: the authenticity of the saying and the meaning of the term παλιγγενεσία.

There is general disagreement regarding whether Matt. 19.28 represents the words of Jesus or the creation of the early church.[72] The term παλιγγενεσία is unique to Matthew. In addition, the saying regarding the twelve appears patently to contradict Mark 10.35-40 (cf. Matt. 20.21-23) where Jesus refuses to grant a prominent positon to the twelve; particularly to James and John. According to Burnett, as an eschatological promise of prominence, vis-à-vis a present position of authority, the evangelist formulated the saying and thus minimized the tendency of community leaders to exalt one disciple over another.[73] However, Jesus did not refuse the twelve a ruling or judging role in the kingdom but simply states that such a place of prominence is reserved for those who have been prepared (Mark 10.40).

---

[71]L/N appropriately distinguish the translation of παλιγγενεσία in Titus as "new birth" and Matt. 19.28 as "new age" (§41.53; cf. §67.147).

[72]Bultmann, e.g., argued that the saying was a post-Easter creation of the early church because "it was there that the twelve were first held to be the judges of Israel in the time of the end." *Synoptic Tradition*, 159.

[73]Fred W. Burnett, "Παλιγγενεσία in Matt. 19.28: A Window on the Matthean Community?" *JSNT* 17 (February 1983): 60-72; cf. Davies, *Gospel and the Land*, 364-65.

Thus while the other disciples are certainly indignant at the request of James and John, Jesus does not rebuff them but only their naivete. Jesus' response, οὐκ οἴδατε τὶ αἰτεῖσθε, reveals that the disciples do not know what their request will entail. Prominence in the kingdom involves participation in the cup and baptism which Jesus must experience on his way to glory (cf. Matt. 20.21-23; Mark 10.35-40). Nevertheless, the precise meaning of the statement regarding the disciples' ruling role in the kingdom remains uncertain. In an attempt to soften the text, Hill has suggested that in keeping with the OT under-standing, the passage does not contain the concept of judgment but that of ruling over Israel.[74] However, the mention of the Son of Man invokes thoughts of the final judgment (Matt. 25.31). It may be noted that the concept of the righteous participating in judgment of the wicked is not alien to apocalyptic (1 Enoch 91.10; 95.3; 38.5; 48.9; 1QS 8.10; Dan. 7.22; cf. Wis. 3.1, 8; 1 Cor. 6.2). What is new in this passage is the reference to Israel itself.

Schlatter argues that the thrust of this passage is the purification of the new Israel in which the disciples play a decisive role and as such it presents a striking contrast to their present situation.[75] The ruling function of the twelve thus may be reflective of Israel as the "true Israel, the redeemed."[76] Whatever the precise meaning of the passage, Beasley-Murray is among those who believe that the saying derives essentially from Jesus' own understanding of his mission to Israel. This promise arises from the role of the twelve as emissaries of Jesus. To accept or reject the message of the disciples was to embrace or repudiate the Christ who sent them. It was this conviction that gave impetus to the role of the twelve in the judgment over Israel.[77] One also may argue that the image of the twelve thrones simply derives from the idea that those who have shared the cup and baptism of Jesus in his ministry on the

---

[74]David Hill, *The Gospel of Matthew*, NCB (Greenwood, SC: Attic, 1972), 284.

[75]Schlatter, *Der Evangelist Matthäus*, 582-83.

[76]Cf. the comments of Ellis, *Luke*, 109, 256.

[77]Beasley-Murray, *Jesus and the Kingdom*, 277.

earth will participate in the same manner at the climax of history.[78] Therefore, it is certainly possible then that this conception belongs essentially to the pre-Easter tradition of Jesus. The task is now to discover Matthew's meaning of παλιγγενεσία.

The term παλιγγενεσία has an interesting tradition-history in Hellenistic texts which at first may make its use in Matthew seem strange. In Plutarch's *Moralia* the word describes the revivified god Osiris (*De Is. et Os.* 364.35; 389.9; 996.7). Philo uses παλιγγενεσία in reference to the resurrection of the soul (*Cher.* 114.9) and the new beginning following the flood in which Noah and his progeny are regarded as the leaders of the παλιγγενεσία καὶ δευτέρας ἀρχηγέται περιόδου (*Vit. Mos.* 2.65). Most often it occurs as a technical term for the Stoic doctrine of ἐκπυρῶσις and the endless cycles of παλιγγενεσία (Philo *Aet. Mun.* 9.3; 47.1; 76.5; 85.1, 6). Josephus designates the return to Palestine under Zerrubabel as τὴν ἀνάκτησιν καὶ παλιγγενεσίαν τῆς πατρίδος (*AJ.* 11.67). Thus, the concept of individual resurrection, rebirth or restoration in general is denoted by the term in various contexts. The term occurs in the NT only in Matthew and in Titus 3.5 where it refers to the individual who participates in the new age through the "washing of regeneration [παλιγγενεσία] and renewing by the Holy Spirit." The parallels--Luke's passage occurs in the context of the Lord's supper--seem to indicate that Matthew's temporal phrase, ἐν τῇ παλιγγενεσία, corresponds to Luke's ἐν τῇ βασιλεία μου (22.30) and Mark's ἐν τῷ αἰῶνι τῷ ἐρχομένῳ (10.30), and thus alludes to the consummation of the age or the kingdom. Moreover, the apocalyptic content of παλιγγενεσία is stressed by the subsequent phrase regarding the Son of Man. It recalls the parousia and judgment scene of Matt. 13.39-42 and is virtually synonymous with ἐν τῇ συντελεία τοῦ αἰῶνος (cf. 24.3; 28.20).

Since there is no explicit mention of the new world, one

---

[78]Eduard Schweizer, *The Good News According to Matthew*, trans. David Green (Atlanta: John Knox, 1975), 389.

must be cautious about definitive statements. However, that Jesus in keeping with apocalyptic conceptions envisioned a cosmic transformation seems a reasonable inference. The statement, then, cannot be limited to national restoration[79] or even individual resurrection.[80] Therefore, although the term has no Hebrew or Aramaic equivalent, it may be regarded as practically identical with the ἀποκαταστάσεως πάντων mentioned by Peter (Acts 3.21)--a thought that has occurred to others.[81] The importance of the term in Hellenistic texts regarding cosmic renewal suggests that Matthew enriched a common term to convey the Jewish-Christian idea of the renewal of heaven and earth with Jerusalem as its crown as in Isa. 65.17-25. That he would do so certainly is in keeping with the Matthean community which constituted a large number of Gentile origin.[82] As Schlatter reminds, and the previous discussion supports, thoughts of the new world for the Jews always turned to their own people. The new world therefore was first and foremost the new Israel.[83]

Paul and the Redemption of Creation

Hope for the Creation (Rom. 8.18-23)

The biblical view of the created order and its redemption is especially indebted to the Pauline writings.[84]   Particularly, scholarly discussion of Rom. 8.18-23 has helped rescue creation from its plight as merely the background and scene for the sal-

[79]Anton Vögtle, *Das Neue Testament und Die Zukunft des Kosmos* (Düsseldorf: Patmos, 1970), 155-56.

[80]J. Duncan M. Derrett, "Palingenesia (Matthew 19.28)," *JSNT* 20 (February 1984): 51-58. Cf. Josephus *AJ* 11.3-9 where παλιγγενεσία and ἀποκαταστάσις are used synonymously.

[81]F. F. Bruce, *The Book of Acts*, rev. ed., TCNTC (Grand Rapids: Eerdmans, 1988), 84 n. 41; Ernst Haenchen, *The Acts of the Apostles*, (Philadelphia: Westminster, 1971), 208. Schlatter has argued that παλιγγενεσία is the Semitic equivalent to שׁדח םלוע. *Der Evangelist Matthäus*, 582.

[82]Jack D. Kingsbury, *Matthew* (Philadelphia: Fortress, 1986), 98-100.

[83]*Der Evangelist Matthäus*, 582-83.

[84]The hymn of Col. 1.15-20 whether appropriated by Paul or perhaps a later disciple nevertheless stands within the Pauline tradition with its view of Christ as the creator *and* redeemer of creation. See below pp. 173-186.

vation-history of humanity. Not all, however, have appreciated the significance of its positive message for the creation. Some have argued that Paul's introduction of the theme of creation into this context does not reflect an interest in the material order itself but serves only an illustrative purpose, namely, to "emphasize the certainty of future salvation for the Christian."[85] Moreover, some have refused to see any reference to the created order in Paul's words. Reumann, following Gager's suggestion that verses 18-23 constitute an earlier apocalyptic tradition, contends that while Paul utilizes a source that originally spoke of the cosmic dimensions of salvation, it has been modified to support anthropological purposes. Therefore, in these verses "there is not a word about the inanimate world of nature, . . . The whole concern is with believers, Christians, 'we who have the first fruits, the Spirit' (v. 23)."[86] However, we contend that the intrusion of the motif of creation is central to the argument and meaning of Rom. 8.18-23. Indeed, it presents humanity's salvation as actually an "outline in miniature" of the larger cosmic redemptive event. Paul's introduction of the topic of creation in the argument of Romans 8 is therefore integral to understanding God's salvific work in a holistic manner. The issue in these verses primarily centers in the interpretation of κτίσις and often is colored by anthropological-soteriological presuppositions perhaps influenced by the scheme of Romans 5-8 which according to some commentators supposedly concerns only the believer's sanctification. It is thus appropriate to determine the meaning of κτίσις in this context as well as the reason for the intrusion of the topic of creation in Rom. 8.18-23.

The term κτίσις in Romans is used of the activity of the creation of the world (1.20), the creative product of that action

---

[85]C. K. Barrett, *A Commentary on the Epistle to the Romans*, HNTC (New York: Harper & Row, 1957), 165. See also Lampe, "Ktisis," 455-56.

[86]John Reumann, *Creation and Redemption: The Past, Present, and Future of God's Creative Activity* (Minneapolis, MN: Augsburg, 1973), 99. John G. Gager, "Functional Diversity in Paul's End-Time Language" *JBL* 89 (September 1970): 325-37. Gager admits that in the original tradition piece κτίσις referred to the entire created order but Paul has modified it to denote the unbelieving human world (328-29).

(1.25), and the individual creature (8.39). That Paul means the "creation" in vv. 18-23 is generally agreed. It is the scope of the word that has prompted vigorous debate. The modern discussion primarily can be simplified into three different understandings of the term κτίσις.[87] Some, noting the πᾶσα κτίσις of verse 22, see Paul's referent in a more comprehensive light. Κτίσις means the entire creation including humanity but more particularly the unbeliever and certainly excluding Satan.[88] Others stressing the personifying language of verse 22 limit κτίσις to the human creation. Manson, for example, observes that it is uncertain whether the word refers only to humanity or nature. If it is the later, "it is not clear how the material order can 'obtain the glorious liberty of the children of God.'"[89]

The majority of modern commentators agree that κτίσις should be limited to the material or "subhuman" creation.[90] This seems to reflect Paul's primary emphasis in this passage for several reasons. The term κόσμος is more often used of the non-believing world in opposition to Christians. Cranfield observes that to use κτίσις in this way would be unnatural since it inherently connotes the idea of relation to God.[91] It is also unlikely that Paul would describe unbelievers as waiting "eagerly for the

---

[87]The history of interpretation reveals that the term has been interpreted variously to mean the entire creation including humanity, both believers and unbelievers, angels, unbelievers only, angels only, believers only, the irrational order with humankind, only the material order, etc. See C. E. B. Cranfield, *The Epistle to the Romans*, ICC (Edinburgh: T. & T. Clark, 1975), 1:411.

[88]See especially Adolf Schlatter, *Gottes Gerechtigkeit: Ein Kommentar zum Römerbrief* (Stuttgart: Calwer, 1935), 269-75; Vögtle, *Zukunft des Kosmos*, 184-89; Foerster, "Κτίζω," 3:1031; Gibbs, *Creation and Redemption*, 39-40.

[89]T. W. Manson, "Romans," in *PCB*, (London: Nelson, 1962), 946.

[90]Ernst Käsemann adduces πᾶσα κτίσις in support of this view. *Commentary on Romans*, trans. Geoffrey W. Bromiley (Grand Rapids: Eerdmans, 1980), 233-33. See also William Sanday and Arthur C. Headlam, *The Epistle to the Romans*, 11th ed., ICC (Edinburgh: T. & T. Clark, 1908), 207, 210-12; Cranfield, *Romans*, 1:411-12; idem "Some Observations on Romans 8.19-21," in *Reconciliation and Hope: New Testament Essays on Atonement and Eschatology*, ed. Robert Banks (London: Paternoster, 1974), 224-30; James D. G. Dunn, *Romans 1-8*, WBC (Dallas: Word, 1988), 469-70.

[91]Cranfield, *Romans*, 1:411; Foerster, "Κτίζω," 3:1029-30.

revelation of the sons of God" (v. 19). Humanity in general cannot be in mind since Paul asserts that the creation was subject to futility "not of its own will" (v. 20). In addition, the aversion to the "poetic" language of Paul, as seen in Manson's comment, fails to comprehend and appreciate the proper background for Paul. Paul's description cannot be considered as purely poetic fancy or the extension of anthropomorphism to nature but reflects, as this study has often noted, that in keeping with the OT and apocalyptic view each part of the natural order was created "capable of its own response to its Creator and Upholder." As Robinson further observes, this Hebrew conception of the natural world marks the biblical record as unique among the ancient writings.[92] Finally, the objection of Gibbs may be noted. Gibbs prefers to regard κτίσις as denoting the "cosmic totality" rather than restricting it to the material or natural order. This precludes any idea of a dualism between nature and human existence and as such underscores the solidarity of creation and humanity.[93] As discussed in the introductory chapter, it is impossible to extricate the relationship of humanity and creation. To speak of one is to infer the other. However, there is no danger of suggesting a nature-humanity dualism as reflected in verses 20-22. The solidarity of humanity and the created order is especially affirmed in this passage by the dominant Adamic themes which recall Gen. 3.17-19.[94] Furthermore, Paul affirms that both humankind and creation are the objects of God's redemptive work and their destinies are interrelated (v. 21). The context must provide the meaning for κτίσις. Käsemann agrees with the more comprehensive idea but recognizes that Paul's *primary* focus in this passage is upon the nonhuman creation.[95] One's view in the matter is influenced by what is intended by Paul's introduction of the theme of creation into this

---

[92]Robinson, *Inspiration and Revelation*, 206, 210-12.

[93]Gibbs, *Creation and Redemption*, 40-41.

[94]See Dunn, *Romans*, 467; Sanday and Headlam, *Romans*, 207.

[95]Käsemann, *Romans*, 233. Matthew Black suggests that vv. 19-20 refers to "man" as a part of creation and v. 22 to the entire creation. *Romans*, NCB (Greenwood, SC: Attic, 1973), 121.

[96]See the discussion of C. E. B. Cranfield, "The Freedom of the Chris-

passage. An understanding of the setting is thus an important consideration.

Romans 8 reflects an eschatological perspective rooted in its main emphasis on the Holy Spirit as a present gift of life and a pledge of ultimate fulfillment. Paul in chapters 6-7 has stressed the enticing and incarcerating impact of sin, death, and the law concluding in 7.25 with a thanksgiving to God for deliverance from this condition through Jesus Christ. He turns in chapter 8 to the issue of the new life in the Spirit. By "the law of the life-giving Spirit" God has done what the law could not, namely, condemn sin in the flesh through his own son thereby providing freedom from the tyranny of the law of sin and death (vv. 1-3). Moreover, new life in the Spirit means not only freedom *from* the law but by the presence and effecting power of the Spirit it means freedom *for* obedience to God's law "that the requirement of the Law might be fulfilled in us" (v. 4).[96] The eschatological tension is heightened in verses 5-11 in which the two ages are brought into striking contrast as Paul describes those who belong to the old order as "according to the flesh" (vv. 4, 5, 6, 8, 9) in opposition to those who are "according to the Spirit" (vv. 4, 5, 6, 9). The terminology, as Ridderbos explains, reflects a corporate view by which Christians are no longer regarded as belonging to the sphere of Adam, that is, to the old order characterized by sin and death, but are "in Christ" by virtue of Christ's salvific work and the gift of the Spirit. Further, this new "realm" is an objective reality which determines one's actions (cf. 5.12-21).[97] Dunn opines correctly that Paul does not intend a strict compartmentalization in these verses as though those who walk according to the Spirit are never influenced by the things of the flesh. The believer, although possessing the gift of the Spirit, nevertheless is in transit. One continues to live between the "already" and the "not yet." Thus, Paul's $\pi\nu\varepsilon\hat{\upsilon}\mu\alpha$-$\sigma\acute{\alpha}\rho\xi$ antithesis–the new and the old age–is sharpened not only to underscore the

tian According to Romans 8.2," in *New Testament Christianity for Africa and the World*, ed. Mark E. Glasswell and Edward W. Fasholé-Luke (London: SPCK, 1974), 91-98.

[97]Hermann Ridderbos, *Paul: An Outline of His Theology*, trans. John Richard De Witt (Grand Rapids: Eerdmans, 1975), 221-22.

eschatological tension but also for parenetical reasons in order to remind his readers that the decisions made in conversion must be affirmed in every day experience.[98] This does not lessen the impact of the decisive transfer of the believer from the realm and power of sin and death to freedom and life. Paul will have no confusion in the matter. There are only two possible spheres of life with decisive consequences (vv. 12-13). Paul thus comes in verses 14-17 to the determinative element which gives the believer understanding for living in the eschatological tension of the "already-not yet."[99] Believers have received the "spirit of adoption" (8.15) and hence are children of God (v. 16), yet they await the full benefits of that relationship. Paul then places this relationship within a cosmic context to provide support in the interim and hope for glory (vv. 18-23).

It is helpful to note at this juncture that a movement from individual to cosmic concerns in Romans 8 mirrors the same emphasis in 5.1-21. As Dunn observes, "from 8.14 onward there is a steadily mounting climax in which the tensions of the present stage of God's saving purpose are set more and more fully within the context of the Creator's purpose for the cosmos as a whole" and is resolved with the assurance that nothing can defeat his purpose determined in Christ.[100] Particularly, Paul's discussion in 8.14-39 continues the central theme of 5.1-11.[101] Both are formulated within the eschatological polarity of present

---

[98]Dunn, *Romans*, 441; idem "Paul's Epistle to the Romans: An Analysis of Structure and Argument," *ANRW*, 25.4, ed. W. Haase (Berlin: de Gruyter, 1988), 2863-64.

[99]Dunn, "Paul's Epistle," 2864.

[100]Ibid., 2857.

[101]That Rom. 8.14-39 contains a fuller elucidation of the themes of 5.1-11 has been noted especially by Nils A. Dahl, "Two Notes on Romans 5," *ST* 5/1 (1952): 37-48. The place of ch. 5 in the argument of chs. 1-8 has prompted considerable debate. It is regarded as either the conclusion of 1.18-4.25 or beginning the new section of chs. 5-8. Once this is settled there is the problem of 5.12-21. There is much to be said for either side. The linguistic affinities with the first section are remarkable. Cf. δικαιοσυνή (2.12; 3.4, 5, 20, 21, 25, 28, 30; 4.2-5; 5.1, 9), δόξα (1.21, 23; 5.2, 8), καυχᾶσθαι (2.17; 5.2, 11). However, cf. πίστις occurring over thirty times in chs. 1-4 and only three times in chs. 5-8 and ζωή/ζάω appearing in the first section twice but twenty-four times in chs. 5-8. Word frequency while helpful is hardly determinative. Perhaps the strongest position is to regard ch. 5 as a transitional chapter

assurance and ultimate victory, present suffering and the hope of glory. Paul in 5.3-4 reminds his readers that suffering is not only a reality but in actuality an occasion for joy and strengthened hope "which does not disappoint" because the love of God has been showered upon the Christian in the Holy Spirit (v. 5). Rom. 8.14-30 develops this theme more fully by arguing that the believer lives in the midst of distress but longs for the "glory that is to be revealed to us" (v. 18). Chapters 5-8 are thus bracketed by the theme of the assurance of glory.[102] The coming glory in 8.17-18 is assured paradoxically by the reality of suffering. No doubt Paul means practically that glory is as certain as suffering. There is, however, for the believer an intimate relationship between suffering and future glory even as there was for Jesus. Sharing in Christ's suffering (συμπάσχομεν) provides meaning for it affirms that the believer will share in his glory (συνδοχασθῶμεν).[103] Present suffering is a necessary, unavoidable, and indispensable pathway to participation in Christ's coming glory.

It is within this context of the suffering-glory, assurance-victory tension that Paul introduces the idea of creation's suffering and glory thus placing the Christian experience within the cosmic context of the Creator's purpose. The Christian's hope of glory is buoyed by revealing that not only the believer but the entire cosmos experiences suffering leading toward the same goal of redemption. Further, the creation's suffering is actually a sign of the rapidly approaching advent. Significantly, the inclu-

---

summarizing the argument thus far in 1.18-4.25 and propelling the argument to a new level regarding eschatological life and hope as a consequence of justification by faith. Cf. Beker, *Paul*, 84-85; Cranfield, *Romans*, 1:252-54; Sanders, *Paul*, 487. Dunn while preferring ch. 5 as the conclusion to the first section nevertheless recognizes it as a "bridging chapter" in which chs. 6-8 and 9-11 develop the conclusion drawn in ch. 5 on an individual level (5.1-11) and a more cosmic level (5.12-21). Thus, 5.1-11 corresponds to chs. 6-8 and 5.12-21 is equivalent to chs. 9-11. "Paul's Epistle," 2856-57.

[102]See Douglas Moo, *Romans 1-8*, WEC (Chicago: Moody, 1991), 302-3.

[103]The preposition σύν affirms unequivocally that "only he who participates on earth in the passion of the Kyrios will participate in his glory." Käsemann, *Romans*, 229.

sion of these statements in the chapter on the Spirit affirms that the present possession of the Spirit as a pledge of the Christian's deliverance points also to the ultimate redemption of all creation. The dominion of the Spirit therefore is not confined to humanity but reaches even to the entire cosmos.[104] God fully intends to bring the entire creation, both human and the nonhuman created order, to fulfillment. This ultimate *telos* of God's original creative intentions is predicated upon his activity as creator *and* redeemer. Paul, then, asserts that the redemption of the Christian is in actuality a part of a much larger creative-redemptive work. This fact by implication affirms the inherent dignity of the creation apart from humankind. Paul's remarks are therefore integral to his argument. A study of the passage reveals important observations regarding the creation and its redemption.

> [18] For I consider that the sufferings of this present time are not worthy to be compared with the glory that is to be revealed to us. [19] For the anxious longing of the creation waits eagerly for the revealing of the sons of God. [20] For the creation was subjected to futility, not of its own will, but because of Him who subjected it, in hope [21] that the creation itself also will be set free from its slavery to corruption into the freedom of the glory of the children of God. [22] For we know that the whole creation groans and suffers the pains of childbirth together until now. [23] And not only this, but also we ourselves, having the first fruits of the spirit, even we ourselves groan within ourselves, waiting eagerly for our adoption as sons, the redemption of our body (Rom. 8.18-23).

Verse 18 serves as the basis for the comment regarding the suffering-glory tension of verse 17. Paul regards the suffering of the present age as insignificant in comparison with the glory "that is to be revealed" (τὴν μέλλουσαν δόξαν ἀποκαλυφθῆ-ναι). Dunn finds in the present participle of μέλλω the idea of the certainty and immanence of the parousia.[105] Note, however,

---

[104]Cf. the statement of Gibbs: "The rule of the Spirit, which is confined to the sphere of humanity, is unthinkable apart from the rule of the Lord in all creation." *Creation and Redemption*, 36.

that the coming glory that will be revealed "in us" (εἰς ἡμᾶς) does not imply a rejection of the Jewish materialist connotations of the new age.[106] The construction denotes not "in us" (ἐν ἡμῖν) but "to us" (NASB, TEV) or better yet "toward us" ("for" cf. NEB) and "suggests that the glory reaches out and includes us in its scope."[107] This is a cosmic concept indeed! Paul then introduces the plight and destiny of the creation in verses 19-23 as the basis for his statements in verse 18.[108]

It is apparent that Paul's primary concern in this passage is not present suffering, although such is not to be dismissed easily as a petty distraction. His central focus is clearly the future glory. The entire section is therefore dominated by the theme expressed in the word ἀποκαραδοκία, the "anxious longing" (NASB), "eager expectation" (NEB), or "eager longing" (NRSV) which is the characteristic outlook of the created order. In this term, which occurs in the NT only here and in Phil. 1.20, Paul ascribes to the creation an attribute of positive and confident anticipation. While the etymology of a word may be misleading, that Paul apparently constructed the word is instructive. The verb, from κάρα ("head") and δέχομαι ("to take," originally "to stretch"), gives the image of "craning the head forward," that is, straining with outstretched head to catch the first glimpse of an object in the distance.[109] The preposition ἀπό may suggest "diversion from other things and concentration on a single object."[110] Notably, the word always appears in close relation with ἐλπίς. This is true especially of Phil. 1.20 where ἀποκαραδοκία and ἐλπίς are linked by the copulative καί. The

---

[105]Dunn, *Romans*, 468-69.

[106]Cf. Leon Morris, *The Epistle to the Romans* (Grand Rapids: Eerdmans, 1988), 320.

[107]Moo, *Romans*, 550. The phrase εἰς ὑμᾶς is more accurately translated as "toward us" or "to us-ward." *RWP*, 4:375.

[108]The following verses introduced by γάρ (vv. 19, 20, 22) continues in logical sequence the explanation of v. 18. See Robertson, *GGNT*, 1190-91; Cranfield, *Romans*, 1:408.

[109]See D. R. Denton, "Ἀποκαραδοκία," *ZNW* 73 (1982): 138-40; *TDNT*, s.v. "Ἀποκαραδοκία," by G. Delling 1:393. Cf. Philip's expressive translation: "The whole creation is on tiptoe. . . ."

[110]Sanday and Headlam, *Romans*, 206.

following verses in Rom. 8.21-22 link decisively the creation's anxious watching with the confident expectation of ultimate deliverance from corruption. Käsemann notes that ἐφ᾽ ἐλπίδι in verse 20 "obviously interprets the ἀποκαραδοκία of v. 19 in Christian terms."[111] This picturesque term thus denotes an intense, confident expectation or hope with no hint of hesitation, anxiety, or uneasiness.[112] The image is strengthened by another compound word ἀπεκδέχεται ("to wait") which as the main verb of ἀποκαραδοκία gives a vivid picture of a confident but *active* expectancy with which creation waits for the coming glory. That for which the creation confidently awaits is the "revealing of the sons of God." There is no suggestion in this statement that the creation, cursed because of humanity's sin, is therefore also *dependent* on humanity's restoration for its redemption.[113] The phrase refers to the time when God's full salvific work will be completed at the parousia. The "revelation" will be the signal for the glorious transformation that will include all creation.[114] The created order will be transformed concomitantly with humanity.

Verses 20-21, which are one sentence in the original, introduces the reason (γάρ) why the creation waits with such eager expectation. The reason, according to Paul, is that the creation itself was subjected τῇ ματαιότητι ("to vanity," KJV). The word ματαιότης, while usually meaning "vanity" or "emptiness" as it does in Ecclesiastes (LXX), is better taken as the opposite of τέλειος. The translation "to futility" (NASB) or "to frustration" (NIV) is an attempt to reflect the obvious reference to Gen. 3.17-18 in which the creation by reason of humanity's sin becomes unable to obtain the goal or fulfill the purpose for which it was created.[115] Bruce suggests that Paul has in mind the subjection in terms of enslavement to "malignant powers" since its cognate

---

[111]Käsemann, *Romans*, 325-36.

[112]Denton, "Ἀποδαραδοκία," 138-39.

[113]Cf. Dunn, *Romans*, 467.

[114]Sanday and Headlam, *Romans*, 207.

[115]Ibid., 208; Cranfield, *Romans*, 413-14.

μάταιος is used in connection with idol worship.[116] That this is not unreasonable is supported by the account of the fall in which evil is presented as an intruder and hence a cosmic power (Gen. 4.7). However, the context favors the primary reference to Adam's sin. The creation was subjected (the aorist points to a specific event--the fall) "not willingly" or through its own fault "but because of Him who subjected it, in hope . . ." (v. 20). The wording of the sentence is awkward. Dunn recommends that the difficulty arises from Paul's attempt to explain too briefly a more complex thought: that the creation subjected to humanity in the beginning by God was also subjected to the effects of humanity's sin.[117] This remark rejects any hint of an inherently fallen creation but recognizes that due to Adam's sin the created order became "impaired" and unable to fulfill its τέλος.

In view of the Genesis motifs commentators generally agree that τὸν ὑποτάξαντα refers to God and affirms that ultimately the plight of creation is due to the divine decree.[118] Paul, moreover, is not detained by the negative perspective but rapidly moves on to a positive message, namely, that the very decree was issued ἐφ' ἐλπίδι. Amazingly, Paul asserts that the subjection included the element of hope.[119] Barth roots the hope in the faithfulness "of the one who subjected it" (no doubt taking ἐφ ' ἐλπίδι as qualifying ὑποτάξαντα, cf. RSV). "Now, He who has subjected the creature is God: and thence emerges hope."[120] The phrase "in hope" qualifies ὑπετάγη as does ἑκοῦσα and indicates

---

[116]F. F. Bruce, *The Epistle to the Romans*, TNTC (Grand Rapids: Eerdmans, 1980), 172; Gibbs, *Creation and Redemption*, 43.

[117]Dunn, *Romans*, 471.

[118]Cf. Lampe who opts for Adam. "Ktisis," 458. While one might have expected διά with the ablative/genitive meaning "through," διά with the accusative appropriately denotes "cause" or "the effective reason," i.e., God's decree. See *BDF*, §222; Cranfield, *Romans*, 1:414. To suggest that the two grammatical constructions may be equivalent in v. 20, while possible (Robertson, *GGNT*, 581), is unnecessary. Cf. Moo, *Romans*, 552.

[119]The decree was given "on the basis," "on the condition" (cf. Gal. 5.13; 1 Thess. 4.7). See Nigel Turner, *Syntax*, vol. 3 of *A Grammar of New Testament Greek*, ed. J. H. Moulton (Edinburgh: T. & T. Clark, 1963), 272.

[120]Barth, *Romans*, 309.

that the very *act* of subjection included an element of hope. Some have suggested that Paul has in mind the *protoevangelium* (Gen. 3.15). Thus, hope for the creation was included in God's promise to humanity even in the beginning.[121] Whatever the specific reference, clearly the subjection of the creation "in hope" was grounded in the understanding of God as creator. The creation always remains under the sovereignty of God, and it is this relationship that brings hope. Notably, that the act of subjection contains a promise of fulfillment affirms a continuity between the old and new creation.[122] God has not given up on his creation. Such language rejects the notion that the present creation may be discarded and replaced by an entirely *new* one.

The hope, according to verse 21, consists in freedom from the bondage to corruption characteristic of this age and the freedom of glory enjoyed by the children of God.[123] Paul again unites creation and humanity in their common plight and glorious destiny. This verse provides additional support against the assertion of some that creation's redemption is *contingent upon* the freedom of the sons of God.[124] Such a view argues that God has an interest in the deliverance of the created order only as a suitable place for the new humanity. Käsemann presents a more cosmic perspective.

---

[121]Moo, *Romans*, 553; Cranfield, *Romans*, 1:414.

[122]Gibbs, *Creation and Redemption*, 44.

[123]If one accepts ὅτι ("that," NASB, NIV), v. 21 states the substance of the hope. If διότι ("because," RSV), v. 21 gives the reason for the hope. Both readings have strong support: ὅτι is read by 𝔓[46] A B C 33 81 *al* and διότι is attested in ℵ D' F G *al*. Cranfield argues for διότι as the *lectio difficilior*. *Romans*, 1:415. This, however, could have arisen due to dittography. In the context ὅτι seems more natural and has the strongest witnesses. See Metzger, *TCGNT*, 517.

[124]Contra Moo: "It is only with and because of the glory of God's children that creation experiences its own full and final deliverance." *Romans*, 554. Cf. Gibbs: "The hope which is justified for creation depends on the freedom which is rooted in the glory of the children of God." *Creation and Redemption*, 44.

> Since Paul understands eschatological freedom as salva-
> tion in a cosmic dimension, he here singularly describes
> the event of the parousia from the standpoint of anthro-
> pology. He could not say that the world was on the way to
> Christ even though he regarded Christ as the designated
> cosmocrater and oriented world history to him. He was
> concerned to show, however, that . . . in the community
> which suffers with Christ, eschatological freedom as sal-
> vation for all creation appears in outline. Hence Chris-
> tianity; which witnesses to sonship and in the fellowship of
> suffering points to Christ as the coming Lord of the world,
> seemed to him to be the great promise for all creation even
> beyond the human sphere. . . .[125]

The freedom of the sons of God therefore presents an "outline in miniature" of the greater cosmic salvation of God. One may not think here in terms of concentric circles in which God's work extends sequentially from believing humanity to the outermost part of the universe. God's salvation embraces the whole. Humanity's salvation is indeed a microcosm of the greater macrocosmic event--the redemption of creation. In fact, one could say that the "sons of God" participate in creation's redemption.[126] Note also that a continuity between the old and new creation is further attested in Paul's promise of "freedom" which clearly implies the idea of transformation rather than annihilation.

Paul continues in logical sequence his argument (γάρ) in verse 22 which also serves as a summary of the previous three verses by returning to the theme of the longing of creation (v. 19). Paul introduces a well known fact ("we know") that every element of creation groans and suffers together until now.[127] The cosmic and eschatological import of this verse is urged by its very language. The "pains of childbirth" reflects apocalyptic

---

[125]Käsemann, *Romans*, 234.

[126]Contra Moo: "It is not so much that Christians are to participate in the renewal of creation, but that the renewal of creation points to, and participates in, the 'glory of the children of God.'" *Romans*, 579.

[127]The preposition σύν with συστενάζω and συνωδίνω indicates "in all the parts of which creation is made up." Sanday and Headlam, *Romans*, 209.

motifs of the messianic woes prior to and leading up to the final advent and cosmic transformation (cf. Jub. 23.22-31; Matt. 24.21). The cosmic dimension of this passage as in other apocalyptic texts is therefore evident in the protrayal of the entire creation in labor, as it were, bringing to birth the new age and new creation. The present tense of the verbs connotes an ongoing process moving toward the eschatological νῦν ("now") of salvation which has already taken place in Christ's work but is yet to be fulfilled.[128] Thus, verse 22 further emphasizes the two age motif so prominent from chapter 5 onwards to portray the cosmos at the very *brink* of the new age. Suffering is not only minimized in view of the coming glory but against this cosmic backdrop suffering actually becomes a sign of hope. It affirms the imminence of the parousia.

As the distress of creation is a signal that it stands on the verge of salvation so the presence of the Spirit serves as a "pledge" of eschatological adoption as sons--the redemption of the body (v. 23). That the redemption of the body is mentioned in this context is not surprising. The hope of the new order of salvation for Paul does not entail an immaterial existence. This is clearly traced to the NT understanding of the incarnation and resurrection of Jesus. In fact, the resurrection affirms the importance of all material existence. Regarding creation, Martin affirms that "the resurrection of Jesus blocks forever the idea that God wills to be glorified by the annihilation of biological life on this planet."[129] The redemption of creation has often been argued on the basis of the resurrection of the body. Thus, a resurrected body demands a new material creation as a suitable habitat.[130] However, in light of the cosmic scope of this passage, is it not more appropriate to assert that God provides a new body fit for the new creation?

Paul's promise of the redemption of creation in Rom. 8.18-23 provides an important witness to God's cosmic salvific

---

[128]In light of the eschatological context, Dunn contends that ἄχρι τοῦ νῦν refers not to the present time but the "now" of eschatological salvation in the process of realization. *Romans*, 473.

[129]Martin, "Cosmic Christ," 33.

[130]See Berkouwer, *Return of Christ*, 211.

plan and hence to the value of the created order itself. In the present context Paul's cosmic perspective provides a source of hope for believers who likewise are anxiously waiting the glorious parousia. Indeed, as a part of a macrocosmic-redemptive event believers long not only for the "revealing of the sons of God" but for the creation's liberation from bondage. Their confidence in the present "already-not yet" eschatological existence is in fact based "on the condition of hope" that they, like all of creation, stand at the brink of glory.

The Reconciliation of "All Things" (Col. 1.15-20)

The cosmic aspect of Christ's redemptive activity is set forth most clearly in Col. 1.15-20. This so-called Christological hymn unites decisively Christ's work in creation and redemption and affirms that God's redemptive purpose in Christ is the reconciliation of "all things." Christ's universal preeminence is asserted powerfully by the phrases "in him" (three times in six verses) and "all things," "all creation" (seven times) and reveals the ultimate goal of God's redemptive plan "in Christ" for creation and the church: "that He himself in all things (material and spiritual) may come to . . . hold the first place" (v. 18).[131] The stress upon "all things" thus avoids any suggestion that redemption is for the writer anything less than universal in scope. Salvation is not an escape from a this-worldly existence but indeed will include a new creation which "forms around the nucleus of a redeemed humanity--the Christian church."[132]

It is necessary to address briefly the issues of literary structure and setting before considering the teaching of the passage. The general scholarly consensus regards the passage as an early pre-Christian hymn which Paul, or more likely a later disciple, inserted in its present context setting forth the preeminence of Christ to counter the prevailing Colossian "heresy."[133] However, that the author has cited a poetic piece has hardly been

---

[131]*RWP*, 4:480.

[132]F. W. Beare, "Colossians," *IB* (New York: Abingdon, 1978), 11:167.

[133]The majority of NT scholars on the basis of language and style regard

proven. It is all but impossible to reconstruct the original hymn. It often becomes necessary to propose elaborate interpolation and emendation theories in order to delineate the precise structure of the hymn and so to determine its original form as well as its *religionsgeschichtliche* background. Most notably, Schweizer argues that the phrase τῆς ἐκκλησίας (v. 18) among others was added to the original reference to Christ as head of the body, that is of the world. This was necessary to correct against the Hellenistic conception of redemption as merely a physical or metaphysical event.[134]   However, as Wright has correctly observed, admitting the prospect of additions allows also the possibility of omissions thereby rendering impossible the ability to establish with assurance the original form of the hymn.[135]   In fact, the difference of opinion between scholars regarding the

---

Colossians, and certainly the hymn, as deutero-Pauline. See, e.g., the discussion of Eduard Schweizer, *The Letter to the Colossians: A Commentary*, trans. Andrew Chester (Minneapolis, MN: Augsburg, 1982), 15-24. This standard, however, is not conclusive. Eduard Lohse states tentatively that "no final decision can be reached" regarding authorship on this basis. His recourse is to the theology of the book which determines it as non-Pauline. *Colossians and Philemon*, Hermeneia, trans. William R. Poehlmann and Robert J. Karris, ed. Helmut Koester (Philadelphia: Fortress, 1971), 91, 177-83. Werner Georg Kümmel is more decisive in his analysis of language and style arguing that "there is no reason to doubt the Pauline authorship of the letter." *Introduction to the New Testament*, rev. ed., trans. Howard Clark Kee (Nashville: Abingdon, 1975), 342. See particularly the recent arguments for Pauline authorship by Peter T. O'Brien, *Colossians, Philemon*, WBC (Waco: Word, 1982), xli-xlix and N. T. Wright, *The Epistles of Paul to the Colossians and to Philemon*, TNTC (Grand Rapids: Eerdmans, 1986), 31-34. We nevertheless will refer to the writer as "Paul" even though the issue has not been satisfactorily resolved.

[134]Eduard Schweizer, "The Church as the Missionary Body of Christ," *NTS* 8 (October 1961): 7-8. Schweizer notes other interpretive additions to this pagan hymn: "all things in heaven and on earth" are interpreted as "thrones or dominions or principalities or authorities" (v. 16), "that in everything he may be preeminent" (v. 18), "making peace by the blood of his cross" (v. 20). Note Schweizer's standard for determining such interpolations: "all clauses exceeding the rhythmical order and the parallelism of the supposed original hymn agree with the theological conceptions of the author of the letter, . . . " (9). See the chart of scholars' conjectured additions and omissions supplied by Pierre Benoit, "L'hymne christologique de Col. 1.15-20," in *Christianity, Judaism and Other Greco-Roman Cults*, ed. Jacob Neusner (Leiden: Brill, 1975), 1:238.

[135]N. T. Wright, "Poetry and Theology in Colossians 1.15-20," *NTS* 36

precise reconstruction of the hymn has led at least one author to state unequivocally that "there is, however, no real evidence in spite of the ingenuity of exegetes, that such a hymn ever existed."[136] Kümmel recommends that the more likely possibility is that Paul constructed the hymn utilizing traditional material.[137]

The poetic quality of the text is readily detectable. The repetition of relative clauses, words and phrases in corresponding parallel positions (cf. ὅς ἐστιν, πρωτότοκος, vv. 15, 18b), the frequent citation of "all," the use of rhetorical devices such as *chiasmus*, antithesis, and *inclusio* reveal that the passage is certainly more than elevated prose. These traits betray, in the often quoted opinion of Hunter, "the hand of an exacting composer."[138] As noted, various proposals for the poetic form of this text has been suggested. The most usual is the bipartite division of two strophes although the exact number of lines and the place of the break is debated. A two stanza structure has been proposed based upon the parallel of ὅς ἐστιν of verse 15 corresponding with the ὅς ἐστιν of verse 18b. Verses 15-18a stress the preeminence of Christ in creation while verses 18b-20 focus on his work of redemption in the church.[139] Some also have suggested a twofold pattern of verses 15-17 and 18-20[140] or even three strophes of verses 15-

---

(July 1990): 445; idem, *Colossians*, 35.

[136]Morna D. Hooker, "Were there False Teachers in Colossae?" in *Christ and Spirit in the New Testament*, ed. Barnabas Lindars and Stephen S. Smalley (Cambridge: Cambridge University, 1973), 316-17.

[137]Kümmel, *Introduction to the New Testament*, 343. Wright has recently resurrected Burney's thesis that the hymn represents Paul's rabbinic midrash on Gen. 1.1 made possible by the identification of wisdom with ראשית in Prov. 8.22. Particularly, in v. 16 Paul exploits the three possible meanings of the ב of בראשית. See C. F. Burney, "Christ as the APXH of Creation," *JTS* 27 (January 1926): 160-77; Wright, "Poetry and Theology in Colossians," 456-58.

[138]A. M. Hunter, *Paul and His Predecessors*, rev. ed. (Philadelphia: Westminster, 1961) 123-26.

[139]See James M. Robinson, "A Form Analysis of Colossians 1.15-20," *JBL* 76 (December 1957): 270-87; Ralph P. Martin, "An Early Christian Hymn," *EvQ* 36 (October-December 1964): 195-205; Lohse, *Colossians*, 44-45.

[140]P. Ellingworth, "Colossians 1.15-20 and Its Context," *ExpTim* 73 (May 1962): 252-53.

16, 17-18a and 18b-20 reflecting the three aspects of creation, preservation, and redemption respectively.[141] However, as mentioned such arrangements often require elaborate interpolation, emendation, and even transposition theories to create perfect symmetry.[142] Since none of the arrangements is entirely satisfactory, it appears more appropriate to recognize general parallels of words, concepts, and phrases. It is therefore fitting to accept the text as it stands without attempting to identify additional glosses or deletions.[143]

In this regard, perhaps the most promising suggestion is that the passage reflects a general chiastic scheme emphasizing certain parallels without the intention of precise uniformity. Beginning with both ends and working towards the central couplet of verses 17-18a--both clauses begin with αὐτός ἐστιν-- the pivot or focal point falls upon the affirmation of Christ's lordship over "all things" uniting his work of redemption in creation and the church.[144] Whether or not Paul intended the reader

---

[141]Schweizer, "Church as the Missionary Body," 6-7; idem, *Colossians*, 55-58. This pattern was later adopted by Ralph P. Martin, "Reconciliation and Forgiveness in Colossians," in *Reconciliation and Hope: New Testament Essays on Atonement and Eschatology*, ed. Robert Banks (London: Paternoster, 1974), 110-16; idem, *Colossians and Philemon*, NCB (Greenwood, SC: Attic, 1974), 63-64; and more recently by Paul Beasley-Murray, "Colossians 1.15-20: An Early Christian Hymn Celebrating the Lordship of Christ," in *Pauline Studies*, ed. Donald A. Hagner and Murray J. Harris (Grand Rapids: Eerdmans, 1980), 169-83 and F. F. Bruce, "The 'Christ Hymn' of Colossians 1.15-20," *BSac* 141 (April-June 1984): 99-111. For additional proposals see O'Brien, *Colossians*, 33-36.

[142]On the difficulty of discovering a perfect arrangement see J. C. O'Neill, "The Source of the Christology in Colossians," *NTS* 26 (October 1979): 88. "Nowhere else in Greek of the time, . . . do we find such monstrous sentences, so loaded with ideas, so badly coordinated" (89).

[143]"The fact is that scholarship has developed no consensus about the number and context of strophes . . . or about possible Pauline additions, so that one may safely speak only of certain parallels. . . . No single reconstruction is fully persuasive." Gibbs, *Creation and Redemption*, 98-99; O'Brien, *Colossians*, 36.

[144]Wright who proposes this structure notes that the parallelism between vv. 15-16 and vv. 18-20 are preserved without elaborate theories of additions or emendations since it highlights basic parallels rather than demanding exact correspondence. The structure follows the chiastic pattern of A (vv. 15-16) B (vv. 17) B (v. 18ab) A (vv. 18c-20). "Poetry and Theology in Colossians 1.15-

to understand the passage according to any particular pattern, there is clearly a movement of thought from Christ's lordship in creation (vv. 15-17) and the church (v. 18) concluding with the reconciliation of "all things" (v. 20) which sums up the hymn with the same universal emphasis with which it began. The thought of the text moves generally from the universal to embrace the church and then back to the universal. Paul thus relates Christ's work within a cosmic worldview.

The cosmic context is made apparent even in the preceding context by the presence of creation and Exodus motifs. For example, the expression of thanksgiving to the Father who has granted the saints an allotment (κλῆρος) and effected their transfer from the domain of darkness to God's kingdom recalls the Exodus and Israel's entrance into Canaan (vv. 12-14; cf. Exod. 6.6).[145] Such motifs to Paul's readers also would no doubt evoke ideas of Isaiah's prophesies of a new Exodus and a new creation. The uniting of Exodus and creation themes here as throughout the scriptures is not accidental. As Lindeskog has noted in reference to Isaiah, the parallel of creation with redemption was drawn not to subordinate creation to redemption but to emphasize the significance of redemption by equating it with the greatest event of the world.[146] Redemption is comprehended only against the basic understanding of God as creator. Paul utilizes these motifs much like Isaiah to remind the readers that the creator *is* the redeemer. Col. 1.15-20 therefore should be read in light of the Jewish monotheistic confessions of God as creator rather than against Gnosticism[147] or Hellenism[148] or even the

___

20," 446-51. See also a similar suggestion by Steven M. Baugh who believes that the text represents a "good example of a Semitic-type chiasm" in its basic structure and content. "The Poetic Form of Col. 1.15-20," *WTJ* 47 (Fall 1985): 227-44.

[145]The entire section, as O'Brien observes, is permeated with echoes of the OT promise of deliverance and the inheritance of the land. *Colossians*, 25-28; Wright, *Colossians,* 60-62.

[146]Gösta Lindeskog, "The Theology of Creation in the Old and New Testaments," in *The Root of the Vine: Essays in Biblical Theology*, ed. Anton Fridrichen (Philadelphia: Westminster, 1953), 5.

[147]Ernst Käsemann, "A Primitive Christian Baptismal Liturgy," in *Essays on New Testament Themes*, trans. W. J. Montague (Naperville, IL: Allenson), 149-68.

more narrow conceptions of Jewish wisdom traditions.[149] Thus, as Wright appropriately observes, Paul's teaching is rooted in the Jewish worldview that

> There is one God; he made the world, and is neither iden-
> tified with it . . . nor detached from it (as in dualism); he is
> in covenant with Israel, and he will in fulfilling that
> covenant, reclaim and redeem his whole creation from that
> which at present corrupts and threatens it.[150]

A further analysis of the passage reveals this emphasis.

> [15] And He is the image of the invisible God, the first-born of
> all creation. [16] For by Him all things were created, both in
> the heavens and on earth, visible and invisible, whether
> thrones or dominions or rulers or authorities all things have
> been created by Him and for Him. [17] And He is before all
> things, and in Him all things hold together. [18] He is also head
> of the body, the church; and He is the beginning, the first-
> born from the dead; so that He Himself might come to have
> first place in everything. [19] For it was the Father's good
> pleasure for all the fullness to dwell in Him, [20] and through
> Him to reconcile all things to Himself, having made peace
> through the blood of His cross; through Him, I say, whether
> things on earth or things in heaven (Col. 1.15-20).

Christ's supremacy in creation and redemption is portrayed in various ways throughout the hymn. Paul presents
Christ as mediator in revelation, creation, and redemption
through the Jewish motif of the divine wisdom. Christ as the
"image of the invisible God, the firstborn over all creation"
(NIV) is ascribed the functions attributed to wisdom in OT and
Hellenistic Jewish literature.[151] Wisdom is described in Prov.

---

[148]Schweizer, "Church as the Missionary Body," 6-7.

[149]W. D. Davies, *Paul and Rabbinic Judaism: Some Rabbinic Elements in Pauline Theology*, 4th ed. (Philadelphia: Fortress, 1980), 147-68.

[150]Wright, "Poetry and Theology in Colossians," 453.

[151]Scholars are generally agreed regarding this background. See Lohse, *Colossians*, 46-47; Gibbs, *Creation and Redemption*, 102; Wright, *Colossians*, 71; O'Brien, *Colossians*, 43-44; et al.

8.22-31 as present with God at the beginning of his work of creation. The sage also writes that "the Lord by wisdom founded the earth; . . ." (Prov. 3.19; cf. Ps. 104.24). Wisdom, which in the OT was merely the personified attribute of God, was given an existence of its own in later Jewish texts (cf. Wis. 18.14). Particularly significant for this passage is that wisdom is described as the "everlasting light, the flawless mirror of the active power of God and the image of his goodness" (Wis. 7.26, NEB). Wisdom thus performs a revelatory role manifesting the goodness of God. Philo's interpretation of OT theophany passages has revealed that wisdom and logos were often hypostatized and appeared in the place of God as his εἰκών. Such concepts, according to Kim, provided the background for Paul's ascription of the attribute of wisdom to Christ. Just as wisdom appeared in theophany as the image of God, so also Christ at Damascus was seen by Paul as having the εἰκών of God. Further, in this event Paul realized that the law--wisdom and law were identified in Jewish writings--no longer revealed the salvation of God. The Damascus Christophany convinced Paul that Christ had superseded the law as the embodiment of wisdom. Paul therefore transferred all the attributes and functions of divine wisdom (and law) to Christ.[152] Paul does not identify Christ with wisdom. There is nothing in Jewish literature approaching the NT affirmation that the wisdom or logos "became flesh" (John 1.14). The statement that Christ is the "image" is thus not so much ontological as functional. The wisdom motif reflects the revelatory and cosmic function of Christ. Yet as God's image Christ is the son who reveals God's cosmic-redemptive purpose.

The second title, πρωτότοκος ("firstborn"), further explains the significance of the first in relation to creation. The term is used often in the LXX in genealogies to indicate temporal priority or status. It is also used of Israel to denote her special relation to God.[153] Beasley-Murray suggests that it is perhaps synonymous with μονογενής thus referring to

---

[152]Seyoon Kim, *The Origin of Paul's Gospel*, WUNT (Tübingen: Mohr, 1981), 104-259; Davies, *Paul and Rabbinic Judaism*, 145-76.

[153]See references in BAGD.

Christ's uniqueness.[154]   This, however, has been asserted by Christ's portrayal as God's image. The intended parallel with verse 18 (πρωτότοκος ἐκ τῶν νεκρῶν) indicates that the temporal concept is not diminished. Against the OT wisdom motif of Prov. 8.22 Christ is pictured as preexistent before all creation. In addition, the NIV translation "over all creation" is an attempt to clarify the genitive construction of πάσης κτίσεως representing Christ as supreme over creation as lord. It can hardly be construed as a partitive genitive denoting Christ as "firstborn among all created things" (NEB, mg.), that is, the first in succession of beings. However, it may be unnecessary to choose between the objective (NIV) or the genitive of comparison denoting priority, "before all creation." The phrase influenced by the wisdom ideas thus has the force of both priority and primacy since the prexistence of wisdom implies preeminence.[155] The two titles of "image" and "firstborn" reflect the significance of God's work in Christ *in* the world, and *for* the world, that is, in redemption.

Paul continues his stress on the preeminence of Christ in creation with further support for what has been said in verse 15 (ὅτι) by describing Christ as the sphere, agent, sustainer, and goal of creation (v. 16). The precise meaning of the phrase ἐν αὐτῷ ("in him") is unclear. It may have an instrumental sense, hence "by or through him." However, this is the focus of the end of verse 16 (δι᾽ αὐτοῦ), and a parallel with v. 19 is clearly intended. Bruce construes it as a locative of sphere denoting Christ as the "sphere" within which the work of creation takes place. God's creation like the election of his people (cf. Eph. 1.4) is accomplished only "in Christ" and not apart from him.[156] The intended parallel with verse 19 (cf. v. 17b) seems to confirm this as the best view. Beasley-Murray finds this reasoning

[154]Beasley-Murray, "Colossians 1.15-20," 171.

[155]In support of this interpretation note that πρωτότοκος carries both the idea of priority and primacy. L/N lists it in connection with Col. 1.15 as a subdomain both of "Existing," hence "to exist before" (§13.79) and "Rank" denoting superiority (§87.47).

[156]Bruce, "Christ Hymn," 102; O'Brien, *Colossians*, 45. Cf. Lohse, *Colossians*, 50.

attractive especially if in verse 20 Christ is seen as in some sense restoring the universe to its original state in his role as the second Adam.[157] All things were created not only "in him" but "though him" and moreover, the creation finds its ultimate goal εἰς αὐτόν ("unto/toward him"). Only "in Christ" does the created order find its fulfillment. Martin remarks that "no Jewish thinker ever rose to these heights in daring to predict that wisdom was the ultimate goal of all creation."[158] Moreover, to state that creation was made for Christ and is fulfilled only in its relationship to him is to reject above all the primary anthropocentric interpretation of texts regarding redemption. The created order is also the object of God's redemptive purposes. Significantly, the correspondence of creation and redemption is expressed remarkably by the use of the same prepositions in verse 20 as the discussion below explains.

Christ is also depicted as the sustaining force of creation as the perfect tense of ἔκτισται (v. 16) and συνέστηκεν (v. 17) reveals. Apart from Christ the world disintegrates. Christ rather than natural laws holds the universe together! This statement also affirms Christ's relation with the creation which exceeds the comprehension of humanity. All things therefore were created and stand created *in*, *through*, and *oriented toward* Christ. Paul by means of *inclusio* leaves no doubt that there are no exceptions. Even the cosmic powers and principalities are included. Whatever the place of the "powers" in the so-called Colossian "heresy," Paul includes angelic powers as well as world rulers as indicated by the phrase "in heaven and on earth." Every power, angelic or human, owes its existence to Christ.[159] The list should not be taken as exhaustive but as indicating the

---

[157]Beasley-Murray, "Colossians 1.15-20," 172.

[158]Martin, *Colossians*, 58.

[159]Scholars historically have interpreted the so-called "powers" in heaven (1.16; 2.8, 15) against the gnosticising worldview that venerated angels. However, it has been argued recently that such was not unknown to Judaism and thus the Colossian "heresy" was none other than Judaism. See Hooker, "Were there False Teachers at Colossae?" 315-31 and Wright, *Colossians*, 23-30. While the concept of angelic powers were part of Paul's apocalyptic conceptual worldview, this study hesitates to address the issue in detail for fear of slipping into angelology.

comprehensive scope of Christ's creative activity--all things visible and invisible.

Verses 17 and 18 provide the pivotal point of the passage uniting the complementary ideas of creation and redemption. Verse 17 serves as a fitting climax and reiteration of the previous two verses affirming Christ's preeminence over all creation (πρὸ πάντων ἐστιν as before denotes time and status)[160] while verse 18a facilitates a transition to Christ's work in the church. Verses 17 and 18a, however, provide more than a summary and transition from creation to redemption in the argument of the hymn. As the focal pivot of the hymn, they bear the primary emphasis, namely, that just as God created the world under the lordship of Christ, so though the death and resurrection he has provided the way by which the creation (τὰ πάντα) might be restored to its rightful place and purpose. God's redemptive plan is universal and embraces the church. The church is thus a salvific abstract and pledge of a greater cosmic purpose of which it is a part. Verses 17-18 actually present an *Urzeit-Endzeit* scheme centered in Christ.[161]

As Christ is head of the creation so is he head of the church. To be sure, Paul is not oblivious to the fact that Christ does not yet reign as unquestioned lord over his creation (1 Cor. 15.25). Nevertheless, this position of lordship over all creation which belongs to Christ *de jure*, will *de facto* become a reality at the consummation of which the resurrection serves as the pledge of its certainty.[162] As noted, most scholars regard the phrase τὰς ἐκκλησίας as an addition to the original hymn. However, Gibbs has argued that it is essential to the text. It reveals the cosmic effects of redemption.

> The cosmos is never described in Pauline literature as the body of Christ in the way the Church is (Col. 1.24), but Christ is "head" in the juridical sense not only of the Church but also of the universe, as is stated also in Col.

---

[160]*RWP*, 4:479.

[161]For the concept, see Dahl, "Christ, Creation and the Church," 434.

[162]Cf. the comments of G. B. Caird, *Paul's Letters from Prison* (Oxford: University, 1976), 180.

2.10 . . . and as implied in the concept of dying with Christ to the στοιχεῖα τοῦ κόσμου. . . . The hymn, no less than its context in Colossians, declares that Christ's lordship over the Church has cosmic implications and Church-existence is inseparable from the rest of the universe.[163]

The passage in verse 18 thus moves from creation to new creation and finally in v. 20 to creation restored to its proper place under Christ as its head. Christ is the beginning, that is, he initiated the new order and new creation by virtue of his resurrection as first from among the dead (v. 18b). The terms ἀρχή and πρωτότοκος often occur together in the LXX to describe the firstborn as the founder of a people (cf. Gen. 49.3; Deut. 21.17). While Paul's main emphasis is the church, no doubt the concept of a new beginning embracing both humanity and creation is suggested by ἀρχή recalling Gen. 1.1. This universal aspect of the new beginning is implied by the statement that the expressed purpose (or the realized result, ἵνα) of the resurrection is that Christ might be first in "all things," and is further accentuated by the intended parallelism of verse 18c with verse 15. Paul's focus is thoroughly cosmic in scope.

The reason for Christ's primacy over everything is because (ὅτι) "it was the Father's good pleasure for all the fullness to dwell in Him" (v. 19). This translation assumes "God" as the implied subject of εὐδόκησεν. However, the original does not include an expressed subject unless πᾶν τὸ πλήρωμα serves as such (NRSV). The latter option is preferred as a circumlocution for "God in his fullness" since πατήρ is too far removed to serve as an implied subject (v. 12). Grammatically πλήρωμα can be taken as a masculine and thus related in sense to εἰς αὐτόν and εἰρηνοποιήσας (v. 20).[164] This is also more satisfactory since εὐδόκησεν and ἀποκαταλλάξαι suggest personal action and agree with the same emphasis in Col. 2.9. Thus, the reason for Christ's primacy is that "it pleased the Father that in him the divine nature should dwell" (TCNT). Once again the statement is not merely ontological. It

[163]Gibbs, *Creation and Redemption*, 105-6.
[164]Lohse, *Colossians*, 56-57; O'Brien, *Colossians*, 51,

also has a functional focus, namely, that in Christ God expressed his redemptive purposes.[165]

Notably, the term πλήρωμα is employed in the LXX in an active sense: "the earth is the Lord's and all it contains" (Ps. 24.1; cf. 1 Chr. 16.32; Jer. 8.16). This use leads Gibbs to regard it in this passage as a *nomen actionis* designating "Christ's eschatological power of bringing the creation to its τέλος."[166] It is thus in and through Christ as the embodiment of πᾶν τὸ πλήρωμα that God's redemptive plan is accomplished thereby restoring creation, both human and nonhuman, according to his original purposes. This moreover is the import of the term ἀποκαταλλάξαι ("reconciliation," v. 20). The term appears unusual in this instance since it is used exclusively by Paul in reference to humanity (cf. Rom. 5.10, 11; 11:15; 2 Cor. 5.18-20). The application of this word to "all things," however, is not as peculiar as first thought. Establishing peace between two quarrelling parties is the basic idea of reconciliation. As Morris has pointed out, the way to reestablish harmony is to deal with the root cause of the hostility, namely, sin.[167] According to Romans 8, which Moule calls the best commentary on this verse,[168] humanity's sin has disrupted the harmony of the created order. In dealing with the sin of humankind God also has dealt with creation's plight. On this view of reconciliation, the entire universe has been returned to its divinely created and intended order through the resurrection. In Christ the universe has been restored under its proper head accomplishing cosmic peace. "This peace which God has established through Christ binds the whole universe together again into unity and underlines that the restored creation is reconciled with God."[169]

Therefore, while commentators believe that the focus in verses 18b-20 is Christ's preeminence in the church, the passage

---

[165]Martin, *Colossians*, 60.

[166]Gibbs, *Creation and Redemption*, 108.

[167]Leon Morris, *The Cross in the New Testament* (Grand Rapids: Eerdmans, 1965), 250.

[168]C. F. D. Moule, *The Epistles of Paul the Apostle to the Colossians*, CGTC (Cambridge: University, 1962), 71.

[169]Lohse, *Colossians*, 59-60.

nevertheless guards against any suggestion that Paul's thoughts have moved beyond the importance of the material (and spiritual) order. The reconciling work of Christ embraces "all things" whether on earth or in heaven (v. 20). Indeed, as noted the use of the same prepositions in verse 20 and in verse 16 stresses that Christ's redemptive work is a creative event. "All things," which originally were created *in, through,* and *for* Christ (v. 16), have been through the death on the cross properly reoriented to him. The life, death, and resurrection of Christ not only set in motion the salvific process for those who believe but also initiated the process by which Christ would ultimately reclaim his entire creation. Christ's death and resurrection pledged that the created order will once again find its fulfillment in its creator.

In summary, the passage moves from universal concerns to embrace the church and back to the cosmos. Paul therefore presents Christ's work of reconciliation in a cosmic context of which the church is a part--a microcosm of the greater macro-cosmic-redemptive event as in Romans 8. Christ is lord over all creation and in the church thus uniting creation and redemption. The concept of Christ's redemption is thus accompanied by the understanding of creation as the foundational thought of Paul's message. The comments of Ridderbos in this regard are worthy to cite in full.

> For Paul the creation and the sustaining of the cosmos by God was the foundation of the entire history of redemption. For this reason the relation of Christ to the cosmos was given with his divine pre-existence. Noetically, the soteriological aspect may take preference, in the sense that the Son of God reveals himself as the Redeemer of the world. On the other hand, however, Christ because he is the Son, is also the Lord of the cosmos in both creation and redemption. What Paul says of Christ's creative work is not a strange cosmological addition to his doctrine of redemption, . . . Nor is it a soteriological postulate, in the sense that according to Paul the world is created by the Son of God because he is also the Redeemer of the world. Rather, in these pronouncements the unity of the divine work of creation and redemption is expressed and therefore nothing in heaven and upon earth withdraws itself

from the redeeming rule of Christ, because the Redeemer
came to *his own* world.[170]

Conflagration and the New Creation in 2 Peter 3

2 Peter 3 is important for discussion not only because of
the reaffirmation of Isaiah's promise of the new heavens and
new earth but as the most explicit statement in the Bible of the
total destruction of the earth by fire. Conclusions regarding the
teaching of the passage are far from evident and are immediately complicated due to text-critical matters and the general worldview of the author.[171] These will be addressed in the course of
the discussion of the text. Significantly, 2 Peter provides an
appropriate vantage point for this study for it addresses three
important aspects central to the concept of creation and cosmic
hope: the creation and constancy of the created order (vv. 4-5),

---

[170]Hermann Ridderbos, *Paul and Jesus: Origin and General Character
of Paul's Preaching of Christ*, trans. David H. Freeman (Grand Rapids: Eerdmans, 1958), 128.

[171]The problem of authorship of 2 Peter does not substantially affect the
results of the discussion. J. N. D. Kelly, represents the scholarly consensus
when he states that "scarcely anyone nowadays doubts that 2 Peter is pseudonymous." *A Commentary on the Epistles of Peter and Jude*, BCNT (London:
Adam & Charles Black, 1969), 235. He admits, however, that those who
defend Petrine authorship do so "with an impressive combination of learning
and ingenuity." Such is characteristic, e.g., of Michael E. Green, *2 Peter
Reconsidered*, rev. ed. (London: Tyndale, 1987); idem, *The Second Epistle of
Peter*, rev. ed. (Grand Rapids: Eerdmans, 1987), 13-39 and Donald Guthrie,
New Testament Introduction, rev. ed. (Downers Grove, IL: InterVarsity, 1990),
820-42. Difference in style, vocabulary, and theological thought from 1 Peter,
dependence upon Jude, anachronisms that reflect a later period, its Hellenistic
character, and most importantly, the problem of the delay of the parousia have
been adduced as evidence against Petrine authorship. See also the most thorough discussion of Richard J. Bauckham who believes that 2 Peter was intended by the author as "entirely *transparent* fiction." *Jude, 2 Peter*, WBC (Waco:
Word, 1983), 131-63. Bo Reicke regards the author as a disciple of Peter and
dates the work along with Bauckham (158) to ca. AD 90. *The Second Epistle
of Peter*, AB (New York: Doubleday, 1964), 143-44. Cf. J. A. T. Robinson who
names Jude as the agent of Peter and dates the work ca. AD 60-62. *Redating
the New Testament* (Philadelphia: Westminster, 1976), 186-99. While the issue
of authorship will remain open for this study, for convenience the author may
be designated as "Peter" without prejudice.

the world's plight and judgment (vv. 6-7, 10-12), and the new creation (v. 13).

> ³ Know this first of all, that in the last days mockers will come with their mocking, . . . ⁴ and saying, "Where is the promise of His coming? For ever since the fathers fell asleep, all continues just as it was from the beginning of creation." ⁵ For when they maintain this, it escapes their notice that by the word of God the heavens existed long ago and the earth was formed out of water and by water, ⁶ through which the world at that time was destroyed, being flooded with water. ⁷ But the present heavens and earth by His word are being kept for the day of judgment and destruction of ungodly men. . . . ¹⁰ But the day of the Lord will come like a thief in which the heavens will pass away with a roar and the elements will be destroyed with intense heat, and the earth and its works will be burned up. ¹¹ Since all these things are to be destroyed in this way, what sort of people ought you to be in holy conduct and godliness, ¹² looking for and hastening the coming of the day of God, on account of which the heavens will be destroyed by burning, and the elements will melt with intense heat! ¹³ But according to His promise we are looking for new heavens and a new earth, in which righteousness dwells (2 Peter 3.5-13).

In response to the taunts of those who see the delay of the parousia as proof positive that judgment will never come, the author adduces the steadfastness of God's word by which the world was created and by which he has determined its ultimate judgment. Peter asserts that all has not continued as normal since the beginning of the world. The world has once before experienced the mighty intervention of God and would do so again.[172] The creation and flood, then, serve as types of judgment and renewal and ensure the reality of the future intervention of God. In the typological understanding of the biblical writers the antitype not only corresponds to the type but the type actually calls the fulfillment into existence. That God will come in judgment in the end is thus predicated upon his activity as

---

[172]Bauckham, *2 Peter*, 294. Cf. Vögtle, *Zukunft des Kosmos*, 131-32.

both creator and judge in the beginning. The verbal parallelism between verses 5 and 7 reveals that this typological emphasis is deliberate. Just as the old world was created by the word of God (τῷ λόγῳ) and perished (ἀπώλετο) in the flood, so also will the present universe experience destruction (ἀπωλείας) by the same word (τῷ λόγῳ).[173] Likewise, the previous generation of Noah (cf. 2.5) corresponds to the present generation of scoffers who likewise deserve judgment (vv. 3-4) while Noah represents a typological model for the righteous. The entire section therefore reveals a typological hermeneutic.[174]

Peter's primary emphasis is upon the certainty of the parousia and the judgment of the wicked. Cosmological speculations reflected in these verses, while secondary, are not totally unrelated. For example, the writer's terminology of the cosmos that existed "then" (ὁ τότε κόσμος, v. 6) and the present world (οἱ νῦν οὐρανοὶ καὶ ἡ γῆ, v. 7) as well as the new creation (v. 13) is not intended to suggest three entirely distinct worlds but reflects the apocalyptic idea of world history divided by two great cosmic upheavals.[175] Notably, the reference to the destruction of the world in the deluge does not connote complete annihilation. In accordance with the OT tradition, it portrays the return of creation to its primeval chaotic state. Further, do verses 5-6 teach that the earth was formed "out of water" (ἐξ ὕδατος, v. 5, NASB, NIV), that is, as the basic element of creation? It is possible that Peter intends a parallel with the Stoic motif of ἐκπύρωσις in which the cosmos dissolved periodical-

---

[173]See Tord Fornberg, *An Early Church in a Pluralistic Society: A Study of 2 Peter*, ConBNT, no. 9 (Lund: Gleerup, 1977), 66-67; Wright, *Second Peter*, 146.

[174]Evald Lövestam, "Eschatologie und Tradition im 2 Petrusbrief," in *The New Testament Age*, ed. William C. Weinrich (Macon, GA: Mercer, 1984), 2:288-96. See also Richard J. Bauckham, "James, 1 and 2 Peter, Jude," in *It is Written: Scripture Citing Scripture*, ed. D. A. Carson and H. G. M. Williamson (Cambridge: Cambridge University, 1988), 314. See also the discussion above on Peter's typological hermeneutic chapter two, p. 67-68.

[175]The flood is called the period of the "first consummation" in 1 Enoch 93.4. Cf. 1 Enoch 10.11-11.2. Cf. also Bauckham, *2 Peter*, 299. On the periodization of history see, e.g., Dan. 2.21; 4.37; 4 Ezra 4.37; 1QS 4.18; 1QM 14.14; Gal. 4.4; Eph. 1.10.

ly into fire (v. 10), the basic element of the universe. The phrase more likely recalls Gen. 1.6, 9 in which God confined the waters that the land might appear. (cf. Ps. 33.7; 104.5-6). The second phrase, δι᾽ ὕδατος, "by means of water" (RSV, NEB) suggests, according to Green, the means by which the earth was sustained, that is, by rain.[176] This, however, is not mentioned in Genesis 1 or 2. Bauckham contends plausibly that the writer has in mind the act of separating the waters.[177] As such the phrase is an alternative to the first and suggests that Peter is drawing upon the *chaoskampf* motif in which creation was wrought *by means of* the defeat of the watery primeval chaos. The problematic plural relative pronoun in verse 7, δι᾽ ὧν, refers to both the word and the waters as the basis and agent of creation and destruction.[178] Significantly, 2 Pet. 3.5-7 maintains that unlike Hellenistic cosmology the world was created and continues to exist by God's effective word (vv. 5, 7). The creation and its destiny therefore are not natural occurrences. Nature in biblical thought is not an autonomous, self-determinative system. Schelkle states appropriately that "the world is not nature, and its history is not natural, but it is creature, and its history is judgment and salvation."[179]

The certainty of universal judgment is assured by Peter's statement that the present heavens and earth "stand reserved" for fire (v. 7). Yet this reality carries an unexpected and sudden quality for the "day of the Lord will come as a thief" (v. 10). God's advent in judgment is accompanied by catastrophic events. The heavens will pass away "with a roar" (v. 10). The word ῥοιζηδόν, an onomatopoeic word, is used in Hellenistic texts to express the whizzing sound produced by rushing motion through air such as the flight of an arrow or a bird's wings, and later by extension the rushing motion itself.[180] Kelly

---

[176]Green, *2 Peter*, 141.

[177]Bauckham, *2 Peter*, 297.

[178]Kelly, *Second Epistle of Peter*, 360. Cf. Bauckham, *2 Peter*, 298.

[179]Karl Hermann Schelkle, *Die Petrus Briefe, Der Judasbrief*, 5th ed., HTKNT (Freiburg: Herder, 1982), 226.

[180]See references and discussion in *LSJ*. Cf. J. B. Mayor, *The Epistles of St. Jude and the Second Epistle of St. Peter* (New York: MacMillan, 1907), 157.

thinks that the word connotes in this context the hissing, crack-ling, or roaring sound of uncontrollable and consuming blazes of fire.[181] This noise also may represent the divine voice which like fire is often a standard element of theophanies (cf. Ps. 18.13-15; Joel 3.16; 1 Thess. 4.16). The event therefore is not merely one of destruction but pictures the arrival of the Lord himself in judgment.[182] Peter also prophesies that the heavens will pass away and the "elements" (στοιχεῖα) will melt with the intense heat (vv. 10, 12). Στοιχεῖα may refer to the four elements of water, fire, air, and earth which in Stoic thought comprised the physical world. The term can also refer to the heavenly bodies. Schelkle suggests that since the στοιχεῖα were sometimes conceived as celestial "powers" (Gal. 4.3), which in apocalyptic are represented by the stars, the writer might have combined the two meanings.[183] However, the paral-lel of the heavens with the earth favors the reference to the heavenly bodies (cf. Isa. 34.4).

The precise effect of the judgment theophany upon the earth is complicated because of the reading of the last word in the verse. Several English versions accept the reading εὑρεθήσεται but translate the verb "will be burned up" (NASB, RSV, NJB) even though it should be rendered "will be found." This is no doubt an accommodation which attempts to understand the meaning of this difficult reading in the context of cosmic conflagration. Metzger declares that "the word seems to be devoid of meaning in this context."[184] While this assessment is true, εὑρεθήσεται seems to be more original as the oldest reading and the one which best explains all the variants.[185] The manuscript evidence reveals that this reading was often modified by additions,[186] omitted

---

[181]Kelly, *Second Epistle of Peter*, 364.

[182]Bauckham, *2 Peter*, 315.

[183]Schelkle, *Petrusbriefe*, 228.

[184]Metzger, *TCGNT*, 706.

[185]Εὑρεθήσεται is read by ℵ B K P 056 424ᶜ 1175 1739ᵗˣᵗ Origen *al.*

[186]𝔓⁷² adds λυόμενα ("The earth . . . will be found dissolved"). The reading οὐχ εὑρεθήσεται appears as a marginal reading in the Harclean ver-sion. Mayor prefers this reading because it makes sense of the context and the accidental omission of οὐκ would explain the origin of the others. *Second*

altogether,[187] or replaced by another verb[188] in an attempt to harmonize the reading with the context. Additional conjectures have been proposed by modern commentators. Metzger, following Hort, suggests the reading of ῥυήσεται or ῥεύσεται ("will waste away") as a scribal corruption of εὑρεθήσεται. The verbs ἀρθήσεται ("will be taken away") and κριθήσεται ("will be judged") also have been recommended.[189]

Other solutions have been offered which attempt to make the passage intelligible while also accepting εὑρεθήσεται as the original reading. Kelly ingeniously recommends punctuating the end of verse 10 as a question: "and the earth and the works it contains--will they be found?"[190] This, however, has not recommended itself to scholars. Danker has argued that the reading is not unnecessarily difficult in the context if the meaning is understood properly. He objects that εὑρεθήσεται has often been regarded as unacceptable because commentators have tended to focus upon the mode of judgment, that is, the utter destruction of the earth. By contrast, the verb describes the judicial process involving the earth's inhabitants and hence the meaning "will be judged." The absolute use of the verb, however, requires Danker to emend the text. In comparison with similar wording in Ps. Sol. 17.10, he conjectures that κατά was replaced by καί through haplography and restores the text to read: "the earth will be found judged according to the deeds done in it."[191] Bauckham and Schelkle accept the basic premise of this argument but without the conjectured emenda-

---

Epistle of St. Peter, 169; Fornberg, *Early Church*, 75-77.

[187]Ψ it[div? z] vg[ww] Pelagius *al.*

[188]C reads ἀφανισθήσονται ("will disappear") and κατακαήσεται ("will be burned up") is read by several late manuscripts including A 048 049 056 0142 33 88 614 *Byz Lect* syr[h] *al.*

[189]See especially Metzger, *TCGNT*, 706 and Bauckham, *2 Peter*, 317-18.

[190]Kelly, *Second Epistle of Peter*, 364-66.

[191]Frederick W. Danker, "II Peter 3.10 and Psalm of Solomon 17.10," *ZNW* 53/1-2 (1962): 82-86. Ps. Sol. 17:10 reads: κατὰ τὰ ἁμαρτήματα αὐτῶν ἀποδώσεις αὐτοῖς, ὁ θεός εὑρεθῆναι αὐτοῖς κατὰ τὰ ἔργα αὐτῶν. Danker's reconstruction of v. 10 requires more than the insertion of κατά: καὶ γῆ κατὰ τὰ ἐν αὐτῇ ἔργα εὑρεθήσεται.

tion.   The entire context centers upon the judgment of the wicked rather than cosmic annihilation which is of interest to the writer only as a means of God's judgment against humanity.   The verse therefore ends on a note describing the exposure of human works.   The wicked and their works "will be found," that is, will be open to God's scrutiny and condemnation.[192]   A view closely related but which does not confine the judgment process to human inhabitants is Wolters' argument that Peter envisioned the day of the Lord as a smelting process from which the world "will be found" or "will emerge purified."   The description of the judgment by verbs meaning "to melt" (πυρόομαι, v. 12) and to burn (καυσόομαι, v. 10, 12) portray the picture of intense heat without burning up completely. In keeping with the OT view of God as a refiner through fire the verb thus connotes "to have survived," "to have stood the test," "to have been found or proved genuine."   Wolters finds support for such an interpretation in 1 Pet. 1.17 where the passive of εὑρίσκω is used absolutely to denote surviving a purifying fire.   The weakness of this view, as he admits, is that this meaning of εὑρίσκω is without lexical support outside the Petrine writings.   This interpretation does, however, attempt to recognize the cosmic dimension of judgment while protecting against a Gnostic worldview which regards the world as expendable.[193]

It is difficult, if not impossible, to determine the best reading and its interpretation in the context.   While there is strong support for the translation, "will be found" in the sense that humanity's works "will be laid bare" (NIV), this view nevertheless seems strained.   It may reflect the thinking of the scribe who at an early stage introduced the reading but whether or not it represents the reading of the author's hand is uncertain. The reading has merit since the *primary* focus of the passage is the judg-

---

[192]Bauckham, *2 Peter*, 318-21.   Schelkle, *Petrusbriefe*, 228, n. 3. Schelkle sees 1 Cor. 3.13-15 as illustrative for his translation of v. 10: "und die Erde und die Werke auf ihr werden im Gericht erfunden werden" (222).   See also William E. Wilson, "Εὑρεθήσεται in 2 Pet. iii.10," *ExpTim* 32 (1920-21): 44-45.

[193]Al Wolters, "Worldview and Textual Criticism in 2 Peter 3.10," *WTJ* 49 (Fall 1987): 405-13.

ment upon the wicked. However, this view drives a wedge
between humankind and the created order. A solidarity between
humanity and the creation is always a basic working assumption
whether or not it is expressed. The author's contemplation of
God's judgment on evil works naturally leads to a consideration
of the effects of that judgment upon the created order. Just as the
decree upon humanity affected the creation according to Genesis 3 so also will God's judgment have cosmic consequences.
Additionally, verses 10-11 imply that the earth will suffer a similar fate as the heavens. This clearly accounts for the reading of
ἀφανισθήσονται. Wolters' interpretation does not necessarily demand the acceptance of εὑρεθήσεται. He could have
arrived at the same basic conclusion from the verb
κατακαήσεται (cf. Mal. 4.1). Wolters' strength is the emphasis upon the OT context, and moreover Bauckham's conjecture
that an apocalyptic source lies behind 2 Peter 3, while plausible,
merely affirms the use of traditional motifs.[194] Particularly
noteworthy is 1 Enoch 1.6 which as noted above by Metzger
also may contain an acceptable solution for the reading.

> And the eternal God will walk upon the earth, on Mount
> Sinai, . . . and the high mountains will be shaken and will
> fall and be dissolved and the high mountains will be made
> low so that the mountains will waste away [τοῦ
> διαρυῆναι] and they will melt like wax before the fire in
> a flame and the earth will be split apart and all the things
> upon the earth will perish (1 Enoch 6.3-7, translated from
> G; cf. Ps. 97.5, Zeph. 1.18).

As noted in our discussion of this passage in chapter three, this
verse like 2 Peter 3 reflects more appropriately the OT theophanic texts which reveal through violent language God's
authority over his creation rather than total dissolution of the
world (cf. Mic. 1.4; Nah. 1.5; Hab. 3.6).[195]

The language of 2 Peter 3 nevertheless has suggested to
some the influence of Greek cosmology. As mentioned, the

---

[194]Bauckham, *2 Peter*, 283-85, 304-5.

[195]See the discussion on 1 Enoch 1.6 above chapter three, pp. 82-83.

Greeks envisioned world history in two movements each punc-
tuated decisively by the destruction of the world by water and
fire. In Plato's *Timaeus* a legend is recounted regarding several
destructions of humanity of which the greatest are by fire and
water and the lesser ones by countless other means (22B-C).
Interestingly, the term ἐκπύρωσις does not appear and the
destruction by fire is described in the same manner as the flood
by which the gods "purged" (καθαίροντες) the earth by water
(22D). That the Stoic doctrine of ἐκπύρωσις was influential in
Judaism even among the more reclusive Qumran sectarians was
noted in the discussion of 1QH 3.29-36. In contrast to Jewish
conceptions, the Stoic idea was based on an impersonal and
mechanical cyclical cosmology in which the cosmos periodically dissolved into fire, its basic element, from which the world
was reborn. Each "new" world, however, was identical to the
former.[196] The context of Peter's teaching indicates that the
conceptual matrix is found in the OT and Jewish apocalyptic traditions. The distinctiveness of the Jewish and Christian concept
of a new creation in contrast to Stoic ideas is thus immediately
apparent. As Riesner states, the Stoic expected a νεός κόσμος
while 2 Peter anticipated a καινός οὐρανός καὶ γῆ καινή.[197]
The uniqueness is likewise evident in the hope of the new creation as the basis of ethical admonitions (v. 11). The worldview
of the writer is therefore that of Jewish Christianity.

Whatever conclusions may be drawn from the passage
regarding creation and cosmic hope, one must realize that 2 Peter
3 is first and foremost a text concerning the certain punishment
of the wicked and reward for the righteous. The cosmic scope of
the destruction no doubt communicated to the scoffers not only
the reality of judgment but that nothing or no one could escape

---

[196]See comments above chapter three, pp. 114-117 and n. 125.

[197]Rainer Riesner, "Die Zweite Petrus-Brief und die Eschatology," in
Zukunftserwartung in biblischer Sicht: Beiträge zur Eschatologie, ed. G. Maier
(Wuppertal: R. Brockhaus, 1984) 139-40. Joseph Chaine in an early but still
useful discussion of Persian and Greek sources arrives at the same conclusion.
"Cosmogonie aquatique et conflagration finale d'après la secunda Petri," *RB*
46 (1937): 207-16. See also Carsten Peter Thiede, "A Pagan Reader of 2 Peter:
Cosmic Conflagration in 2 Peter and the *Octavius* of Minucius Felix," *JSNT* 26
(February 1986): 79-96.

the wrath of God. Furthermore, the anticipation of the day of the Lord functioned primarily to encourage righteous living in preparation for the "new heavens and new earth in which righteousness dwells" (vv. 13, 14). In this regard, Peter's hesitancy to describe the new creation in vivid and picturesque detail betrays the NT concern more for *who* is coming rather than *what* is to come.[198] This statement, however, does not diminish the importance of the new creation for the *who* of the *eschaton* will be no other than the creator God.

The passage nevertheless reveals important information regarding the concept of the future of creation. The heavy barrage of words such as ἀπώλειας, ἀπολέσθαι (vv. 7, 9), πῦρ, πυρούμενοι (vv. 7, 12), κρίσεως (v. 7), λύω (vv. 10, 11, 12), καυσούμενα (vv. 10, 12), and τήκεται (v. 12) reveal the violence of the devastation. An ultraliteral reading of such language, however, fails to recognize that Peter portrays the advent of God in typical theophanic language reflecting the terrible effects of God's wrath upon the wicked that even will reach cosmic proportions. Nonetheless, this picture discloses a radical discontinuity between the old and the new world more than any other passage previously encountered in this study of the OT or NT. However, that the passage rejects the idea of total annihilation is evident from the author's typological hermeneutic. The flood motif as a type of future judgment and deliverance for humanity and creation suggests that the author does not envision total destruction and a new creation *ex nihilo*, but as in God's first intervention there will be a purging primarily related to sinful humanity. Further, a total and final desolation of the creation not only implies a Gnostic view which denigrates the present created order but also denies the redemptive aspect even in the judgment of God. Judgment is not the last word; it is merely the prelude to the new heavens and new earth.[199] Notably, the overwhelming influence of the OT in 2

---

[198]Schelkle notes that righteousness is a mark of the messianic era in the OT and Jewish writings. *Petrusbriefe*, 230. Further, the description of the new world as the abode of righteousness like 4 Ezra reflects the writer's contrast to the present godlessness rather than a spiritual-material dualism.

[199]R. Larry Overstreet unfortunately has overlooked the redemptive element in God's judgment in his argument for total annihilation in this passage.

Peter 3, as a glance at the NA[26] reveals, makes it clear that Peter does not depart from the OT hope of a new creation which especially in Isaiah 65 reflects a continuity with the old creation.[200]

2 Peter thus speaks of a radical discontinuity and continuity. The old world purged from corruption through the refining fires of God has given way to a new order. This hope of the new heavens and new earth rejects Käsemann's assertion that 2 Peter evinces "the relapse of Christianity into Hellenistic dualism." According to Käsemann, the writer stands apart from the Pauline doctrine of redemption "in a materialist sense." 2 Peter reflects the believer's longing for escape from the corruption of this world and the attainment of his ultimate destiny, namely, the participation in the divine φύσις--apotheosis (cf. 1.4).[201] On the contrary, the writer of 2 Peter has not altered the Pauline doctrine of redemption which includes all creation. Peter has no disdain for this world. He, like the other apocalyptists has a concern for the present created order. The "materialist" promise of the new heavens and new earth is opposed to a dualistic escape from the present world to another eternal, ethereal existence. 2 Peter 3 is entirely in accord with Paul's concept of the freedom of creation (Rom. 8.21). In fact, although this passage represents a more radical break with the old world than does Romans 8, Beker's statement with reference to Paul applies also to 2 Peter for both writers draw upon the same biblical and apocalyptic worldview that renounces the Gnostic contempt for this world and affirms the importance of the created

"A Study of 2 Peter 3.10-13," *BibSac* 137 (October-December 1980): 354-71.

[200]2 Peter 3.5-13 represents an implicit midrash on several "summary" texts or allusions with one citation (v. 8). See E. Earle Ellis, "How the New Testament uses the Old," in *New Testament Interpretation: Essays on Principles and Methods*, ed. I. Howard Marshall (Grand Rapids: Eerdmans, 1977), 205.

[201]Ernst Käsemann, "An Apologia for Primitive Christian Eschatology," in *Essays on New Testament Themes*, trans. W. J. Montague (London: SCM, 1964), 179-84. Cf. Al Wolters who argues that θεία φύσις, translated with the genitive of κοινωνός as "partakers of the divine nature," should be rendered "partners of God" since the phrase appears as a periphrasis for "God" in Philo and thus denotes a covenant idea rather than apotheosis. "'Partners of the Deity': A Covenantal Reading of 2 Peter 1.4," *CTJ* 25 (April 1990): 28-44.

order. God will not negate his creation.

> Although the glory of God will break into our fallen world,
> it will not annihilate the world but only break its present
> structure of death, because it aims to transform the cosmos
> rather than to confirm its *ontological nothingness* (empha-
> sis mine).[202]

Creation and Redemption in Revelation

Creation as the Fundamental Theme of Revelation

If the apocalyptists expressed disdain for the creation it
would be abundantly evident in the NT apocalyptic writing concerned with the end of the world. Specific references to the
material world in Revelation center primarily in its elements as
instruments in God's judgement. In chapters 6-16, for example,
the transitory nature of the created order and its relationship with
humanity is suggested in the cycles of judgment represented by
the seals, trumpets, and bowls that include the release of natural
disasters upon the earth. However, one should not press too literally the theophanic language which particularly in the case of
the trumpet judgments utilizes Exodus motifs as types of God's
eschatological judgment upon wicked humanity. Notably, the
restriction of the plagues to one third of the earth in 8.6-13
implies that human sin not the creation is the focus of God's
wrath.[203] The value of the created order is not depreciated in the
NT apocalypse. Indeed, so important is the theme of creation to
the writer that it permeates the entire message of Revelation
from the opening vision in chapter 1 to the vision of the new
heavens and new earth in Revelation 21-22. In fact, as one
writer states, the motif "seems virtually to be dragged into some
other contexts" (cf. 10.5-6; 14.7).[204]

---

[202]Beker, *Paul the Apostle*, 149.

[203]G. R. Beasley-Murray argues that the restriction of the plagues to one
third of the earth rather than the whole permits the opportunity for humanity to
repent. *The Book of Revelation*, NCB (Grand Rapids: Eerdmans, 1981), 156-57.

[204]M. Eugene Boring, "The Theology of Revelation: 'The Lord Our
God Almighty Reigns,'" *Interp* 40 (July 1986): 68.

The opening vision presents God as lord over his creation and history. John proclaims God as the "first and last," that is, the one who directs this world and its history from creation to consummation according to his purposes (1.8, 17; 21.6; 22.13; cf. Isa. 41.4; 44.6; 43.12). This statement attests that the world is not an autonomous, mechanical "entity." God is the ground and the goal of its existence (cf. Col. 1.16). The affirmation of the maintenance of the cosmos and its ultimate deliverance from evil, both cosmic and political, is further qualified by the title "the Lord God, Almighty" (1.8). The phrase κύριος ὁ θεός, ὁ παντοκράτωρ renders the Hebrew צבאות יהוה ("Lord God, of hosts"). The OT meaning of צבאות has been variously interpreted as the earthly hosts or army of God, the heavenly host, that is, angels, and the stars as representative of the entire universe. The use of this designation in Isaiah and elsewhere leads Koehler to contend that the phrase denotes the stars or the cosmos and all it contains. Implicit in this title was the rejection of the Babylonian view of the heavenly bodies as angelic beings. Moreover, the formation of the Greek word παντοκράτωρ, from κρατεῖν, "to exercise control," designates the "one who controls or rules over all things." It does not express merely the possession of might, as the English translation "Almighty" suggests, but the active sovereignty over the universe.[205] As John's favorite title for God, it thus reflects appropriately God's reign over the entire cosmos.[206]

Further, that God rules the cosmos and history and is committed to restoring all of creation according to his original intentions is verified in the throne vision prior to the revelation of his wrath. Chapter 4 thus forms the basis for the presentation of the ultimate triumph (4.1-11.19). That John's belief in God as creator and lord underlies his entire message is seen in the placement of chapter 4 in the structure of the book. As the initial vision of

---

[205]Koehler, *Old Testament Theology*, 49-51; C. H. Dodd, *The Bible and the Greeks* (London: Hodder & Stroughten, 1935), 19.

[206]With the exception of 2 Cor. 6.18, which is a citation of Isa. 43.6, παντοκράτωρ occurs in the NT only in Revelation (1.8; 4.8; 11.17; 15.3; 16.7; 16.14; 19.6, 15; 21.22).

a new major section stretching from Revelation 4 to 22.5 it reveals "something of the important convictions that determine the content of that section."[207] The centrality of this vision in the book with its emphasis on the *throne* of the "Almighty" serves to remind the readers that God's rule includes also the political world. As Mussner observes, the entire horizon of the Apocalypse is entirely one of universal, cosmic reach. It encompasses the heavens and the earth because God as creator reigns as universal lord over the universe, and Christ by virtue of his resurrection rules over the "kings of the earth" (1.5). John's emphasis upon God's reign over creation thus embraces both the cosmic and political realms and answers the question, "who will ultimately rule the world?"[208] This focus reveals the primary role of creation language in the book which surfaces in regard to the growing threat of persecution of the church by the state.[209]

The primary question concerning the recipients of the letter, "who is on the throne?" or "who will rule the world?" draws forth the author's use of the creation motif. Creation language in Revelation is reminiscent of its role in the days of Second Isaiah as Israel lay destitute and dying in the grip of a pagan nation. Two crucial questions plagued the Israelites. "Has God deserted his people?" "Does he have the power to help his people?" The prophet utilizes creation language to affirm that God's power extends over the entire creation. "Do you not know?

---

[207]L. W. Hurtado, "Rev. 4-5 in Light of Jewish Apocalyptic Analogies," *JSNT* 25 (1985): 110.

[208]Franz Mussner, "'Weltherrschaft' als eschatologischie Thema der Johannesapokalypse," in *Glaube und Eschatologie*, ed. Erich Grässer and Otto Merk (Tübingen: Mohr, 1985), 217-222. He also notes the political overtones of the titles for God and Christ in contrast to the emperor cult (219-22). Boring observes that in almost every instance the term "Almighty" is related to the title "Lord" which properly belongs to God but has been usurped by the emperors. "Theology of Revelation," 259.

[209]Evidence of widespread persecution of Christians by the Roman state is slight during the reign of Domitian. John mentions only one who had suffered martyrdom for his faith (2.13). However, the growing prospect of confrontation between the church and state promoted primarily by the emperor cult prompted John to pen Revelation in order to prepare the church for what it was "about to suffer" (2.10; 3.10). Boring, *Revelation*, 13-19; Leon Morris, *The Book of Revelation*, rev. ed., TNTC (Grand Rapids: Eerdmans, 1987), 36-37.

Have you not heard? The everlasting God, the Lord, the creator of the ends of the earth does not become weary or tired?" (Isa. 40.28). The supposedly powerful astral deities of Babylon were even created by Israel's God (Isa. 40.25-26). The faithful there-fore could be certain of God's enduring faithfulness.[210] As in Second Isaiah, the role of creation language functions to offer comfort and nurture hope. In the face of the Babylon of John's day it affirmed that contrary to the reality of the Christians' experience God is still lord over the world and its history.[211]

Further, like Second Isaiah, John unites the concepts of creation and redemption to affirm that the creator *is* the redeemer. This is accomplished effectively in John's placement of the two hymns of Rev. 4.1-11 and 5.1-14 representing respec-tively God's work in creation and his creative work of redemp-tion through the lamb.[212] The concept of creation and redemp-tion in chapters 4-5 proclaims that only God can bring the world and history to a final and purposeful conclusion. The context of the visions in these chapters concerns the choice of the one wor-thy to open the scroll to reveal God's plan to restore order out of chaos (5.1-14). Even though the opening of the sealed scroll unleashes violent, catastrophic forces upon the world (6.12-16.21), one must remember that the release of God's wrath does not primarily have destructive intentions but is actually a "clear-ing of the decks for a new order" and thus includes a redemptive element.[213] The lamb's acceptance of the scroll sets him apart as

---

[210]See the comments of Westermann, *Isaiah*, 25.

[211]Most commentators agree that Babylon was a symbolic name for Rome (cf. 14.8; 16.19; 17.5; 18.2, 10, 21). The parallel of Isaiah and Revela-tion is appropriate since Rome like Babylon destroyed the Temple and Jerusalem. Such identification had become traditional by the end of the first century AD. See Adela Yarbro Collins, "Myth and History in the Book of Rev-elation," in *Traditions in Transformation: Turning Points in Biblical Faith*, ed. Baruch Halpern and Jon D. Levenson (Winona Lake, IL: Eisenbrauns, 1981), 382.

[212]See David R. Carnegie, "Worthy is the Lamb: The Hymns in Revela-tion," in *Christ the Lord: Studies in Christology presented to Donald Guthrie*, ed. Harold H. Rowdon (Downers Grove, IL: InterVarsity, 1982), 248-49.

[213]J. P. M. Sweet, *Revelation*, WPC (Philadelphia: Westminster, 1979), 143.

eschatological regent who will as in the days of the Exodus exe-
cute the plagues and accomplish a new Exodus. As such he
reigns as eschatological ruler: "We give Thee thanks, O Lord
God, The Almighty, who art and who wast, because Thou hast
taken Thy great power and hast begun to reign" (11.17). Notice-
ably, the usual phrase, "who is to come," is absent in this verse
(cf. 1.8; 4.8). As such it serves as a proleptic vision of the
certainty of victory. The world is already ruled by God and his
Christ even though the final battle has yet to be fought. The ultimate triumph and establishment of his rule is seen in the defeat
of Satan and his representatives and the establishment of a new
heaven and earth devoid of all oppressive forces that seek to
usurp the creator's rule (19.1- 22.5). It is thus incomprehensible
to John that the God who had created the world and his people
would leave them to face "an endless battle against sin and death
as the powers sovereign over this world; that he should not finally overcome all his enemies and reign as unquestioned Lord of
his creation."[214] God will not abandon his own world. Indeed,
the redemptive work of Christ assures that God's aims are
already in the process of realization. John's message of hope for
the dilemma of this age then reverberates in the divine
pronouncement, "Behold, I make all things new" (21.5).

Mythical Pictures of Creation's Redemption

In the great throne scene of Revelation 4, John is swept up
to the court of heaven and beholds a vision of the sovereign creator God. The reality of this vision reflects in contrast to the
Christian's experience of the moment a world under complete
control. For John, only God is worthy to occupy the throne and
to receive the designation of "Lord." Arrayed in splendor and
attended by heavenly worshippers, God is praised as worthy "to
receive glory and honor and power; for Thou didst create all
things, and because of Thy will they existed, and were created"
(v. 11). As the παντοκράτωρ, he rules the universe. John's

---

[214]The observation of Käsemann in reference to the theology of Paul
and Revelation. "An Apologia," 182.

language reveals a treasury of mental images as he describes the crystal sea before the throne, the rainbow, and the living creatures representing "organic nature."[215] While some scholars see the description of the sea merely as window dressing for the scene, this writer believes John was drawing upon ancient myths to express the magnificence of the sovereign creator God.[216] The idea of the "sea" or "waters" evoked a variety of meanings to the Israelites.   As mentioned previously, the theme of the *chaoskampf* played an important role in Israel's understanding of the creator. The motif of a struggle over the demonic foes of the deep symbolized the powers which violently opposed God and thus threatened the "meaningfulness of history" if the world returned to its precreation chaotic state. The Genesis account portrays God as holding back, as it were, the monsters of the deep as he continually maintains the boundaries of the waters with the firmament.   Thus, the waters of chaos were not destroyed but held at bay with the result that humanity's world occupied the precarious position between the "waters above" and the "waters below." The waters took on historical significance as they symbolized Israel's enemies. Further, by extending the motif, the descent into the deep also represented the concept of death.[217] The symbol of the sea, as Caird observes, stands as a stark reminder that the whole creation has been corrupted by evil.[218] Yet this does not negate God's lordship.

God is sovereign creator whose power holds sway over the powers of the sea. Its calm appearance reflects his maintenance of both creation and history. John's vision projected hope to a people anticipating the prospect of a "descent into the watery depths of death" for their faith. Their feeling of estrange-

---

[215]Foerster, "Κτίζω," 3:1030.

[216]R. H. Charles thinks that by the time of the New Testament the mythical concept of the sea had been forgotten. *Revelation of St. John*, 1:118. Robert H. Mounce contends that it merely adds to the splendor of the scene. *The Book of Revelation*, NICNT (Grand Rapids: Eerdmans, 1977), 36. But cf. George B. Caird, *The Revelation of St John the Divine*, HNTC (New York: Harper & Row, 1966), 65-68.

[217]See also *IDB*, s.v. "Water," by Bernhard W. Anderson, 4:808-9 and comments above in chapter 2, pp. 73-74.

[218]Caird, *Revelation of St. John*, 68.

ment in this tumultuous time no doubt also reminded this new Israel (1.6; 5.10) of the waters which separated Israel from its promised homeland in days of old. John affirms God's presence in the midst of their troubles. The picture of a serene sea attests that while war may rage fiercely on the earth in their everyday experience, nevertheless God is still creator and lord over his creation. The great demonic forces of evil embodied in the Roman power while very much alive must still submit to his sovereignty. God's creative power therefore embraces both the historical and cosmic dimensions. Only he is worthy to be praised as creator. The mention of the rainbow (v. 3) reminds of the symbol of God's covenant with all creation (Gen. 9.11). Furthermore, John's vision of the rainbow just prior to the eschatological woes represents a sign of hope that God intends to deliver his creation *through* judgment and bring it to fulfillment.[219]

Therefore, drawing from the prophetic visions of Isaiah 6 and Ezekiel 1, John places the emphasis of the vision upon the *throne*. God is depicted as arrayed in splendor, and acclaimed in the trisagion as holy. He will vindicate his holiness in the triumph over evil through the cross as chapter 5 affirms. In the praise to the lamb, the universal reach of Christ's reconciling work is displayed. As in the Pauline tradition, Christ's death on the cross provides the means of reconciling to God "every created thing which is in heaven and on the earth and under the earth and on the sea, and all things in them" (5.13; cf. Col. 1.20; Phil. 2.9-11). This universal sweep is suggested, according to Swete, by the entire animate nature as represented in the animals which surround the throne and attests that both humanity and creation unite in the worship of the creator.[220] The assurance of this redemptive event is rooted in the conviction that what is a reality in heaven will be accomplished upon the earth. Thus, victory and hope is guaranteed because God has through the lamb calmed the chaotic sea and accomplished peace. Indeed, when Christ receives the scroll the entire creation joins already

---

[219]Boring, *Revelation*, 105.
[220]H. B. Swete, *The Apocalypse of St. John*, 3d ed. (London: Macmillan, 1911), 71 and Foerster, "Κτίζω," cited above in n. 212.

in worship of his sovereignty. This is the ultimate work for the one who is the beginning and goal of creation (3.14; 22.13). The hymn affirms God's creation as good and promises its ultimate fulfillment. John therefore rejects any suggestion of a dualistic view.

> John, inspired by the Spirit and caught up into the other world, hears there a constant song of praise to God as the creator of *this* world. John, like apocalyptic generally, is not otherworldly; he is the opposite of those who reject this world for some other. His fervent eschatological faith is not an alternative to faith in God as the loving creator of this world but the outcome of this faith. In a situation of persecution or threat, John has no interest in a dualistic escape hatch; he insists on the rigorous faith and theology demanded by faith in one God who is the creator of all.[221]

The eschatological promise invoked in Rev. 4.8 of the "one who is to come" and his redemptive work through "the Lamb that was slain" (5.12) thus clearly serves to unite the concept of God as creator and redeemer.[222]

The relation of creation and redemption is likewise portrayed vividly though the use of the *chaoskampf* in Revelation 12. The author utilizes OT traditions of the defeat of the Leviathan by God in primordial times and the Exodus motif in the portrayal of the woman clothed with the sun. The use of the term "dragon" for the monster associates the beast with the OT sea monster Leviathan (δράκων, LXX, cf. Isa. 27.1;) which is portrayed as God's opponent in the *chaoskampf* who must be vanquished by the chief god in order to restore order out of chaos.[223] As in Isaiah 51 and other passages God is the one who not only created the cosmos and triumphed over the threat of chaos, but he now "re-creates" a people delivered from a new element of bondage. Through mythical language chaos is portrayed as conquered and order is restored. Likewise through the

---

[221]Boring, *Revelation*, 107-8.

[222]See also Hurtado, "Rev. 4-5," 115.

[223]Adela Yarbro Collins, *The Combat Myth in the Book of Revelation* (Missoula: Scholars, 1976), 76, 117-19.

triumph over the dragon (chaos) the people can expect deliverance. The sweeping of the stars from heaven by the dragon or chaos connotes evil's disruption of the cosmic order expressed in Rome's religious idolatry (vv. 3-4). The dragon attempts to devour the child in order to forestall his rise to power (v. 4). The messianic figure arises (v. 5; cf. Ps. 2.9) and an angelic mediator appears and casts the dragon from heaven restoring order "for the kingdom of our God and the authority of his Christ have come" (v. 10).[224] Notably, the earth as God's good creation is repulsed at the violence of Satan. The earth unlike its inhabitants rejects Satan and comes to the aid of the woman (v. 16; cf. 13.4, 8). The portrayal of the woman's rescue from the waters and subsequent refuge in the wilderness assures the expectation of a new eschatological Exodus. The readers are convinced that after a brief sojourn in the wilderness the Messiah will appear to accomplish liberation from Roman rule.[225] Once again creation motifs serve as a promise of eschatological salvation. Significantly, the Exodus background helps explain the appropriation of Isaiah's promise of the new heavens and new earth. John envisions the ultimate deliverance from Satan and the Roman persecution in terms of a new Exodus--a creative event--which includes the reestablishment of God's people, the new Israel, with Jerusalem as its center representing the very presence of God. Like Isaiah 65 this deliverance will be cosmic in scope.

The "New Heavens and New Earth"

The negative effects of God's wrath upon evil and its representatives gives way to a positive message of "re-creation" or renewal in Revelation 21-22. The victory is won. The earth and its inhabitants can no longer stand before the throne (20.11). God has cast all wickedness into the lake of fire (20.14-15). The threatening sea and its horde of devilish beasts is no more. There is a new heaven and earth and a new capital city--the new Jerusalem (21.1-2). All alienation has been resolved. Now God dwells with humanity and once more there shall be a joyous inti-

[224]Ibid., 60-61.
[225]Collins, *Combat Myth*, 60.

mate fellowship as in the beginning. There will be no feeling of estrangement for they shall be exclusively his people (21.3). Every distress of life will flee at God's presence. All things have become new because the "first things" have passed away (21.4). Such is the climactic message of John.

A collage of images are brought together by John in an attempt to portray the magnificence of God's ultimate redemptive act. The patchwork of traditional OT images from Isaiah and Ezekiel provides the seer with a common stock of images and vocabulary.[226] The mention of the new heavens and new earth has often been used along with 2 Peter 3 as the basis for the view of the annihilation of the present world.[227] John has previously presented the earth as suffering under the judgment of God. Notably, the breaking of the sixth seal by the lamb results in catastrophic upheavals on the earth: "there was a great earthquake; and the sun became black as sackcloth . . . and the whole moon became like blood; and the stars of the sky fell to the earth, . . ." (6.12-13; cf. 16.17-21). These verses represent in typical OT theophanic terminology the day of the Lord (Isa. 13.10; 34.4; Joel 2.10, 30-31; Mic. 1.4; Mark 13.24-27).[228] That the earth is not to be completely destroyed is evident since following the earthly catastrophe the kings of the earth are depicted as fleeing from the presence of God (vv. 15-16). The impact

---

[226]The issue of the unity of chs. 20-22 has been raised by the imagery marked by repetition and conceptual incongruities. Charles, for example, inquires that if the new world is devoid of all evil and sin how does one explain the mention of dogs, sorcerers, and immoral persons outside the city gates of the new Jerusalem (22.15) or the purpose of leaves that provide healing for the nations (22.2)? In light of the general and orderly development of chs. 1-20.3, he conjectures that after the death of John a "faithful but unintelligent disciple" gathered together chs. 20-22, which existed as independent documents, "in the order which he thought was best." *Revelation of St. John*, 2:144-54. However, it is characteristic of apocalyptic language that logical consistency often yields to evocative imagery. Moreover, Matthias Rissi has demonstrated that Rev. 21.1-22.15 presents "a clear, formal articulation." *The Future of the World: An Exegetical Study of Revelation 19:11-22:15*, SBT, 2d series, no. 23 (Naperville, IL: Allenson, 1972), 52-54.

[227]See Berkouwer, *Return of Christ*, 219-25.

[228]See Richard J. Bauckham, "The Eschatological Earthquake in the Apocalypse of John," *NovT* 19 (July 1977): 224-33.

of the theophanic language describing the effect upon the creation as well as humanity reveals most importantly that nothing can stand before the presence of God (v. 17). A literal interpretation clearly destroys the overall impact of the imagery. This is also true of chapter 20 where John records that the heavens and earth "have fled away" from the presence of God (v. 11). This verse is followed by the portrayal of the final judgment scene at which time the "sea gave up the dead" and "they were judged everyone of them according to their deeds" (20.13). Obviously, John is not implicitly describing the destruction of the material universe. That John was unaware of this discrepancy only further complicates the matter. More likely the focus as in chapters 6 and 8 is not upon geological or astronomical transformation but the presence of God in judgment.[229]

The opening vision of chapter 21 draws upon Isa. 65.17-25 as the most vivid and meaningful of all OT images for expressing the eschatological hope of salvation for John which embraces both humanity and the universe. That John interprets Isaiah's promise for his present audience is clear from the verbal and conceptual correspondences.

Isaiah 65.17-25	Rev. 21.1-5
new heavens and new earth (v. 17)	new heavens and new earth (v. 1)
former troubles forgotten (v. 17)	first heaven and earth and first things passed away (vv. 1, 4)
"I create Jerusalem" (v. 18)	new Jerusalem descending from heaven (v. 2)
communion with God (v. 24)	God dwells among saints (v. 3)
no weeping or crying (v. 19)	no tears or mourning (v. 4)
long and productive life (v. 20)	no death (v. 4)
serpent cursed (v. 25)	no more sea (v. 1)

Significantly, the differences between the two passages clearly reflect that John recognizes a transcendent aspect to the new world not evident in Isaiah. The new Jerusalem descends, death is abolished, and the sea is no more. Such themes reveal a radical distinction between this world and the world to come. Yet *complete* discontinuity between the old and the new is not advo-

---

[229]Beasely-Murray, *Revelation*, 300.

cated. The old is not a superfluous commodity.

Three primary reasons attest that John envisions a fulfillment rather than the destruction of the old world. First, the life in the new world is described as in 4 Ezra and Isaiah 65 in negative terms. The concern of the author is primarily that of a new world in which evil, death, suffering, and corruption of every kind have been banished. There is no spiritual-material dualism. Even the statement that the first heaven and earth and the "first things" have passed away does not suggest the complete destruction of the old and the creation *ex nihilo* of the new. The "first things," like Isaiah's "former troubles," includes the totality of life's ambivalences vanquished at the presence of God. Thus, the "new" involves more than merely a temporal understanding. What qualifies the new order as "new" for John is primarily a *new relationship* rather than a new *appearance*. God himself dwells among his people (21.3). The distinction between the old order and the new is the community relationship between God and his people.[230] Indeed, the presence of God will prohibit any need for the luminaries, "Because the Lord God shall illumine them and they shall reign forever and ever" (22.5). Second, God's pronouncement, "I am making all things new," reminds the readers, as in the visions of chapters 4 and 5, that renewal is already in process in the old. God makes *all things new* rather than *all new things!*[231] There is no myth of the eternal return. Third, a continuity is underscored by the depiction of the new age in a this-worldly manner. Certainly, Boring is correct that this is due in part to the fact that the "other" world can be understood only in terms of the language of this world.[232] Yet this language affirms the importance of the present world. The return of Paradise is clear in Rev. 22.1-5. The imagery is that of the OT with the river of paradise of Gen. 2.10 interpreted as the water of life. The tree of paradise drawing upon Ezek. 47.2, 12 is a picture of a renewed land. This is a time of great fruitfulness.

---

[230]Paul S. Minear, "The Cosmology of the Apocalypse," in *Current Issues in the New Testament*, ed. William Klassen and Graydon F. Snyder (New York: Harper, 1962), 27.

[231]The observation of Boring, *Revelation*, 220. Cf. Caird, *Revelation of St. John*, 265.

[232]Boring, *Revelation*, 220.

There no longer will be any curse on the earth and humanity's conflict with the natural world will be resolved. It is true that there is no explicit mention of the resolution of such conflict, but in John's use of Isaiah 65 this idea must have been assumed (cf. Isa. 65.25). In brief, the new creation, whatever it may entail specifically, will surely retain the constituent elements of the original creation. Soil, trees, oceans, mountain ranges, the world of insects and beasts; all of these components of creation are a part of God's original and ultimate plan. John's use of the paradisal motif therefore affirms that the one who is the first and last will restore his creation to conform to his original design. It reflects God's intention that his creation reach its τέλος. To dismiss the material aspect of redemption is to reject God as creator as affirmed in the throne vision of chapter 4 and indeed throughout the entire book.

> The salvation of individual souls is not, however, enough to vindicate the purposes of God. God is the Creator. . . . Merely to destroy what he has made would be a confession of failure, a negation of omnipotence. . . . The purpose of the Creator can be complete only when "the whole creation, everything in heaven and on earth and in the sea" joins in the worship of the heavenly choir (5.13).[233]

---

[233]Caird, *Revelation of St. John*

CHAPTER V
CREATION, REDEMPTION,
AND THE CHURCH

Summary and Conclusions

The thesis of this study affirms that the apocalyptic motif of the "new heavens and new earth" or cosmic redemption preserves an important and positive role for the present created order. The apocalyptists and biblical writers anticipated the renewal of creation. However, this hope did not reflect negatively upon the *present* natural order. Indeed, it actually affirmed its significance as a part of God's redemptive plan.

The discussion in the previous chapters has demonstrated that an overwhelming positive perspective toward the present creation prevails in apocalyptic and biblical writings. The OT writings witness that in the beginning God created the natural order "perfectly" good. However, due to humanity's transgression the creation has been impaired in some way and is thus unable to fulfill its original purpose. The impact of creation's plight is manifested especially in eschatological contexts which depict its suffering due to human sin and experiencing along with humanity the judgment of God. That the OT writers do not relegate the created order to a secondary status in God's redemptive work is witnessed most notably in the prophecies of Isaiah. It is significant, for example, that when Second Isaiah anticipates a new redemptive event for Israel, the dimensions of which are incomprehensible, he enlists creation language to express the meaning of the new and greater Exodus. Such does not suggest a subsidiary role to history. On the contrary, as Lindeskog suggested, the parallel between creation and redemption is drawn by Second Isaiah in order to emphasize the significance of the new Exodus by equating it with the greatest of God's acts--the creation of the world.[1] Thus creation even when brought together with redemptive history has its own singular significance. One could therefore say that Israel affirmed God as redeemer because only the creator and lord of both cosmos and history could once again bring order out of the present political chaos. This also clarifies how creation could serve as a *type* of God's new *creative* redemptive event. In fact, understood in this light, one might argue that in this case history actually serves creation (or at least complements it). Israel's deliverance from Exile as a new creation was a token of God's intention for the ultimate redemption of the created order from chaos (cf. Isa. 51; 65.17). Israel now is viewed not against the backdrop of history but is reintegrated into the order of God's creation.[2] Significantly, Isaiah 65 presents in the most vivid and comprehensive pictures God's salvation which embraces both humankind and the created order. This passage affirms that the creation has not become superfluous in light of individual or national deliverance.

The apocalyptic writings likewise maintain a positive interest in the created order. Contrary to popular opinion, the apocalyptists do not long to exchange the present world for some other. The writings of 1 Enoch, particularly chapters 1-5, reveal a concern more for righteous living in the present than an escape beyond the bounds of history. The writers are especially knowledgeable of the elements of creation and even point to their obedience as an example of proper conduct. Indeed, the creation is the only stable, obedient, and faithful aspect of a world otherwise gone awry. The apocalyptists, then, do not regard the cre-

---

[1] Lindeskog, "The Theology of Creation in the Old and New Testaments," , 5; Isa. 40.12-14, 21-23; 41.18-20; 43.15-21; 45.7-13; etc. Cf., Ph. B. Harner, "Creation Faith in Deutero-Isaiah," *VT* 17 (July 1967): 298-306. The NT writers certainly recognized that the best analogy to redemption was creation (2 Cor. 5.17; Gal. 6.15).

[2] Knierim, "Cosmos," 98.

ated order as hopeless but affirm it as above all "perfectly" good. This rejects the notion of an inherently fallen creation. The longing for a new creation, however, is due to the recognition that the creation has been impaired in some way by human and/or supernatural acts of rebellion and is thus unable to fulfill its τέλος. The visionaries stand within the OT dialectic of a good yet perverted creation. The hope for a new creation therefore reflects a healthy respect for God's creation and the desire to see it return to its proper place and role in God's plan.

Accordingly, the presence of creation motifs in eschatological passages accentuates the importance of creation. The writers often depict life in the new world in a this-worldly manner. However, this is more than merely the use of stock traditions in order to portray reality beyond the present world. The paradisal motifs attest that God intends to restore his creation according to his original design. Even works such as 4 Ezra, which displays a more radical break between this age and the age to come, often manifest a *material* continuity with the present creation. It is thus clear that the writers are not disposed toward a dualistic worldview. The emphasis upon the renewal of creation among the apocalyptists should not be surprising since, like the biblical writers, this conviction is predicated upon the doctrine of God as creator. God is both creator *and* redeemer who has not abandoned his creation but fully intends to bring it to fulfillment.

No one would argue that the NT writers intended to disparage the creation. However, this has been the natural consequence in light of the tendency of modern NT scholars to focus on anthropological issues at the expense of cosmic considerations. The NT writers believed that the natural order even in its impaired condition remained God's good creation. Furthermore, the motif of the "new heavens and new earth" or new creation in the NT attests that the creation has not become inconsequential in view of the emphasis on spiritual salvation. The full realization of the believer's new life in Christ is not limited to personal salvation in heaven. It also includes the cosmic reach which was rooted in the OT and apocalyptic understanding of God as creator who would not negate his creative artistry.

The NT authors' anticipation of the renewal or fulfillment

of creation therefore also reflects the abiding conviction that God is both creator *and* redeemer. The apocalyptic idea of cosmic hope, modified by the emphasis on Jesus the Christ as the agent in creation and redemption, served to evoke in the minds of the writers the expectation of God's holistic salvation embracing both humanity and the created order. Redemption therefore has a cosmic purpose, namely, that God will "reconcile all things to Himself, having made peace through the blood of the cross; . . . whether things on earth or things in heaven" (Col. 1.20). Indeed, no greater affirmation of creation can be stated than Paul's assertion that the created order, which was made *in*, and *by* Christ, has been through the cross reconciled and reoriented *toward* him. Therefore, the natural order finds fulfillment only in its divinely ordered relationship with its creator (Col. 1.16, 20). Furthermore, to state that the inauguration of the kingdom set in motion not only humanity's salvific process but that of the creation as well may sound eccentric to some but in fact the resurrection of Christ serves as the pledge that God has already begun to reclaim his creation.

The Church and the Creation

Christians who take seriously their participation in God's *cosmic* work of salvation must so order their lives in accordance with this universal scope of redemption. Such a view has far reaching implications concerning the present conservation of the environment. God's creation is worth preserving, and whatever the transformation of the new heavens and new earth may involve, it includes primarily a cleansing of all that opposes God and perverts creation's purpose. A longing for the new creation therefore does not indicate the rejection of a "this worldly" existence. This is certainly not the tradition of the Hebrew and Christian scriptures. Earthly existence is good. Contrary to Greek dualism which viewed salvation as an escape from earthly life, the biblical and apocalyptic writers always place redeemed humanity on a renewed earth rather than in a celestial realm far removed from an earthly habitation.[3] Indeed, theolo-

---

[3]George E. Ladd, *A Commentary on the Revelation of John* (Grand

gies which overemphasize the future heavenly existence of the believer tend to lessen one's sense of responsibility for the present natural order. It is therefore evident that the world and its ultimate redemption must not be neglected, for as Rissi appropriately observes, "with the elimination of the hope for a future re-creation of the world, the whole biblical belief in the creation in its all-embracing significance collapses."[4] Such an *eschatological* ecological perspective of creation will lead to a radical change in one's attitude toward the present *and* future creation.[5] One implication noted by Gowan is that if one takes seriously the scripture's vision of the future "as the key to what God wants, then any arbitrary or irresponsible hurting or destroying of anything *in this world* must surely be judged as contrary to what God is doing."[6] God's creation is good and as creator he is committed to bringing both creation as well as humankind's history to fulfillment. In fact, as seen especially in the discussion on Romans 8 and Colossians 1 and even the NT Apocalypse, their destinies are dynamically interrelated.

Decisions for the Christian no longer relate merely to spiritual matters; they include the material as well. Therefore, if God is both creator *and* redeemer, then Christian commitment involves, among other things, effective evangelism *and* responsible environmentalism. Any other response in effect rejects the goodness of God's creation and dishonors the Christ through whom "all things" were made (John 1.3; Heb. 1.2) and reconciled (Col. 1.20). Further, irresponsible attitudes and actions toward the created order ultimately robs humanity of its own dignity as created in God's image to inhabit this world and hence to "image" God's will and design (Gen. 1.26, 27).

Rapids: Eerdmans, 1972), 275.
  [4]Rissi, *The Future of the World*, 104 n. 165.
  [5]See the comments of Moltmann, "Creation and Redemption," 119-34.
  [6]Gowan, *Eschatology*, 109 (emphasis mine).

SELECTED BIBLIOGRAPHY

Primary Sources

Biblical Sources

Aland, Kurt, Matthew Black, Bruce Metzger, and Allen Wikgren, eds. *The Greek New Testament*. 3d cor. ed. New York: United Bible Society, 1975.

Elliger, K. and W. Rudolf, eds. *Biblia Hebraica Stuttgartensia*. Stuttgart: Deutsch Biblestiftung, 1966.

Nestle, Eberhard, Erwin Nestle, and Kurt Aland, eds. *Novum Testamentum Graece*. 26th ed. Stuttgart: Deutsch Bibelstiftung, 1979.

Rahlfs, Alfred, ed. *Septuaginta*. 2 vols. Stuttgart: Württembergische Bibelanstalt, 1935.

Weavers, John H., ed. *Genesis*. Septuaginta. Vetus Testamentum Graecum Autoritate Academiae Scientiarum Gottingensis editum. Göttingen: Vandenhoeck & Ruprecht, 1974.

Ziegler, Joseph, ed. *Duodecim Prophetae*. Septuaginta. Vetus Testamentum Graecum Autoritate Academiae Scientiarum Gottingensis editum. Göttingen: Vandenhoeck & Ruprecht, 1943.

_____, ed. *Isaias*. Septuaginta. Vetus Testamentum Graecum Autoritate Academiae Scientiarum Gottingensis editum. Göttingen: Vandenhoeck & Ruprecht, 1983.

Jewish Sources

Black, Matthew. *Apocalypsis Henochi Graece: Fragmenta Pseudepigraphorum quae supersunt Graeca*. Pseudepigrapha Veteris Testamenti Graece, no. 3. Leiden: Brill, 1970.

_____. *The Book of Enoch or 1 Enoch: A New English Edition*. With an Appendix on the "Astronomical Chapters" (72-82) by Otto Neughbaur. Studia in Veteris Testamenti Pseudepigrapha, no. 7. Leiden: Brill, 1985.

Box, G. H. *The Ezra-Apocalypse*. London: Pitman, 1912.

Cathcart, Kevin, Michael Maher, and Martin McNamara, ed. *The Aramaic Bible: The Targums*. Wilmington, DE: Glazier,

1987.

Charles, R. H. *The Book of Jubilees or the Little Genesis.* London: Adam & Charles Black, 1902.

_____. *The Book of Enoch or 1 Enoch.* 2d ed. Oxford: Clarendon, 1912.

_____. *The Apocrypha and Pseudepigrapha of the Old Testament.* 2 vols. Oxford: Clarendon, 1913.

Charlesworth, James H., ed. *The Old Testament Pseudepigrapha.* 2 vols. New York: Doubleday, 1983-85.

Dupont-Sommer, André. *The Essene Writings from Qumran.* Translated by Geza Vermes. Oxford: Basil Blackwell, 1961.

Josephus. *The Life, Against Apion, and the Jewish War.* 10 vols. Edited and translated by H. St. J. Thackery. Loeb Classical Library, Greek Series. Cambridge: Harvard University, 1976.

Klijn, A. F. J., ed. *Der Lateinische Text Der Apokalypse Des Esra.* Mit einem Index Grammaticus von Gerard Mussies. Texte und Untersuchungen, no. 131. Berlin: Akademie, 1983.

Knibb, Michael A. *The Ethiopic Book of Enoch: A New Edition in Light of the Aramaic Dead Sea Fragments.* 2 vols. Oxford: Clarendon, 1978.

Leaney, A. R. C. *The Rule of Qumran and Its Meaning: Introduction, Translation, and Commentary.* New Testament Library. Philadelphia: Westminster, 1966.

Lohse, Eduard, ed. *Die Text aus Qumran.* 4th ed. Munich: Kösel, 1986.

Milik, J. T., ed., Matthew Black, collaborator. *The Books of Enoch: Aramaic Fragments of Qumran Cave 4.* Oxford: Clarendon, 1976.

Philo of Alexandria. *Works.* 10 vols. Translated by F. H. Colson and G. H. Whitaker. Loeb Classical Library, Greek Series. Cambridge: Harvard University, 1929-62.

Sukenik, E. L., ed. *The Dead Sea Scrolls of the Hebrew University.* Jerusalem: Magnes, 1955.

Uhlig, Siegbert. *Das äthiopische Henochbuch.* Jüdische Schriften aus hellenistisch-römimischen Zeit, no. 5. Gütersloh: Mohn, 1984.

VanderKam, James C. *The Book of Jubilees: A Critical Text and Translation*. 2 vols. Corpus scriptorium christianorum orientalium, nos. 510-11. Leuven: Peeters, 1989.

Vermes, Geza. *The Dead Sea Scrolls in English*. 3d ed. London: Penguin, 1987.

Early Christian Sources

Hennecke, Edgar. *The New Testament Apocrypha*. 2 vols. Edited by Wilhelm Schneemelcher. Translated by R. McL. Wilson. Philadelphia: Westminster, 1963.

Lake, Kirsopp, trans. *The Apostolic Fathers*. 2 vols. Loeb Classical Library, Greek Series. New York: Putnam, 1976-77.

Marcovich, Miroslav, ed. *Hippolytus, Refutatio Omnium Haeresium*. Patristische Texte und Studien. New York: de Gruyter, 1986.

Greek and Hellenistic Sources

Arnim, J. von. *Stoicorum Veterum Fragmenta*. Indices by M. Adler. 4 vols. Leipzig: Teubner, 1921-24.

Berkowitz, Luci and K. A. Squitter. *Thesaurus Linguae Graecae: Canon of Greek Authors and Works*. 3d ed. New York: Oxford, 1990.

Plutarch. *Moralia*. 16 vols. Translated by Frank Cole Babbitt, Harold Chreniss, W. C. Helmbold, Paul A. Clement, Herbert B. Hoffleit, Edwin L. Minar, Jr., F. H. Sandbach, Lionel Pearson, Harold North Fowler, Benedict Einarson, and Phillip H. De Lacy. Loeb Classical Library, Greek Series. Cambridge: Harvard University, 1962-76.

Plato. *Timaeus, Critias, Cleitophon, Menexenus Epistles*. Vol. 9. Translated by R. G. Bury. Loeb Classical Library, Greek Series. Cambridge: Harvard University, 1929.

Thesaurus Linguae Graecae Pilot CD ROM #C. Irvine: University of California, 1987.

Reference Works

Aland, Kurt. *Vollständige Konkordanz zur Griechischen Neuen*

Testament. 3 vols. Berlin: de Gruyter, 1978-83.

_____. *Synopsis Quattuor Evangeliorum.* 13th ed. Stuttgart: Deutsche Bibelanstalt, 1985.

Blass, F. and A. Debrunner. *A Greek Grammar of the New Testament.* Translated and Revised by Robert W. Funk. Chicago: University of Chicago, 1961.

Denis, Albert-Marie, ed., and Yvonne Janssens, collaborator. *Concordance Grecque des Pseudépigraphes D'Ancien Testament.* Louvain: Université catholique, 1987.

Gesenuis, Wilhelm. *Gesenuis' Hebrew Grammar.* 2d English ed. Edited by E. Kautzsch. Translated by A. E. Cowley. Oxford: Clarendon, 1910.

Kuhn, Karl Georg, ed. *Konkordanz zum den Qumrantexten.* Göttingen: Vandenhoeck & Ruprecht, 1960.

Lisouwsky, Gerhard. *Kornkordanz zum Hebräischen Alten Testament.* Stuttgart: Privi-legierte Württembergische Bibelanstalt, 1958.

Louw, Johannes P. and Eugene A. Nida. *Greek-English Lexicon of the New Testament Based on Semantic Domains.* 2 vols. New York: United Bible Societies, 1988-89.

Metzger, Bruce M. *A Textual Commentary on the Greek New Testament.* New York: United Bible Societies, 1971.

Robertson, A. T. *A Grammar of the Greek New Testament in the Light of Historical Research.* 4th ed. Nashville: Broadman, 1938.

Turner, Nigel. *Syntax.* Vol 3. *A Grammar of New Testament Greek.* Edited by James H.Moulton. Edinburgh: T. & T. Clark, 1963.

Secondary Sources

Monographs

Anderson, Bernhard W. *Creation Versus Chaos: The Reinterpretation of Mythical Symbolism in the Bible.* New York: Association, 1967.

Austin, Richard Cartwright. *Hope for the Land: Nature in the Bible.* Environmental Theology Book Series, no. 3. Atlanta: John Knox, 1988.

Bandstra, A. J. *The Law and the Elements of the World: An Exegetical Study in Aspects of Paul's Teaching*. Kampen: H. H. Kok, 1964.

Barr, James. *Semantics of Biblical Language*. London: SCM, 1961.

Barrett, C. K. *The Holy Spirit in the Gospel Tradition*. 2d ed. London: SPCK, 1966.

Barth, Karl. *Church Dogmatics*. 4 vols. Translated by G. W. Bromiley. Edited by G. W. Bromiley and T. F. Torrance. Edinburgh: T. & T. Clark, 1975.

Beasley-Murray, G. R. *Jesus and the Kingdom of God*. Grand Rapids: Eerdmans, 1986.

Beker, J. Christiaan. *Paul the Apostle: The Triumph of God in Life and Thought*. Philadelphia: Fortress, 1984.

————. *Paul's Apocalyptic Gospel: The Coming Triumph of God*. Philadelphia: Fortress, 1982.

Berkouwer, G. C. *The Return of Christ*. Translated by James van Oosterom. Studies in Dogmatics. Grand Rapids: Eerdmans, 1972.

Black, Matthew. *An Aramaic Approach to the Gospels and Acts*. 3d ed. Oxford: Clarendon, 1967.

————. *The Scrolls and Christian Origins: Studies in the Jewish Background of the New Testament*. Brown Judaic Studies, no. 48. New York: Scribner, 1961; reprint, Chico, CA: Scholars, 1983.

Bousset, Wilhelm. *Die Religion des Judentums im neutestamentlichen Zeitalter*. Handbuch zum Neuen Testament, no. 21. Edited by Hugo Gressmann. Berlin: Reuter & Reichard, 1906.

Brueggemann, Walter. *The Land: Place as Gift, Promise, and Challenge in Biblical Faith*. Overtures to Biblical Theology. Philadelphia: Fortress, 1977.

Bultmann, Rudolf. *Jesus Christ and Mythology*. New York: Scribner, 1958.

————. *The History of the Synoptic Tradition*. rev. ed. Translated by John Marsh. New York: Harper & Row, 1963.

Burney, C. F. *The Aramaic Origin of the Fourth Gospel*. Oxford: Clarenden, 1922.

Caird, G. B. *The Language and Imagery of the Bible*.

Philadelphia: Westminster, 1980.

Charles, R. H. *Religious Development Between the Old and New Testaments*. New York: Holt, 1914.

_____. *Eschatology: The Doctrine of a Future Life in Judaism and Christianity: A Critical History*. New York: Schocken, 1963.

Charlesworth, James H., ed. *The Pseudepigrapha and Modern Research with a Supplement*. Society of Biblical Literature Series in Septuagint and Cognate Studies, no. 7S. Missoula, MT: Scholars, 1976; reprint, Chico, CA: Scholars, 1981.

Charlesworth, James H. and James R. Muell. *The New Testament Apocrypha and Pseudepigrapha: A Guide to Publications, with Excurses on Apocalypses*, ed. James H. Charlesworth and James R. Mueller, 19-51. Atla Bibliography, no. 17. Metuchen, NJ: American Theological Library Association and Scarecrow, 1987.

Childs, S. Brevard. *Myth and Reality in the Old Testament*. London: SCM, 1960.

_____. *Introduction to the Old Testament as Scripture*. Philadelphia: Fortress, 1979.

Clements, Ronald E. *God's Chosen People: A Theological Interpretation of the Book of Deuteronomy*. London: SCM, 1968.

Cobb, John B. Jr. *Is It Too Late? A Theology of Ecology*. Beverly Hills, CA: Bruce, 1972.

Collins, Adela Yarbro. *The Combat Myth in the Book of Revelation*. Missoula, MT: Scholars, 1976.

_____. *Crisis and Catharsis: The Power of the Apocalypse*. Philadelphia: Westminster, 1984.

Collins, John J. *Sibylline Oracles of Egyptian Judaism*. Society of Biblical Literature Dissertation Series, no. 13. Missoula, MT: Scholars, 1974.

_____. *The Apocalyptic Imagination: An Introduction to the Jewish Matrix of Christianity*. New York: Crossroad, 1984.

Collins, John J., ed. *Apocalypse: The Morphology of a Genre*. Semeia, no. 14. Missoula, MT: Scholars, 1979.

Court, John M. *Myth and History in the Book of Revelation*. Atlanta: John Knox, 1979.

Crenshaw, James L. *Studies in Ancient Israelite Wisdom*. New York: KTAV, 1976.

_____. *Old Testament Wisdom: An Introduction*. Atlanta: John Knox, 1981.

Cross, Frank Moore. *The Ancient Library of Qumran and Modern Biblical Studies*. rev. ed. New York: Doubleday, 1961; reprint, Grand Rapids: Baker, 1980.

Cullmann, Oscar. *Christ and Time: The Primitive Christian Conception of Time and History*. rev. ed. Translated by Floyd V. Filson. Philadelphia: Westminster, 1964.

Davenport, Gene L. *The Eschatology of the Book of Jubilees*. Studia Post-Biblica, no. 20. Leiden: Brill, 1971.

Davies, W. D. *The Gospel and the Land: Early Christianity and Jewish Territorial Doctrine*. Berkeley: University of California, 1974.

_____. *The Territorial Dimensions of Judaism*. Berkeley: University of California, 1982.

_____. *Paul and Rabbinic Judaism: Some Rabbinic Elements in Pauline Theology*. 4th ed. Philadelphia: Fortress, 1980.

_____. *The Setting of the Sermon on the Mount*. Brown Judaic Studies, no. 186. Atlanta: Scholars, 1989; reprint, Cambridge: Cambridge University, 1966.

Davies, W. D. and David Daube, ed. *The Background of the New Testament and Its Eschatology*. Cambridge: University, 1956.

Day, John. *God's Conflict with the Dragon and the Sea*. Cambridge: Cambridge University, 1985.

De Vries, Simon J. *The Achievements of Biblical Religions: A Prolegomenon to Old Testament Theology*. New York: University Press of America, 1983.

Dexinger, Ferdinand. *Henochs Zehnwochenapokalypse und Offene Probleme der Apokalyptikforschung*. Studia Post-Biblica. Leiden: Brill, 1977.

Dodd, C. H. *The Bible and the Greeks*. London: Hodder & Stroughten, 1935.

Dumbrell, William J. *The End of the Beginning: Revelation 21-22 and the Old Testament*. Grand Rapids: Baker, 1985.

Dunn, James D. G. *Baptism in the Holy Spirit*. Studies in Bibilical Theology, no. 15. Naperville, IL: Allenson, 1970.

_____. *Unity and Diversity in the New Testament*. 2d ed. London: SCM, 1990.

Eichrodt, Walter. *Theology of the Old Testament*. 2 vols. Translated by J. A. Baker. Philadelphia: Westminster, 1961-67.

Eliade, Mircea. *The Myth of the Eternal Return*. Translated by Willard Trask. Bollingen Series, no. 46. New York: Pantheon, 1954.

Farrer, Austin. *A Rebirth of Images: The Making of St. John's Apocalypse*. Boston: Beacon, 1963.

Fornberg, Tord. *An Early Church in a Pluralistic Society: A Study of 2 Peter*. Coniectanea Biblica, New Testament Series, no. 9. Lund: Gleerup, 1977.

Fuller, Reginald H. *Interpreting the Miracles*. Philadelphia: Fortress, 1963.

Funk, Robert W. *Parables and Presence: Forms of the New Testament Tradition*. Philadelphia: Fortress, 1982.

Galloway, Allen D. *The Cosmic Christ*. New York: Harper & Bros., 1951.

Gaster, Theodor H. *The Dead Sea Scriptures*. New York: Doubleday, 1956.

Gibbs, John G. *Creation and Redemption: A Study in Pauline Theology*. Leiden: Brill, 1971.

Gilkey, Langdon. *Maker of Heaven and Earth: A Study of the Christian Doctrine of Creation*. New York: Doubleday, 1959.

Glasson, Thomas F. *His Appearing and His Kingdom: The Christian Hope in the Light of Its History*. London: Epworth, 1953.

_____. *Greek Influence in Jewish Eschatology: With Special Reference to the Apocalypses and Pseudepigraphs*. London: SPCK, 1961.

_____. *Jesus and the End of the World*. Edinburgh: St. Andrew, 1980.

Green, E. M. B. *2 Peter Reconsidered*. rev. ed. London: Tyndale, 1987.

Goldingay, John. *Theological Diversity and the Authority of the Old Testament*. Grand Rapids: Eerdmans, 1987.

Goppelt, Leonhard. *Typos: The Typological Interpretation of the Old Testament in the New*. Translated by Donald H. Madvig. Grand Rapids: Eerdmans, 1982.

_____. *Theology of the New Testament*. 2 vols. Edited by John Alsup. Translated by Jürgen Roloff. Grand Rapids: Eerdmans, 1981-82.

Gowan, Donald E. *Eschatology in the Old Testament*. Philadelphia: Fortress, 1986.

Gunkel, Hermann. *Schöpfung und Chaos in Urzeit und Endzeit: Eine religionsgeschichtliche Untersuchung über Gen. 1 und Ap. Joh. 12*. Gottingen: Vandenhoeck & Ruprecht, 1895.

Hahm, David E. *The Origins of Stoic Cosmology*. Columbus: Ohio State University, 1977.

Hasel, Gerhard F. *Old Testament Theology: Basic Issues in the Current Debate*. rev. ed. Grand Rapids: Eerdmans, 1975.

Hanson, Paul D. *The Dawn of Apocalyptic: The Historical and Sociological Roots of Jewish Apocalyptic Eschatology*. rev. ed. Philadelphia: Fortress, 1979.

Harrelson, Walter. *From Fertility Cult to Worship*. Garden City, NY: Doubleday, 1969.

Hartman, Lars. *Asking for a Meaning: A Study of 1 Enoch 1-5*. Coniectanea Biblica, New Testament Series, no. 12. Lund: Gleerup, 1979.

Hayes, John H. and Frederick Prussner. *Old Testament Theology: Its History and Development*. Atlanta: John Knox, 1985.

Hays, Zachary. *What Are They Saying About Creation?* New York: Paulist, 1980.

Heim, Karl. *The World: Its Creation and Consummation*. Translated by Robert Smith. London: Oliver & Boyd, 1962.

Hellholm, David, ed. *Apocalypticism in the Mediterranean World and the Near East*. Tübingen: Mohr, 1983.

Hendry, George S. *Theology of Nature*. Philadelphia: Westminster, 1980.

Hengel, Martin. *Judaism and Hellenism: Studies in Their Encounter in Palestine During the Early Hellenistic Period*. Translated by John Bowden. 1 vol. ed. Philadelphia: Fortress, 1981.

Hoekema, Anthony A. *The Bible and the Future*. Grand Rapids: Eerdmans, 1979.

Holm-Nielsen, Svend. *Hodayot: Psalms from Qumran*. Aarhus:

Universitetsforlaget, 1960.

Hooker, Morna D. *Jesus and the Servant: The Influence of the Servant Concept of Deutero-Isaiah in the New Testament.* London: SPCK, 1959.

_____. *The Son of Man in Mark.* Montreal: McGill University, 1967.

Jacob, Edmond. *Theology of the Old Testament.* Translated by Arthur W. Heathcote and Philip J. Allcock. New York: Harper and Bros., 1958.

Jeremias, Joachim. *New Testament Theology.* Vol. 1. Translated by John Bowden. New York: Scribner, 1971.

Jeremias, Jörg. *Theophanie: Die Geschichte einer Alttestamentlichen Gattung.* Wissen-schaftliche Monogragraphien zum Alten und Neuen Testament. Neukirchen-Vluyn: Neukirchener, 1965.

Johnson, A. R. *Sacral Kingship in Ancient Israel.* Cardiff: University of Wales, 1955.

Johnson, Dan G. *From Chaos to Restoration: An Integrative Reading of Isaiah 24-27.* Journal for the Study of the Old Testament Supplement Series, no. 61. Sheffield: University of Sheffield, 1988.

Kallas, James. *The Significance of the Synoptic Miracles.* Greenwich, CT: Seabury, 1961.

Kim, Seyoon. *The Origin of Paul's Gospel.* Wissenschaftliche Untersuchungen zum Neuen Testament. Tübingen: Mohr, 1981.

Kittel, Bonnie Pedrotti. *The Hymns of Qumran: Translation and Commentary.* Society of Bibilical Literature Dissertation Series, no. 50. Chico, CA: Scholars, 1975.

Koch, Klaus. *The Rediscovery of Apocalyptic.* Translated by Margaret Kohl. Naperville, IL: Allenson, 1970.

Koehler, Ludwig. *Old Testament Theology.* Translated by A. S. Todd. Philadelphia: Westminster, 1957.

Kuhn, H. W. *Enderwartung und Gegenwärtiges Heil: Untersuchungen zu den Gemeindeliedern von Qumran mit einem Anhang über Eschatologie und Gegenwart in der erkündigung Jesu.* Studien zur Umwelt des Neuen estaments, no. 4. Göttingen: Vandenhoeck & Ruprecht, 1966.

Kümmel, Werner Georg. *Promise and Fulfillment: The Escha-*

tological Message of Jesus. Translated by Dorothea M. Barton. rev. ed. London: SCM, 1957.

_____. *The Theology of the New Testament*. Translated by John E. Steely. Nashville: Abingdon, 1973.

_____. *Introduction to the New Testament*. rev. ed. Translated by Howard Clark Kee. Nashville: Abingdon, 1975.

Ladd, George Eldon. *The Presence of the Future: The Eschatology of Biblical Realism*. rev. ed. Grand Rapids: Eerdmans, 1974.

LaSor, William S., David A. Hubbard and Frederic Wm. Bush. *Old Testament Survey*. Grand Rapids: Eerdmans, 1983.

Leaney, A. R. C. *The Rule of Qumran and Its Meaning*. New Testament Library. Philadelphia: Westminster, 1966.

Levenson, Jon D. *Creation and Persistence of Evil: The Jewish Drama of Divine Omnipotence*. San Francisco: Harper & Row, 1988.

Lindeskog, Gösta. *Studien zum Neutestamentlichen Schopfungsgedanken*. Vol. 1. Uppsala: Lundequistika, 1952.

Lücke, Friedrich. *Versuch einer vollständingen Einleitung in die Offenbarung Johannisund in die gesamte apokalyptische Literature*. Bonn: Weber, 1832.

Manson, T. W. *The Sayings of Jesus*. London: SCM, 1949.

Mayer, Rudolf. *Die biblische Vorstellung vom Weltbrand: Eine Untersuchung über die Beziehungen zwischen Parismus und Judentum*. Bonn: Bonn University, 1956.

Merrill, Eugene H. *Qumran and Predestination: A Theological Study of the Thanksgiving Hymns*. Studies on the Texts of the Desert of Judea, no. 8. Leiden: Brill, 1975.

Millar, William R. *Isaiah 24-27 and the Origin of Apocalyptic*. Harvard Semitic Mono-graphs, no. 11. Missoula, MT: Scholars, 1976.

Minear, Paul S. *New Testament Apocalyptic*. Interpreting Biblical Texts. Nashville: Abingdon, 1981.

Moltmann, Jürgen. *Theology of Hope*. New York: Harper & Row, 1965.

_____. *God in Creation: A New Theology of Creation and the Spirit of God*. Translat-ed by Margaret Kohl. San Francisco: Harper & Row, 1985.

Monsoor, Menahem. *The Thanksgiving Hymns: Translation and*

Annotation with an Introduction. Studies on the Texts of the Desert of Judea, no. 3. Grand Rapids: Eerdmans, 1961.

Morris, Leon. *The Cross in the New Testament.* Grand Rapids: Eerdmans, 1965.

_____. *Apocalyptic.* Grand Rapids: Eerdmans, 1972.

Moule, C. F. D. *Man and Nature in the New Testament.* London: Athlone, 1964.

Mowinckel, Sigmund. *He That Cometh.* Translated by G. W. Anderson. New York: Abingdon, 1956.

_____. *The Psalms in Israel's Worship.* 2 vols. Translated by A. R. Ap-Thomas. New York: Abingdon, 1962.

Nickelsburg, George W. E. *Jewish Literature Between the Bible and the Mishnah.* Philadelphia: Fortress, 1981.

Perrin, Norman. *Jesus and the Language of the Kingdom: Symbol and Metaphor in New Testament Interpretation.* Philadelphia: Fortress, 1976.

Plöger, Otto. *Theocracy and Eschatology.* Translated by S. Rudman. Richmond: John Knox, 1968.

Rad, Gerhard von. *Old Testament Theology.* 2 vols. Translated by D. M. G. Stalker. New York: Harper, 1962-65.

Reumann, John. *Creation and Redemption: The Past, Present, and Future of God's Creative Activity.* Minneapolis, MN: Augsburg, 1973.

Ridderbos, Hermann. *Paul and Jesus: Origin and General Character of Paul's Preaching of Christ.* Translated by David H. Freeman. Grand Rapids: Eerdmans, 1958.

_____. *Paul: An Outline of His Theology.* Translated by John Richard De Witt. Grand Rapids: Eerdmans, 1975.

Ringgren, Helmer. *The Faith of Qumran: Theology of the Dead Sea Scrolls.* Translated by Emilie T. Sander. Philadelphia: Fortress, 1963.

Rissi, Mathias. *The Future of the World: An Exegetical Study of Revelation 19:11-22:15.* Studies in Biblical Theology, 2d series, no. 20. Naperville, IL: Allenson, 1972.

Robertson, A. T. *Word Pictures in the New Testament.* 6 vols. Nashville: Broadman, 1931.

Robinson, H. Wheeler. *Inspiration and Revelation in the Old Testament.* Oxford: Clarendon, 1946.

Robinson, J. A. T. *In the End, God: A Study of the Christian Doc-*

trine of the Last Things. New York: Harper & Row, 1968.

Rogerson, J. W. *Myth in Old Testament Interpretation*. Beihefte zur Zeitschrift für die alttestamentliche Wissenschaft, no. 134. Berlin: De Gruyter, 1974.

Rowland, Christopher. *The Open Heaven: A Study of Apocalyptic in Judaism and Early Christianity*. New York: Crossroad, 1982.

Rowley, H. H. *The Relevance of Apocalyptic: A Study of Jewish and Christian Apocalypses from Daniel to the Revelation*. 2d ed. New York: Association, 1963.

_____. *Worship in Ancient Israel: Its Forms and Meaning*. Philadelphia: Fortress, 1967.

_____. *Jewish Apocalyptic and the Dead Sea Scrolls*. London: Althone, 1957.

Russell, D. S. *The Method and Message of Jewish Apocalyptic, 200 B.C.-A.D. 100*. Old Testamant Library. Philadelphia: Westminister, 1976.

_____. *Apocalyptic: Ancient and Modern*. Philadelphia: Fortress, 1978.

Rust, Eric. C. *Nature and Man in Biblical Thought*. London: Lutterworth, 1953.

_____. *Nature--Garden Or Desert? An Essay in Environmental Theology*. Waco: Word, 1971.

Sanders, E. P. *Paul and Palestinian Judaism: A Comparison of Patterns of Religion*. Philadelphia: Fortress, 1977.

Santmire, H. Paul. *Brother Earth: Nature, God and Ecology in Time of Crisis*. New York: Nelson, 1972.

_____. *The Travail of Nature: The Ambiguous Ecological Promise of Christian Theology*. Philadelphia: Fortress, 1985.

Schnackenburg, Rudolf. *God's Rule and Kingdom*. New York: Herder & Herder, 1963.

Shürer, Emil. *The History of the Jewish People in the Age of Jesus Christ (175 B.C.- A.D. 135)*. 3 vols. A new English Version revised and edited by Geza Vermes, Fergus Millar, Matthew Black, and Martin Goodman. Edinburgh: T. & T. Clark, 1979-87.

Sittler, Joseph A. *Essays on Nature and Grace*. Philadelphia: Fortress, 1972.

Sloan, Robert B. *The Favorable Year of the Lord: A Study of Jubilary Theology in the Gospel of Luke*. Austin: Schola, 1977.

Stadelmann, Luis I. J. *The Hebrew Conception of the World: A Philological and Literary Study*. Analecta Biblica, no. 39. Rome: Pontifical Biblical Institute, 1970.

Stauffer, Ethelbert. *New Testament Theology*. Translated by J. Marsh. New York: MacMillan & Co., 1955.

Steck, Odil H. *Der Schöpfungsbericht Der Priesterschrift*. Forschungen zur Religion und Literatur des Alten und Neuen Testaments, no. 15. Göttingen: Vandenhoeck und Ruprecht, 1975.

_____. World and Environment. Biblical Encounter Series. Nashville: Abingdon, 1980.

Stewart, Claude Y. Jr. *Nature in Grace: A Study in the Theology of Nature*. National Association of Baptist Professors of Religion Dissertation Series, no. 3. Macon, GA: Mercer University, 1983.

Stone, Michael E. *The Features of the Eschatology of IV Ezra*. Harvard Semitic Studies, no. 35. Atlanta: Scholars, 1989.

Testuz, Michael. *Les Idées Religieuses du Livre des Jubiles*. Geneva: Droz, 1960.

Tillich, Paul. *Theology of Culture*. Edited by Robert C. Kimball. New York: Oxford University, 1959.

VanderKam, James C. *Textual and Historical Studies in the Book of Jubilees*, Harvard Semitic Monographs, no. 14. Missoula, MT: Scholars, 1977.

_____. *Enoch and The Growth of an Apocalyptic Tradition*. Washington, DC: The Catholic Biblical Association of America, 1984.

Vögtle, Anton. *Das Neue Testament und die Zukunft des Kosmos*. Düsseldorf: Patmos, 1970.

Vriezen, Th. C. *An Outline of Old Testament Theology*. 2d. ed. rev. Newton, MA: Branford, 1970.

Weiss, Hans-Friedrich. *Untersuchungen zur Kosmologie des hellenistischen und palästinensischen Judentums*. Texte und Untersuchungen, no. 97. Berlin: Akademie, 1966.

Westermann, Claus. *The Genesis Accounts of Creation*. Translated by Norman E. Wagner. Philadelphia: Fortress, 1964.

_____. *Beginning and End in the Bible*. Translated by Keith
    Crim. Philadelphia: Fortress, 1972.
_____. *Blessing: In the Bible and the Life of the Church*.
    Translated by Keith Crim. Philadelphia: Fortress, 1978.
_____. *Elements of Old Testament Theology*. Translated by
    Douglas W. Scott. Atlanta: John Knox, 1982.
Wheelwright, Philip. *Metaphor and Reality*. Bloomington, IN:
    Indiana University, 1962.
Wolters, Albert M. *Creation Regained: Biblical Basics for a
    Reformational Worldview*. Grand Rapids: Eerdmans, 1985.
Wright. G. Ernest. *God Who Acts: Biblical Theology as Recital*.
    Studies in Biblical Theology. London: SCM, 1952.
_____. *The Old Testament and Theology*. New York: Harper
    & Row, 1969.
Yoder, John H. *The Politics of Jesus*. Grand Rapids: Eerdmans,
    1972.
Zimmerli, Walther. *Old Testament Theology in Outline*. Translat-
    ed by David E. Green Atlanta: John Knox, 1978.

Essays and Journal Articles

Aalen, Sverre. "'Reign' and 'House' in the Kingdom of God in
    the Gospels." *New Testament Studies* 8 (April 1962): 215-
    40.
Achtemeier, Paul J. "Person and Deed: Jesus and the Storm-
    Tossed Sea." *Interpretation* 16 (April 1962): 169-76.
Andersen, F. I. "2 Enoch." In *The Old Testament Pseude-
    pigrapha*. Vol. 1, *Apocalyptic Literature and Testaments*,
    ed. James H. Charlesworth, 91-100. New York: Doubleday,
    1983.
Anderson, Bernhard W. "The Earth is the Lord's." *Interpretation*
    9 (January 1955): 3-20.
_____. "Exodus Typology in Second Isaiah." In *Israel's
    Prophetic Heritage*, ed. Bernhard W. Anderson and Walter
    Harrelson, 177-95. New York: Harper & Bros., 1962.
_____. "Human Dominion over Nature." In *Biblical Studies
    in Contemporary Thought*, ed. Miriam Ward, 27-45.
    Somerville, MA: Greeno Hadden, & Co., 1975.
_____. "A Stylistic Study of the Priestly Creation Story." In

Canon and Authority: Essays on Old Testament Religion and Theology, ed. George W. Coats and Burke O. Long, 148-62. Philadelphia: Fortress, 1977.

_____. "Creation and Ecology." In *Creation in the Old Testament*, ed. Bernhard W. Anderson, 152-71. Issues in Religion and Theology, no. 6. Philadelphia: Fortress, 1984.

_____. "Cosmic Dimensions of the Genesis Account." *Drew Gateway* 56 (Spring 1986): 1-13.

Anderson, G. W. "Isaiah XXIV-XXVII Reconsidered." In the *Congress Volume*, 118-26. Supplements to Vetus Testamentum, no. 9. Leiden: Brill, 1963.

Bald, Hans. "Eschatological or Theocentric Ethics? Notes on the Relationship between Eschatology and Ethics in Jesus' Preaching." In *The Kingdom of God in the Teaching of Jesus*, ed. Bruce Chilton, 133-53. Issues in Religion and Theology, no. 5. Philadelphia: Fortress, 1984.

Barker, Margaret. "Slippery Words: Apocalyptic." *Expository Times* 89 (July 1978): 324-29.

Barnard, L. W. "The Judgement in II Peter iii." *Expository Times* 68 (July 1958): 302.

Barr, James. "Man and Nature--the Ecological Controversy and the Old Testament." *Bulletin of the John Rylands University Library of Manchester* 55 (Autumn 1972): 9-32.

_____. "The Question of Religious Influence: The Case of Zoroastrianism, Judaism, and Christianity." *Journal of the American Academy of Religion* 53 (March 1985): 201-35.

Bauckham, Richard J. "The Eschatological Earthquake in the Apocalypse of John." *Novum Testamentum* 19 (July 1977): 224-33.

_____. "The Rise of Apocalyptic." *Themelios* 3 (January 1978): 10-23.1

_____. "First Steps to a Theology of Nature." *Evangelical Quarterly* 58 (July 1986): 229-44.

Baumgarten, Joseph M. "The Calendar of the Book of Jubilees and the Bible" In *Studies in Qumran Law*, 101-14. Studies in Judaism in Late Antiquity, no. 24. Leiden: Brill, 1977.

Beasley-Murray, Paul. "Colossians 1.15-20: An Early Christian Hymn Celebrating the Lordship of Christ." In *Pauline Studies*, ed. Donald A. Hagner and Murray J. Harris, 169-

83. Grand Rapids: Eerdmans, 1980.

Benoit, Pierre. "L'hymne christologique de Col. 1.15-20." In *Christianity, Judaism and Other Greco-Roman Cults*, 4 vols., ed. Jacob Neusner, 1:226-63. Leiden: Brill, 1975.

Betz, Hans D. "On the Problem of the Religio-Historical Understanding of Apocalypticism." In *Apocalyptism*, ed. R. W. Funk, 134-56. Journal for Theology and the Church, no. 5. New York: Herder & Herder, 1969.

Black, Matthew. "The New Creation in 1 Enoch." In *Creation, Christ and Culture*, ed. Richard W. A. McKinney, 13-21. London: T. & T. Clark, 1976.

_____. "The Eschatology of the Similitudes of Enoch." *Journal of Theological Studies*, n.s. 3 (April 1952): 1-10.

_____. "The Apocalypse of Weeks in Light of 4QEn^g." *Vetus Testamentum* (October 1978): 464-69.

Boring, M. Eugene. "The Theology of Revelation: 'The Lord Our God Almighty Reigns.'" *Interpretation* 40 (July 1986): 257-69.

Box, G. H. "IV Ezra." In *The Apocrypha and Pseudepigrapha of the Old Testament*. Vol. 2, *Pseudepigrapha*, ed. R. H. Charles, 542-624. Oxford: Clarendon, 1913.

Bruce, F. F. "The Christ Hymn of Colossians 1.15-20." *Bibliotheca Sacra* 141 (April-June 1984): 99-111.

Bultmann, Rudolf. "The New Testament and Mythology." In *Kerygma and Myth: A Theological Debate*. Vol. 1. Edited by Hans Werner Bartsch. New York: Harper & Bros., 1961.

Burnett, Fred W. "Παλιγγενεσία in Matt. 19.28: A Window on the Matthean Community?" *Journal for the Study of the New Testament* 17 (February 1983): 60-72.

Burney, C. F. "Christ as the ΑΡΧΗ of Creation." *Journal of Theological Studies* 27 (January 1926): 160-77.

Carmignac, Jean. "Qu'est-ce que l'Apocalyptique? Son emploi à Qumrân." *Revue de Qumran* 37 (September 1979): 3-34.

Carnegie, David R. "Worthy is the Lamb: The Hymns in Revelation." In *Christ the Lord: Studies in Christology presented to Donald Guthrie*, ed. Harold H. Rowdon, 243-56. Downers Grove, IL: InterVarsity, 1982.

Chaine, Joseph. "Cosmogonie aquatique et conflagration finale d'après la secunda Petri." *Revue Biblique* 46 (1937):

207-16.

Charlesworth, James H. "The Apocalypse of John--Its Theology
and Impact on Subsequent Apocalypses." In *The New Testament Apocrypha and Pseudepigrapha: A Guide to Publications, with Excurses on Apocalypses*, ed. James H.
Charlesworth and James R. Mueller, 19-51. Atla Bibliography, no. 17. Metuchen, NJ: American Theological Library
Association and Scarecrow, 1987.

Clements, Ronald E. "The Unity of the Book of Isaiah." *Interpretation* 36 (April 1982): 117-29.

_____. "Beyond Tradition-History: Deutero-Isaianic Develop-
ment of First Isaiah's Themes." *Journal for the Study of the
Old Testament* 31 (February 1985): 95-113.

Coggins, R. J. "The Problem of Isaiah 24-27." *Expository Times*
90 (August 1979): 328-33.

Collins, Adela Yarbro. "'What the Spirit Says to the Churches':
Preaching the Apocalypse." *Quarterly Review* 4 (Fall
1984): 69-84.

_____. "Myth and History in the Book of Revelation." In
*Traditions in Transformation: Turning Points in Biblical
Faith*, ed. Baruch Halpern and Jon D. Levenson, 377-403.
Winona Lake, IL: Eisenbrauns, 1981.

Collins, John J. "Cosmos and Salvation: Jewish Wisdom and
Apocalyptic in the Hellenistic Age." *History of Religions*
17 (November 1977): 121-42.

_____. "Methodological Issues in the Study of 1 Enoch:
Reflections on the Articles of Paul D. Hanson and G. W.
Nickelsburg," in *Society of Biblical Literature Seminar
Papers*, ed. Paul J. Achtemeier, 311-315. Missoula, MT:
Scholars, 1978.

_____. "Patterns of Eschatology at Qumran." In *Traditions in
Transformation: Turning Points in Biblical Faith*, ed.
Baruch Halpern and Jon D. Levenson, 351-75. Winona
Lake, IL: Eisenbrauns, 1981.

_____. "The Genre Apocalypse in Hellenistic Judaism." In
*Apocalypticism in the Mediterranean World and the Near
East*, ed. David Helholm, 531-48. Tübingen: Mohr, 1983.

_____. "The Sibylline Oracles." In *The Old Testament
Pseudepigrapha*. Vol. 1, *Apocalyptic Literature and Testa-*

ments, ed. James H. Charlesworth, 317-472. New York: Doubleday, 1983.

————. "Apocalyptic Eschatology as the Transcendence of Death." In *Visionaries and Their Apocalypses*, ed. Paul D. Hanson, 61-84. Philadelphia: Fortress, 1983.

————. "The Kingdom of God in the Apocrypha and Pseudepigrapha." In *The Kingdom of God in 20th Century Interpretation*, ed. Wendell Willis, 81-96. Peabody, MA: Hendrickson, 1987.

Coughenour, R. A. "The Wisdom Stance of Enoch's Redactor." *Journal for the Study of Judaism* 13 (December 1982): 47-56.

Cranfield, C. E. B. "Some Observations on Romans 8.19-21." In *Reconciliation and Hope: New Testament Essays on Atonement and Eschatology*, ed. Robert Banks, 224-30. London: Paternoster, 1974.

————. "The Freedom of the Christian According to Romans 8.2." In *New Testament Christianity for Africa and the World*, ed. Mark E. Glasswell and Edward W. Fasholé-Luke, 91-98. London: SPCK, 1974.

Cross, Frank Moore. "The Redemption of Nature." *Princeton Seminary Bulletin*, n.s. 10 (July 1989): 94-104.

Cullmann, Oscar. "The Connection of Primal Events and End Events with the New Testament Redemptive History." In *The Old Testament and Christian Faith*, ed. Bernhard W. Anderson, 115-23. New York: Harper & Row, 1963.

Dahl, Nils A. "Two Notes on Romans 5," *Studia Theologica* 5/1 (1952): 37-48.

————. "Christ, Creation, and the Church." In *The Background of the New Testament and Its Eschatology*, ed. W. D. Davies and David Daube, 422-43. Cambridge: University Press, 1954.

Danker, F. W. "II Peter 3.10 and Psalm of Solomon 17.10." *Zeitschrift für neuetesta-mentliche Wissenschaft* 53/1-2 (1962): 82-86.

Dantine, W. "Creation and Redemption: An Attempt at a Theological Interpretation in the Light of the Contemporary Understanding of the World." *Scottish Journal of Theology* 18 (June 1965): 129-47.

Davies, Philip R. "Eschatology at Qumran." *Journal of Biblical Literature* 104 (March 1985): 39-55.

Davis, C. "The End of the World: New Heavens and the New Earth." *Worship* 34 (May 1960): 305-8.

Denton, D. R. "Ἀποκαραδοκία." *Zeitschrift für neuetestamentliche Wissenschaft* 73 (1982): 138-40

Derrett, John Duncan M. "Palingenesia (Matthew 19.28)." *Journal for the Study of the New Testament* 20 (February 1984): 51-58.

_____. "New Creation: Qumran, Paul, the Church, and Jesus." *Revue de Qumran* 13 (October 1988): 597-608.

Dunn, James D. G. "Demythologizing--The Problem of Myth in the New Testament." In *New Testament Interpretation: Essays on Priniciples and Methods*, ed. I. H. Marshall, 285-30. Grand Rapids: Eerdmans, 1977.

_____. "Paul's Epistle to the Romans: An Analysis of Structure and Argument." In *Aufstieg und Niedergang der römerische Welt*. Vol. 25.4. Edited by W. Haase, 2856-67. Berlin: de Gruyter, 1988.

Eichrodt, Walter. "In the Beginning: A Contribution to the Interpretation of the First Word of the Bible." In *Creation in the Old Testament*, ed. Bernhard W. Anderson, 65-73. Issues in Religion and Theology, no. 6. Philadelphia: For-tress, 1984.

Epp, Eldon Jay. "Mediating Approaches to the Kingdom: Werner Georg Kümmel and George Eldon Ladd." In *The Kingdom of God in 20th Century Interpretation*, ed. Wendell Willis, 35-52. Peabody, MA: Hendrickson, 1987.

Gager, John G. "Functional Diversity in Paul's End-Time Language." *Journal of Biblical Literature* 89 (September 1970): 325-37.

Georgi, Dieter. "Die Vision von himmlischen Jerusalem in Apk. 21 und 22." In *Kirche: Festschrift fur Günther Bornkamm zum 75. Geburtstag*, ed. Dieter Luhrmann and Georg Strecker, 351-72. Tübingen: Mohr, 1980.

Gibbs, John G. "The Relation Between Creation and Redemption According to Phil. II. 5-11." *Novum Testamentum* 12-13 (July 1970): 270-83.

_____. "Pauline Cosmic Christology and Ecological Crisis."

Journal of Biblical Literature 90 (December 1971):
466-79.

_____. "The Cosmic Scope of Redemption According to
Paul." *Biblica* 56/1 (1975): 13-29.

Gowan, Donald E. "Fall and Redemption of the Material World
in Apocalyptic Literature." *Horizons in Biblical Theology* 7
(December 1985): 83-103.

Greenfield, Jonas C. and Michael E. Stone. "The Enochic Pentateuch and the Date of the Similitudes." *Harvard Theological Review* 70 (January-April 1977): 51-66.

Guelich, Robert A. "The Matthean Beatitudes: 'Entrance
Requirements' or Eschatological Blessings?" *Journal of
Biblical Literature* 95 (September 1976): 415-34.

Gundry, R. H. "The New Jerusalem: People as Place, not Place
for People." *Novum Testamentum* 29 (July 1987): 254-64.

Hamerton-Kelley, R. G. "The Temple and the Origins of Jewish
Apocalyptic." *Vetus Testamentum* 20 (January 1970): 1-15.

Hanson, Paul D. "Rebellion in Heaven: Azazel and Euhemeristic
Heroes in 1 Enoch 6-11." *Journal of Biblical Literature* 96
(June 1977): 195-233.

_____. "Old Testament Apocalyptic Reexamined." In *Vision-
aries and their Apocalypses*, ed. Paul D. Hanson, 27-60.
Philadelphia: Fortress, 1983.

_____. "Apocalyptic Literature." In *The Hebrew Bible and Its
Modern Interpreters*, ed. Douglas M. Knight and Gene M.
Tucker, 465-88. Philadelphia: Fortress, 1985.

_____. "Biblical Apocalypticism: The Theological Dimen-
sions." *Horizons in Biblical Theology* 7 (December 1985):
1-20.

Harris, R. Laird. "The Last Days in the Bible and Qumran." In
Jesus of Nazareth, Savior and Lord, ed. Carl F. H. Henry,
73-85. Grand Rapids: Eerdmans, 1966.

Hasel, Gerhard F. "Recent Translations of Genesis 1.1: A Critical
Look." *Bible Translator* 22 (October 1971): 154-67.

Hasel, Gerhard F. "The Polemic Nature of the Genesis Cosmology." *Evangelical Quarterly* 46 (April-June 1974): 82-102.

Hay, Donald A. "Christians in the Global Greenhouse." *Tyndale
Bulletin* 41.1 (May 1990): 109-127.

Hendry, George S. "Faith and the Cosmos." *Princeton Seminary*

Bulletin, n.s. 10 (July 1989): 84-93.

Hengel, Martin. "Qumran und der Hellenismus." In *Qumrân: Sa piété, sa théologie et son milieu*, ed. M. Delcor, 333-72. Bibliotheca ephemeridum theologicarium lovaniensium, no. 46. Duculot: Louvain University, 1978.

Hermisson, Hans-Jürgen. "Observations on the Creation Theology in Wisdom." In *Creation in the Old Testament*, ed. Bernhard W. Anderson, 118-34. Issues in Religion and Theology, no. 6. Philadelphia: Fortress, 1984.

Himmelfarb, Martha. "From Prophecy to Apocalypse: The Book of the Watchers and Tours of Heaven." In *Jewish Spirituality: From the Bible Through the Middle Ages*, ed. Arthur Green, 145-65. New York: Crossroad, 1986.

Hooker, Morna D. "Were there False Teachers in Colossae?" In *Christ and Spirit in the New Testament*, ed. Barnabas Lindars and Stephen S. Smalley, 315-31. Cambridge: Cambridge University, 1973.

Hurtado, L. W. "Rev. 4-5 in Light of Jewish Apoocalyptic Analogies." *Journal for the Study of the New Testament* 25 (October 1985): 105-24.

Isaac, Ephraim. "1 Enoch." In *The Old Testament Pseudepigrapha*. Vol. 1, *Apocalyptic Literature and Testaments*, ed. James H. Charlesworth, 5-12. New York: Doubleday, 1983.

Käsemann, Ernst. "An Apologia for Primitive Christian Eschatology." In *Essays on New Testament Themes*. Translated by W. J. Montague, 160-95. Studies in Biblical Theology, no. 41. London: SCM, 1964.

_____. "The Beginnings of Christian Theology." In *New Testament Questions of Today*. Translated by W. J. Montague, 82-107. Philadelphia: Fortress, 1969.

Kaufman, Gordan D. "A Problem for Theology: The Concept of Nature." *Harvard Theological Review* 65 (July 1972): 337-66.

_____. "Nuclear Eschatology and the Study of Religion." *Journal of the American Academy of Religion* 51 (March 1983): 3-14.

Keck, Leander E. "The Spirit and the Dove." *New Testament Studies* 17 (October 1970): 41-67.

Kee, Howard Clark. "The Terminology of Mark's Exorcism Stories." *New Testament Studies* 14 (January 1968): 232-46.

Knibb, Michael A. "The Exile in the Literature of the Intertestamental Period." *Heythrop Journal* 17 (1976): 253-72.

_____. "The Date of the Parables of Enoch: A Critical Review." *New Testament Studies* 25 (April 1979): 345-59.

_____. "Apocalyptic and Wisdom in 4 Ezra." *Journal for the Study of Judaism* 13 (December 1982): 56-74.

Knierim, Rolf. "Cosmos and History in Israel's Theology." *Horizons in Biblical Theology* 3 (June 1981): 59-123.

Kolenkow, A. B. "The Genre Testament and Forecasts of the Future in the Hellenistic Jewish Milieu." *Journal for the Study of Judaism* 6 (June 1975): 57-71.

Kraus, Hans Joachim. "Schöpfung und Weltvollendung." *Evangelische Theologie* 24 (June 1964): 462-85.

Kvanvig, Helge S. "The Relevance of the Biblical Visions of the End Times: Hermeneutical Guidelines to Apocalyptical Literature." *Horizons in Bibilcal Theology* 11 (January 1989): 35-58.

Lampe, G. W. H. "The New Testament Doctrine of 'Ktisis'." *Scottish Journal of Theology* 17 (December 1964): 449-62.

Lample, Alfred. "Das neue Jerusalem, Die Eschatologie der Offenbarung des Johannes." *Bibel und Kirche* 39 (1984): 75-81.

Lanchester, H. C. O. "The Sibylline Oracles." In *The Apocrypha and Pseudepigrapha of the Old Testament*. Vol. 2, *Pseudepigrapha,* ed. R. H. Charles, 368-406. Oxford: Clarendon, 1913.

Landes, George M. "Creation as Liberation Theology." In *Creation in the Old Testament*, ed. Bernhard W. Anderson, 135-51. Issues in Religion and Theology, no. 6. Philadelphia: Fortress, 1984.

Lapidge, Michael. "Stoic Cosmology." In *The Stoics*, ed John M. Rist, 161-85. Berkeley: University of California, 1978.

Lattke, Michael. "On the Jewish Background of the Synoptic Concept 'the Kingdom of God.'" In *The Kingdom of God in the Teaching of Jesus*, ed. Bruce Chilton, 92-106. Issues in Religion and Theology, no. 5. Philadelphia: Fortress, 1984.

Laurin, Robert B. "The Question of Immortality in the Qumran 'Hodayot,'" *Journal of Semitic Studies* 3 (October 1958): 344-55.

Lenhard, H. "Ein Beitrag zur Uebersetzung von 2 Pet. 3:10d." *Zeitschrift für neuetestamentliche Wissenschaft* 52 (1961): 128-29.

_____. "Noch einmal zu 2 Petr. 3:10d." *Zeitschrift für neuetestamentliche Wissenschaft* 69 (1978): 136.

Licht, J. "The Doctrine of the Dead Sea Scrolls," *Israel Exploration Journal* 6/1-2 (1956): 1-13; 89-101.

Lindeskog, Gösta. "The Theology of Creation in the Old and New Testaments." In *The Root of the Vine*, ed. Anton Fridrichsen, 1-22. London: Dacre, 1953.

Lövestam, Evald. "Eschatologie und Tradition im 2 Petrusbrief." In *The New Testament Age*. Vol. 2. Edited by William C. Weinrich, 287-300. Macon, GA: Mercer, 1984.

Luck, Ulrich. "Das Weltverständis jüdischen Apocalyptic: Dargestellt am Äthiopishen Henoch und am 4 Esra." *Zeitschrift für Theologie und Kirche* 73 (September 1976): 283-305.

Lyonnet, Stanislas. "The Redemption of the Universe." In *Contemporary New Testament Studies*, ed. M. R. Ryan, 423-36. Collegeville, MN: Liturgical, 1965.

McCarthy, Dennis. "'Creation' Motifs in Ancient Hebrew Poetry." In *Creation in the Old Testament*, ed. Bernhard W. Anderson, 74-89. Issues in Religion and Theology, no. 6. Philadelphia: Fortress, 1984.

McCown, W. "The Hymnic Structure of Colossians 1.15-20." *Evangelical Quarterly* 51 (July-September 1979): 156-62.

McCullough, W. S. "Israel's Eschatology from Amos to Daniel." In *Studies on the Ancient Palestinian World*, ed. J. W. Wevers and D. B. Redford, 86-101. Toronto: University of Toronto, 1972.

McNamara, M. "The Unity of Second Peter: A Reconsideration." *Scripture* 12 (1960): 13-19.

Maier, Gerhard. "Die biblische Zukunftsewartung." In *Zukunftservartung in biblischer Sicht: Beitrag zum Eschatologie*, ed. G. Maier, 52-67. Wuppertal: R. Brockhaus Verlag, 1984.

Malchow, Bruce V. "Contrasting Views of Nature in the Hebrew Bible." *Dialog* 26 (Winter 1987): 40-43.

Maly, Eugene H. "Creation in the New Testament." In *Biblical Studies in Contemporary Thought*, ed. Miriam Ward, 104-12. Somerville, MA: Greeno, Hadden, & Co., 1975.

Maori, Yeshayahu. "The Approach of Classical Jewish Exegetes to *Peshat* and *Derash* and Its Implication for the Teaching of the Bible." *Tradition* 21 (Fall 1984): 40-53.

Marshall, I. H. "Son of God or Servant of Yahweh?: A Reconsideration of Mark 1.11." *New Testament Studies* 15 (April 1969): 326-36.

_____. "Slippery Words: Eschatology." *Expository Times* 89 (June 1978): 264-69.

_____. "Is Apocalyptic the Mother of Christian Theology?" In *Tradition and Interpretation in the New Testament*, ed. Gerald F. Hawthorne and Otto Betz, 33-41. Grand Rapids: Eerdmans, 1987.

_____. "The Hope of the Age: The Kingdom of God in the New Testament." In *Jesus the Saviour: Studies in New Testament Theology*, 211-38. Downers Grove, IL: InterVarsity, 1990.

Martin, James Perry. "Cosmic Christ and Cosmic Redemption: An Essay in Interpretation." *Affirmation* 1 (July 1967): 4-31.

Martin, Ralph P. "An Early Christian Hymn." *Evangelical Quarterly* 36 (October-December 1964): 195-205.

Mauser, Ulrich. "Isaiah 65:17-25." *Interpretation* 36 (April 1982): 181-86.

Mearns, Christopher L. "Dating the Siumilitudes of Enoch." *New Testament Studies* 25 (April 1979): 360-69.

Miller, Patrick D. Jr. "The Gift of the Land: The Deuteronomic Theology of the Land." *Interpretation* 23 (October 1969): 451-65.

Minear, Paul S. "The Cosmology of the Apocalypse." In *Current Issues in the New Testament*, ed. William Klassen and Grayden F. Snyder, 23-37. New York: Harper, 1962.

Moltmann, Jürgen. "Creation and Redemption." In *Creation, Christ and Culture*, ed. Richard W. A. Mckinney, 119-34. Edinburgh: T. & T. Clark, 1976.

Mounce, Robert H. "Synoptic Self Portraits." *Evangelical Quarterly* 37 (October-Decem-ber 1965): 212-17.

Murry, John Middleton. "Metaphor." In *Essays on Metaphor*, ed. Warren Shibles, 21-36. Whitewater, WI: Language, 1972.

Mussner, Franz. "'Weltherrschaft' als eschatologischie Thema der Johannesapokalypse." In *Glaube und Eschatologie*, ed. Erich Grässer and Otto Merk, 209-27. Tübingen: Mohr, 1985.

Newsom, C. A. "The Development of 1 Enoch 6-19: Cosmology and Judgement." *Catholic Biblical Quarterly* 42 (July 1980): 310-29.

Nickelsburg, George W. E. "Apocalyptic and Myth in 1 Enoch 6-11." *Journal of Biblical Literature* 96 (June 1977): 383-405.

_____. "The Apocalyptic Message of 1 Enoch 92-105." *Catholic Biblical Quarterly* 39 (July 1977): 309-28.

O'Neill, J. C. "The Source of the Christology in Colossians." *New Testament Studies* 26 (December 1979): 87-100.

Orlinsky, Harry M. "The Biblical Concept of the Land." In *The Land of Israel: Jewish Perspectives*, ed. Lawrence A. Hoffman, 27-64. Notre Dame: University of Notre Dame, 1986.

Ouderslys, Richard C. "Israel, the Land and the Scriptures." *Reformed Review* 33 (Autumn 1979): 3-15.

Overstreet, R. L. "A Study of 2 Peter 3:10-13." *Bibliotheca Sacra* 137 (October-December 1980): 354-71.

Perrin, Norman. "Eschatology and Hermeneutics: Reflections on Method in the Interpretation of the New Testament." *Journal of Biblical Literature* 93 (March 1974): 3-14.

Pryke, John. "Eschatology in the Dead Sea Scrolls." In *The Scrolls and Christianity*, ed. Matthew Black, 45-57. London: SPCK, 1969.

Pythian-Adams, W. J. "The Mystery of the New Creation." *Church Quarterly Review* 142 (1946): 61-77.

Rad, Gerhard von. "Typological Interpretation of the Old Testament." In *Essays on Old Testament Hermeneutics*, ed. Claus Westermann, trans. James Luther Mays, 17-39. Richmond: John Knox, 1964.

_____. "The Theological Problem of the Old Testament Doctrine of Creation." In *The Problem of the Hexateuch and*

Other Essays, trans. by E. W. Trueman Dicken, 131-43.
New York: McGraw Hill, 1966.

_____. "Some Aspects of the Old Testament World-View." In
The Problem of the Hexatuech and Other Essays, trans. by
E. W. Trueman Dicken, 144-65. New York: McGraw Hill,
1966.

_____."The Promised Land and Yahweh's Land in the Hexa-
teuch." In *The Problem of the Hexateuch and Other
Essays*, trans. by E. W. Trueman Dicken, 79-93. New York:
McGraw Hill, 1966.

Reicke, Bo. "Creation, Determination, and Consummation in the
View of the New Testament." *Abba Salama* 9 (1978):
299-308.

_____. "Positive and Negative Aspects of the World in the
New Testament." *Westminster Theological Journal* 49 (Fall
1987): 351-67.

Ricoeur, Paul. "Biblical Hermeneutics." In *Paul Ricoeur on Biblical Hermeneutics*, ed. John D. Crossan, 29-107. Semeia,
no. 4. Missoula, MT: Scholars, 1975.

Riesner, Rainer. "Der zweit Petrus-Brief und die Eschatologie."
In *Zukunftservartung in biblischer Sicht: Beitrag zum
Eschatologie*, ed. G. Maier, 124-43. Wuppertal: R. Brock-
haus Verlag, 1984.

Ringgren, H. "Der Weltbrand in den Hodajot." In *Bibel und
Qumran: Beiträge zur Erforschung der Beziehungen zwischen Bibel-und Qumranwissenschaft*, ed. S. Wagner,
177-82. Berlin: Haupt-Bibelgesellschaft, 1968.

Roberts, J. W. "A Note on the Meaning of II Peter 3:10d."
Restoration Quarterly 6 (1962): 32-33.

Rogerson, J. W. "The Old Testament View of Nature: Some Preliminary Questions." In *Instruction and Interpretation:
Studies in the Hebrew Language, Palestinian Archaeology
and Biblical Exegesis*, 67-84. Leiden: Brill, 1979.

Rodgers, Margaret. "Luke 4.16-30; A Call for a Jubilee Year?"
Reformed Theological Review 40 (September-December
1981), 72-82.

Rubinstein, Arie. "Observations on the Slavonic Book of Enoch."
Journal of Jewish Studies 13/1 (1962): 1-22.

Russell, Brian. "A Nuclear End 'Would God Let It Happen?'" In

    Theology Against the Horizon, ed. Alan Race, 103-16.
    London: SCM, 1988.

Safrai, Shmuel. "The Heavenly Jerusalem." *Ariel* 23 (1969):
    11-16.

Saldarini, A. J. "Apocalypses and 'Apocalyptic' in Rabbinic Lit-
    erature and Mysticism." In *Apocalypse: The Morphology
    of a Genre*, ed. J. J. Collins, 187-205. Semeia, no. 14. Mis-
    soula, MT: Scholars, 1979.

Sanders, E. P. "The Genre of Palestinian Jewish Apocalypses." In
    *Apocalypticism in the Mediterranean World and the Near
    East*, ed. David Helholm, 447-59. Tübingen: Mohr, 1983.

Sanders, James A. "From Isaiah 61 to Luke 4." In *Christianity,
    Judaism, and Other Greco-Roman Cults*. Vol. 1. Edited by
    Jacob Neusner, 75-106. Leiden: Brill, 1975.

Santmire, H. Paul. "Toward a New Theology of Nature." *Dialog*
    25 (Winter 1986): 43-50.

Schmid, H. H. "Creation, Righteousness, and Salvation: 'Creat-
    ion Theology' as the Broad Horizon of Biblical Theology."
    In *Creation in the Old Testament*, ed. Bernhard W. Ander-
    son, 102-17. Issues in Religion and Theology, no. 6.
    Philadelphia: Fortress, 1984.

Schweizer, Eduard. "The Church as the Missionary Body of
    Christ." *New Testament Studies* 8 (October 1961): 1-11.

Sehmsdorf, Eberhard. "Studien zur Redaktionsgeschichte von
    Jesaja 56-66 (I): (Jes. 65.16b-25; 66.1-4; 56.1-8)."
    Zeitschrift für die Alttestamentliche Wissenschaft 84
    (1972): 517-76.

Shaked, S. "Eschatology and the Goal of the Religious Life in
    Sasanian Zoroastrianism." In *Types of Redemption*, ed. R.
    J. Zwi Werblowsky and C. Jouco Bleeker, 223-30. Leiden:
    Brill, 1970.

Simon, Uriel. "The Religious Significance of *Peshat*." *Tradition*
    23 (Winter 1988): 41-63.

Smith, Morton. "On the History of APOKALUPTW and
    APOKALUYIS." In *Apocalypticism in the Mediterranean
    World and the Near East*, ed. David Helholm, 9-20. Tübin-
    gen: Mohr, 1983.

Stegemann, Hartmut. "Die Bedeutung der Qumranfunde für die
    Erforschung der Apokalyptik." In *Apocalypticism in the*

Mediterranean World and the Near East, ed. David Hellholm, 495-530. Tübingen: Mohr, 1983.

Stone, Michael E. "Lists of Revealed Things in the Apocalyptic
Literature." In *Magnalia Dei: The Mighty Acts of God*,ed.
Frank Moore Cross, 414-52. New York: Doubleday, 1976.

_____. "Coherence and Inconsistency in the Apocalypses:
The Case of 'The End' in 4 Ezra." *Journal of Biblical Literature* 102 (June 1983): 229-43.

_____. "Apocalyptic Literature," In *Jewish Writings of the
Second Temple Period*. Vol. 1, *Apocrypha, Pseudepigrapha, Qumran Sectarian Writings, Philo, Josephus*, ed.
Michael E. Stone, 383-442. Compendia Rerum Iudaicarum
ad Novum Testamentum. Section II. Philadelphia: Fortress,
1984.

_____. "The Parabolic Use of Natural Order in Judaism of the
Second Temple Age." In *Gilgul: Essays on Transformation, Revolution and Permanence in the History of Religions*, ed. S. Shaked, D. Shulman, and G. G. Stroumsa,
298-308. Leiden: Brill, 1987.

Stuhlmueller, Carroll. "Theology of Creation in Second Isaiah."
Catholic Biblical Quarterly 21 (October 1959): 429-67.

_____. "'First and Last' and 'Yahweh-Creator'." *Catholic
Biblical Quarterly* 29 (July 1967): 189-205.

Stuhlmacher, Peter. "Behold I Make All Things New." *Lutheran
World*. 15 (1968): 3-15.

Suter, David. "Weighed in the Balance: The Similitudes of Enoch
in Recent Discussion." *Religious Studies Review* 7 (July
1981): 217-21.

Talmon, Shemaryahu. "Waiting for the Messiah--The Conceptual
Universe of the Qumran Covenanters." In *The World of
Qumran From Within*, 294-300. Leiden: Brill, 1989.

Testa, P. E. "La distruzione del mondo per il fuoco nell 2 ep. di
Pietro iii. 7, 10, 13." *Rivista Biblica* 10 (1962): 252-81.

Thiede, Carsten Peter. "A Pagan Reader of 2 Peter: Cosmic Conflagration in 2 Peter and the *Octavius* of Minucius Felix."
Journal for the Study of the New Testament 26 (February
1986): 79-96.

Tillich, Paul. "Dynamics of Faith." In *Writings on Religion*. Vol.
5. Edited by Robert P. Scharlemann, 231-89. Berlin: de

Gruyter, 1988.

Travis, Stephen H. "The Value of Apocalyptic." *Tyndale Bulletin* 30 (1979): 52-56.

VanderKam, James C. "The Theophany of Enoch 1.3b-7, 9." *Vetus Testamentum* 23 (April 1973): 129-50.

_____. "The Origin, Character, and Early History of the 364-Day Calendar: A Reassessment of Jaubert's Hypothesis." *Catholic Biblical Quarterly* 41 (July 1979): 390-411.

_____. "The 364-Day Calendar in the Enochic Literature." In *Society of Biblical Literature Seminar Papers*, ed. Kent Harold Richards, 157-65. Chico, CA: Scholars, 1983.

_____. "The Prophetic-Sapiential Origins of Apocalyptic Thought." In *A Word in Season*, ed. James D. Martine and Philip R. Davies, 163-176. Journal for the Study of the Old Testament Supplement Series, no. 42. Sheffield: JSOT, 1986.

Villiers, P. G. R. de. "Wisdom and the World in the Similitudes of Enoch." In *Studies in 1 Enoch and the New Testament*, 50-68. Neotestamentica 17. Stellenbosch, South Africa: University of Stellenbosch, 1983.

Viviano, B. T. "The Kingdom of God in the Qumran Literature." In *The Kingdom of God in 20th-Century Interpretation*, ed. Wendell Willis, 97-107. Peabody, MA: Hendrickson, 1987.

Vögtle, Anton. "Röm 8,19-22: Eine Schöpfungstheologische oder Anthropologisch-Soteriologische Aussage?" In *Mélanges Bibliques en hommage au R. R. Béda Rigaux*, 351-66. Gembloux, Belgium: Duculot, 1970.

Wald, George. "Decision and Destiny; the Future of Life on Earth." *Zygon* 5 (June 1970): 159-71.

Westermann, Claus. "God and His Creation." *Union Seminary Quarterly Review* 18 (March 1963): 197-209.

Wheelwright, Philip. "Semantics and Ontology." In *Essays on Metaphor*. Edited by Warren Shibles. Whitewater, WI: Language, 1972.

Widengren, Geo. "Iran and Israel in Parthian Times with Special Regard to the Ethiopic Book of Enoch." In *Religious Syncretism in Antiquity*, ed. Birger A. Pearson, 85-129. Missoula, MT: Scholars, 1975.

Wintermute, O. S. "Jubilees." In *The Old Testament Pseude-*

pigrapha. Vol. 2, *Expansions of the 'Old Testament' and Legends, Wisdom and Philosophical Literature, Prayers, Psalms, and Odes, Fragments of Lost Judeo-Hellenistic Works,* ed. James H. Charlesworth, 35-51. New York: Doubleday, 1985.

Wilkenson, Loren. "Cosmic Christology and the Christian's Role in Creation." *Christian Scholars Review* 11 (Fall-Spring 1981): 18-40.

Williams, G. W. "Christian Attitudes Toward Nature." *Christian Scholar's Review* 2 (Fall-Spring 1971-72): 3-35; 112-26.

Wilson, R. R. "This World--and the World to Come." *Encounter* 38 (Spring 1977): 117-24.

Wilson, William E. "Εὑρεθήσεται in 2 Pet. iii.10." *Expository Times* 32 (1920-1921): 44-45.

Wolters, Albert M. "Worldview and Textual Criticism in 2 Peter 3:10." *Westminster Theological Journal* 49 (Fall 1987): 405-13.

Wright, N. T. "Poetry and Theology in Colossians 1.15-20." *New Testament Studies* 36 (July 1990): 444-68.

Wright, J. H. "What Happened Every Seven Years in Israel?" *Evangelical Quarterly* 56 (April-October): 129-38; 193-202.

Zeitlin, Solomon. "The Judaean Calendar During the Second Commonwealth and the Scrolls," 194-211. In *Studies in The Early History of Judaism*. Vol.1. New York: KTAV, 1973.

Encyclopedia and Dictionary Articles

Encyclopedia of Religions. 16 vols. Edited by Mircea Eliade. New York: MacMillan, 1987. S.v. "Naturalism," by Jeffrey Stout.

Interpreter's Dictionary of the Bible. 4 vols. Edited by George Arthur Buttrick. Nashville: Abingdon, 1962-76. S.v. "Apocalypticism," by M. Risk.

_____. S.v. "Creation," by Bernhard W. Anderson.

_____. S.v. "Fire," by M. E. Goodman.

_____. S.v. "New Earth, New Heaven," by J. W. Bowman.

_____. S.v. "Water," by Bernhard W. Anderson.

_____. Supplementary Volume. Edited by Keith Crim. Nashville: Abingdon, 1976. S.v. "Apocalypse, Genre;" "Apocalypticism," by Paul D. Hanson.

_____. S.v. "Revelation in History," by James Barr.

International Standard Bible Encyclopedia. 4 vols. rev. ed. Edited by Geoffrey W. Bromiley, Everett F. Harrison, Roland K. Harrison, and William S. LaSor. Grand Rapids: Eerdmans, 1979-88. S.v. "Isaiah," by R. K. Harrison and G. L. Robinson.

New Bible Dictionary. 2d ed. Edited by J. D. Douglas, F. F. Bruce, J. I. Packer, N. Hillyer, D. Guthrie, A. R. Millard, and D. J. Wiseman. Wheaton: Tyndale, 1982. S.v. "Isaiah, Book of," by H. N. Ridderbos.

Theological Dictionary of the New Testament. 10 vols. Edited by Gerhard Kittel and Gerhard Friedrich. Translated by Geoffrey W. Bromiley. Grand Rapids: Eerdmans, 1964-74. S.v. "Αἰών," by Hermann Sasse.

_____. S.v. " Ἀποκαραδοκία," by G. Delling.

_____. S.v. "Γῆ," by Hermann Sasse.

_____. S.v. "Καινός," by Johannes Behm.

_____. S.v. "Καλός," by G. Bertram.

_____. S.v. "Κτίζω," by W. Foerster.

_____. S.v. "Οὐρανός," by G. von Rad.

_____. S.v. "Παλιγγενεσία," by F. Büchsel.

_____. S.v. "Φύσις," by H. Köster.

_____. S.v. "Πῦρ," by F. Lang.

Theological Dictionary of the Old Testament. 5 vols. Edited by G. Johannes Botterweck and Helmer Ringgren. Translated by John T. Willis. Grand Rapids: Eerdmans, 1974. S.v. "אבל," by A. Baumann.

_____. S.v. "ארץ," by J. Bergman and M. Ottosson

_____. S.v. "ברא," by K.-H. Bernhardt, G. Botterweck, and H. Ringgren.

_____. S.v. "חדש," by C. R. North.

Commentaries

Anderson, Francis I. and David Noel Freedman. *Hosea.* Anchor Bible. New York: Doubleday, 1980.

Barth, Karl. *The Epistle to the Romans.* Translated by Edwyn C. Hoskyns. London: Oxford University, 1957.

Bauckham, Richard J. *Jude, 2 Peter.* Word Biblical Commentary. Waco: Word, 1983.

Beasley-Murray, G. R. *The Book of Revelation.* New Century Bible. Greenwood, SC: Attic, 1974.

Bigg, C. A. *A Critical and Exegetical Commentary on the Epistles of St. Peter and St. Jude.* International Critical Commentaries. 2d ed. Edinburgh: T. & T. Clark, 1902.

Boring, M. Eugene. *Revelation.* Interpretation. Louisville: John Knox, 1989.

Bruce, F. F. *The Epistle to the Romans.* Tyndale New Testament Commentaries. Grand Rapids: Eerdmans, 1980.

_____. *The Book of Acts.* rev. ed. Tyndale New Testament Commentaries. Grand Rapids: Eerdmans, 1988.

Bright, John. *Jeremiah.* Anchor Bible. New York: Doubleday, 1965.

Caird, George B. *The Revelation of St. John the Divine.* Harper's New Testament Commentaries. New York: Harper & Row, 1966.

_____. *Paul's Letters from Prison.* Oxford: University, 1976.

Carroll, Robert P. *Jeremiah.* Old Testament Library. Philadelphia: Westminster, 1986.

Charles, R. H. *The Revelation of St. John.* 2 vols. International Critical Commentary. New York: Scribner, 1920.

Clements, Ronald E. *Isaiah 1-39.* New Century Bible Commentaries. Grand Rapids: Eerdmans, 1980.

Cranfield, C. E. B. *I and II Peter and Jude.* Torch Bible Commentaries. London: SCM, 1960.

_____. *The Epistle to the Romans.* 2 vols. International Critical Commentary. Edinburgh: T. & T. Clark, 1975.

Davies, W. D. and Dale C. Allison. *The Gospel According to Saint Matthew.* Vol 1. International Critical Commentary. Edinburgh: T. & T. Clark, 1988.

Dunn, James D. G. *Romans 1-8.* Word Biblical Commentary. Dallas: Word, 1988.

Ellis, E. Earle. *The Gospel of Luke.* 2d. ed. Greenwood, SC: 1974.

Eichrodt, Walther. *Ezekiel: A Commentary.* Old Testament

Library. London: SCM, 1966.

Geldenhuys, Norval. *Commentary on the Gospel of Luke*. New International Commentary on the New Testament. Grand Rapids: Eerdmans, 1952.

Goldingay, John E. *Daniel*. Word Biblical Commentary. Dallas: Word, 1989.

Green, Michael E. *The Second Epistle of Peter and the Epistle of Jude*. rev. ed. Tyndale New Testament Commentaries. Grand Rapids: Eerdmans, 1986.

Gundry, Robert H. *Matthew: A Commentary on His Literary and Theological Art*. Grand Rapids: Eerdmans, 1982.

Haenchen, Ernst. *The Acts of the Apostles*. Philadelphia: Westminster, 1971.

Hill, David. *The Gospel of Matthew*. New Century Bible. Greenwood, SC: Attic, 1972.

Kaiser, Otto. *Isaiah 13-39*. Translated by R. A. Wilson. Old Testament Library. Philadelphia: Westminster, 1974.

Käsemann, Ernst. *Commentary on Romans*. Translated by Geoffrey W. Bromiley. Grand Rapids: Eerdmans, 1980.

Kelly, J. N. D. *A Commentary on the Epistles of Peter and Jude*. Black's New Testament Commentaries. London: Adam & Charles Black, 1969.

Kissane, Edward J. *The Book of Isaiah*. Vol. 1. Dublin: Richview, 1941.

Knight, G. A. F. *Deutero-Isaiah: A Theological Commentary on Isaiah 40-55*. New York: Abingdon, 1965.

_____. *The New Israel: A Commentary on the Book of Isaiah 56-66*. International Theological Commentary. Grand Rapids: Eerdmans, 1985.

Ladd, George E. *A Commentary on the Revelation of John*. Grand Rapids: Eerdmans, 1972.

Lohse, Eduard. *Colossians and Philemon*. Hermeneia. Translated by William R. Poehlmann and Robert J. Karris. Edited by Helmut Koester. Philadelphia: Fortress, 1971.

Luz, Ulrich. *Matthew 1-7: A Commentary*. Minneapolis, MN: Augsburg, 1985.

McKenzie, John. L. *Second Isaiah*. Anchor Bible. Garden City, NY: Doubleday, 1968.

Marshall, I. H. *The Gospel of Luke*. New International Greek Testament Commentary. Grand Rapids: Eerdmans, 1978.

Martin, Ralph P. *Colossians and Philemon*. New Century Bible. Greenwood, SC: Attic, 1974.

Mays, Luther L. *Hosea: A Commentary*. Old Testament Library. Philadelphia: Westminster, 1969.

Mayor, J. B. *The Epistles of St. Jude and the Second Epistle of St. Peter*. New York: Macmillan, 1907.

Minear, Paul S. *I Saw a New Earth: An Introduction to the Visions of the Apocalypse*. Washington, DC: Corpus, 1968.

Moo, Douglas. *Romans 1-8*. Wycliffe Exegetical Commentary. Chicago: Moody, 1991.

Morris, Leon. *The Book of Revelation*. rev. ed. Tyndale New Testament Commentaries. Grand Rapids: Eerdmans, 1987.

_____. *The Epistle to the Romans*. Grand Rapids: Eerdmans, 1988.

Mounce, Robert H. *The Book of Revelation*. New International Commentary on the New Testament. Grand Rapids: Eerdmans, 1977.

Myers, Jacob M. *I and II Esdras*. New York: Doubleday, 1974.

Newport, John P. *The Lion and the Lamb*. Nashville: Broadman, 1986.

Nolland, John. *Luke 1-9.29*. Word Biblical Commentary. Dallas, Word, 1989.

O'Brien, Peter T. *Colossians, Philemon*. Word Biblical Commentary. Waco: Word, 1982.

Oesterley, W. O. E. *II Esdras: The Ezra Apocalypse*. London: Methuen, 1933.

Oswalt, John N. *The Book of Isaiah: Chapters 1-39*. New International Commentary on the Old Testament. Grand Rapids: Eerdmans, 1986.

Rad, Gerhard von. *Genesis: A Commentary*. rev. ed. Old Testament Library. Translated by John Marks. Philadelphia: Westminster, 1972.

Reicke, Bo. *The Epistles of James, Peter, and Jude*. Anchor Bible. Garden City, NY: Doubleday, 1964.

Sanday, William and Arthur C. Headlam. *The Epistle to the Romans*. 11th ed. International Critical Commentary. New York: Abingdon, 1906.

Sarna, Nahum M. *Genesis*. Jewish Publication Society Torah

Commentary. Philadelphia: Jewish Publicaton Society, 1989.

Schelkle, Karl Hermann. *Die Petrus Briefe, Der Judasbrief.* Herder Theologischer Kommentar zum Neuen Testament. 5th ed. Freiburg: Herder, 1982.

Schlatter, Adolf. *Der Evangelist Matthäus.* Stuttgart: Calwer, 1959.

_____. *Gottes Gerechtigkeit: Ein Kommentar zum Römerbrief.* Stuttgart: Calwer, 1935.

Schweizer, Eduard. *The Good News According to Matthew.* Translated by David Green.Atlanta: John Knox, 1975.

_____. *The Letter to the Colossians: A Commentary.* Translated by Andrew Chester. Minneapolis, MN: Augsburg, 1982.

Skinner, John. *A Critical and Exegetical Commentary on Genesis.* International Critical Commentary. Edinburgh: T. & T. Clark, 1910.

Stone, E. Michael. *Fourth Ezra: A Commentary on the Book of Fourth Ezra.*Minneapolis, MN: Fortress, 1990.

Strecker, Georg. *The Sermon on the Mount: An Exegetical Commentary.* Translated by O. C. Dean Jr. Nashville: Abingdon, 1988.

Stuart, Douglas. *Hosea-Jonah.* Word Biblical Commentary. Waco: Word, 1987.

Sweet, J. P. M. *Revelation.* Westminster Pelican Commentaries. Philadelphia: Westminster, 1979.

Swete, H. B. *The Apocalypse of St. John.* 3d ed. London: Macmillan, 1911.

Taylor, Vincent. *The Gospel According to St. Mark.* London: Macmillan, 1957.

Walvoord, John F. *The Revelation of Jesus Christ.* Chicago: Moody, 1966.

Watts, John D. W. *Isaiah 1-33.* Word Biblical Commentary. Waco: Word, 1985.

_____. *Isaiah 34-66.* Word Biblical Commentary. Waco: Word, 1987.

Wenham, Gordan J. *Genesis 1-15.* Word Biblical Commentary. Waco: Word, 1987.

Westermann, Claus. *Genesis 1-11: A Commentary.* Translated by

John J. Scullion. Minneapolis, MN: Augsburg, 1984.

_____. *Isaiah 40-66: A Commentary*. Old Testament Library. Translated by D. M. G. Stalker. Philadelphia: Westminister, 1969.

Whybray, R. N. *Isaiah 40-66*. New Century Bible. Greenwood, SC: Attic, 1975.

Wolff, Hans Walter. *Hosea*. Translated by Gary Stansell. Hermeneia. Philadelphia: Fortress, 1974.

Wright, N. T. *The Epistles of Paul to the Colossians and to Philemon*. Tyndale New Testament Commentaries. Grand Rapids: Eerdmans, 1986.

Young, Edward J. *Isaiah*. 3 Vols. New International Commentary on the Old Testament. Grand Rapids: Eerdmans, 1969-72.

Unpublished Materials

Coughenour, Robert A. "Enoch and Wisdom: A Study of the Wisdom Elements in the Book of Enoch." Ph.D. dissertation, Case Western

INDEX OF ANCIENT SOURCES

SCRIPTURE

PSEUDEPIGRAPHA and APOCRYPHA

QUMRAN LITERATURE

MODERN AUTHOR INDEX